Elemental Design Patterns

Elemental Design Patterns

Jason McC. Smith

♦♦ Addison-Wesley

Upper Saddle River, NJ • Boston • Indianapolis • San Francisco
New York • Toronto • Montreal • London • Munich • Paris • Madrid
Capetown • Sydney • Tokyo • Singapore • Mexico City

Many of the designations used by manufacturers and sellers to distinguish their products are claimed as trademarks. Where those designations appear in this book, and the publisher was aware of a trademark claim, the designations have been printed with initial capital letters or in all capitals.

The author and publisher have taken care in the preparation of this book, but make no expressed or implied warranty of any kind and assume no responsibility for errors or omissions. No liability is assumed for incidental or consequential damages in connection with or arising out of the use of the information or programs contained herein.

The publisher offers excellent discounts on this book when ordered in quantity for bulk purchases or special sales, which may include electronic versions and/or custom covers and content particular to your business, training goals, marketing focus, and branding interests. For more information, please contact:

U.S. Corporate and Government Sales
(800) 382-3419
corpsales@pearsontechgroup.com

For sales outside the United States, please contact:

International Sales
international@pearson.com

Visit us on the Web: informit.com/aw

Library of Congress Cataloging-in-Publication Data

Smith, Jason McC. (Jason McColm)
    Elemental design patterns / Jason McC. Smith.
        p. cm.
    Includes bibliographical references and index.
    ISBN 0-321-71192-0 (hardcover : alk. paper) 1. Software patterns.   2. Software architecture
3. System design.   I. Title.
    QA76.76.P37S657 2012
    005.1—dc23

                                                                    2012001271

ISBN 13: 978-0-321-71192-2
ISBN 10:   0-321-71192-0

Text printed in the United States on recycled paper at Courier in Westford, Massachusetts.
First printing, March, 2012

For B.
You were there at the beginning of this journey,
I wish you'd been able to see the end.

Contents

Figures

Tables

Listings

Foreword

There's a wonderful scene in the movie *2001: A Space Odyssey* that comes to mind.

Having spent several months alone on the derelict ship *Discovery*—and that after having earlier lobotomized the errant Hal—Dr. David Bowman approaches a monolith that draws him in to a new world. His final message back to earth ends "It's full of stars!"

Software-intensive systems are new worlds that we create with our own mental labor. Whereas the world that Bowman saw was formed from atoms and thus full of stars, our worlds are formed from bits...and are full of patterns.

Whether intentional or not, all well-structured, software-intensive systems are full of patterns. Identifying the patterns in a system serves to raise the level of abstraction in reasoning about that system; imposing patterns on a system serves to bring even further order, elegance, and simplicity to that system. In my experience, patterns are one of the most important developments in software engineering in the past two decades.

I've had the pleasure of working with Jason as he evolved his work on SPQR, and let me assure you that he has contributed greatly to the advance of the understanding and practice of patterns. *Elemental Design Patterns* will help you think about patterns in a new way, a way that will help you apply patterns to improve the software worlds that you create and evolve. If you are new to patterns, this is a great book to start your journey; if you are an old hand with patterns, then I expect you'll learn some new things. I certainly did.

Grady Booch
IBM Fellow
February, 2012

Preface

This book is an introduction to a new class of design pattern, the Elemental Design Patterns, which form a foundation for the study and application of software engineering design patterns. Its foundations are in research into the very fabric of software programming theory, but it is intended to be practical and pragmatic. It is intended for both the beginning programmer and the seasoned developer. It should help students engage with the software industry and give researchers new points to ponder.

In short, this book is meant to be *used*.

By the end of it, you should have a new set of tools in your toolbelt, a richer understanding of some of the basic concepts of programming that we all use every day, and knowledge of how they relate and interact with one another to do amazing things. The Elemental Design Patterns, or EDPs, are a collection of fundamental programming ideas that we use reflexively and probably don't think twice about when doing so. This body of work gives them explicit descriptions, regularized names to use in discussions, and a framework for using them in concert and for comparing them on their own merits. If you're a new student, you'll learn that instead of facing the ever-growing design patterns literature as a collection of daunting all-or-nothing blocks, you have a chance to take them on piece by piece and gradually understand the literature in a methodical way. If you're an old hand at software design and patterns, you'll find new ways to look at old approaches and see new opportunities for our discipline.

This book assumes you have a passing familiarity with design patterns as a field but have not used or studied them in detail. Knowing that they exist and having a brief colloquial knowledge of what they are is enough to start the discussion. The book does not assume you have a background in programming theory, language design, or even a strong one in object-oriented programming, just a desire to learn how to think critically about software design. These subjects will be touched on but only as a starting point for those interested in diving deeper into them through the provided references. The Unified Modeling Language is used to describe small examples, and I suggest either [20] or [33] as references if you do not already know UML. You should have a basic foundation in programming, either procedural or object oriented. The latter will help, but it's not absolutely required—this text provides much of the necessary information to explain object-oriented programming in easily digestible chunks. Developers experienced with object-oriented systems may still be surprised at finding new perspectives on concepts that they thought they had mastered long ago and a greater appreciation for object-oriented programming as a whole.

Many programmers see the "design patterns community" as an esoteric body of experts and one that they themselves are not a part of. By giving you a new perspective on what can constitute a design pattern, this book should convince you that *every* programmer is a member of the design patterns community, whether they know it or not. Every single programmer uses design patterns every time they write a line of code, even if don't think of it that way. Nor are they likely to realize the options they have at their disposal. Design patterns are the shared conceptual space in which we write the electronic dreams that shape our world. It's time we had a map of the landscape in which we work and play.

Following the example of the seminal Gang of Four text [21], this book is divided into two sections. First is a discussion of why this book was written and who it is written for and an explanation of what EDPs are, where they came from, and why they're important. This section explains the rationale, the *why*, behind the EDPs. Next is an introduction to the Pattern Instance Notation, a diagramming system for working with patterns at many levels of granularity and in a multitude of environments. Wrapping up this first section is a discussion of how EDPs can be used to build up to, and in conjunction with, the greater design patterns literature. The second section of the book is a collection of design patterns, starting with the EDPs and working through examples of how they combine to form Intermediate patterns, and finally, a selection of the Gang of Four patterns recast as EDP compositions. The EDPs presented here are only a portion of the EDP Catalog, a collection of the first round of defined and described fundamental patterns. The software engineering community will continue to define and refine additional EDPs as the underlying concepts take root. I hope you decide to help in the endeavor.

Welcome, it's good to have you join us.

Acknowledgments

I have many people to thank for this book coming to life. In not quite chronological order...

From the University of North Carolina at Chapel Hill, David Stotts, my Ph.D. advisor who oversaw the birth of SPQR and the EDPs over many years; also my committee, who, even though they were convinced it was probably infeasible, thought it would be an interesting journey and let me go for the brass ring anyway: Jan Prins, David Plaisted, Al Segars, and Sid Chatterjee. You each added invaluable help at critical times.

From my years at IBM Watson Research in New York, Sid Chatterjee again, who convinced me to come play in the Big Blue Playpen; Clay Williams, who gave me free rein to pursue these crazy ideas further and with whom I still miss having coffee; Peter Santhanam, who championed those ideas and from whom I learned a greater appreciation for legacy systems; Brent Hailpern, from whom I learned many valuable lessons in management, the dark humor of corporate life and simple humanity; Edith Schonberg, who put up with my shenanigans more than any manager should have to; and many others who listened to me maniacally talk about this body of work at every turn. My friends, I miss you all.

Also from IBM but deserving a special mention, Grady Booch, who took me under his wing for a wild ride that I wouldn't have traded for anything. Grady, your guidance, mentoring, and advocacy have been immeasurable, and I look forward to future collaborations and continued friendship.

From The Software Revolution, Inc., in Kirkland, Washington, where I am now Senior Computer Scientist, I have to thank everyone for being understanding and supportive of my need to commit this information to paper. It has been a true pleasure working with all of you, and I am eager to see where we can take our company.

To my many reviewers, your advice and comments were highly insightful and helpful. You made this book a much better product, and you have my deepest thanks: Lee Ackerman, Lars Bishop, Robert Bogetti, Robert Couch,

Bernard Farrell, Mary Lou Hines Fritts, Gail Murphy, Jeffrey Overbey, Ethan Roberts, Carlota Sage, Davie Sweis, Peri Tarr, and Rebecca Wirfs-Brock. Elizabeth Ryan, Raina Chrobak, Chris Zahn, and Chris Guzikowski at Addison-Wesley were the model of compassionate support during the trials of this process—my thanks to you and the rest of the crew there, with a special thanks to Carol Lallier, whose expert polish on this book was invaluable.

On a personal note, I thank my friends and family, who have been incredibly patient while I have put in seemingly endless hours on this, even though they were hoping to see more of me now that I've moved back to the Seattle area.

Finally, my wife Leah. You have supported me in so many large and small ways throughout our time together. You have given your time, your patience, and your love, and you have my immense love and gratitude. Thank you. Words are simply inadequate.

Thank you all. Every one of you contributed in some way to the refinement of these ideas and this text. This may have been my baby, but it had many midwives.

— Jason McC. Smith
Seattle
September 4, 2011

About the Author

Jason McC. Smith received his Ph.D. in computer science in 2005 from the University of North Carolina at Chapel Hill, where the Elemental Design Patterns were born as part of the System for Pattern Query and Recognition project. Dr. Smith has been awarded two U.S. patents for research performed at UNC-CH, one for technologies related to SPQR and one for the FaceTop distributed document collaboration system.

Prior to that, Dr. Smith spent many years in industry as a physics simulation engineer and consultant building off of dual B.Sc. degrees in physics and mathematics from the University of Washington. Projects of note included sonar and oceanic environment simulation, electronic engineering simulation, commercial and military aircraft flight simulation, and real-time graphical training systems.

Four years at IBM Watson Research provided Dr. Smith with an opportunity to apply the lessons of SPQR and the EDP catalog and compositional approach to immense bodies of software, both legacy and modern.

Dr. Smith is currently Senior Research Scientist at The Software Revolution, Inc., in Kirkland, Washington, where he continues to refine the EDP catalog and look for ways to enhance the company's goal of automated modernization and transformation of legacy systems.

Introduction to Design Patterns

1

Design patterns are one of the most successful advances in software engineering, by any measure. The history of design patterns is a strange one though, and somewhere along the way, much of their original utility and elegance has been forgotten, misplaced, or simply miscommunicated. This book can fill in some possible gaps for those who have experience with design patterns and can provide students new to the literature a better way of consuming it bite by bite. When it comes down to it, the design patterns literature as it stands is a collection of rather large nuggets of information of varying degrees of digestibility. This text is a foundation that provides a practitioner familiar with design patterns a methodology for placing those nuggets into a larger system of understanding and provides the student new to design patterns an approach for learning them from basic principles and in smaller pieces that make sense individually. The Elemental Design Patterns are truly elemental in that they form a foundation for design patterns as a discipline.

The collective wisdom of the software engineering community is one of our most valuable assets, and we still have much to learn from each other. This book and the research on which it is based are an attempt to bring to light some of what we have lost regarding design patterns. In the process, it helps fulfill the original intent of design patterns by establishing a better mechanism for shared discussions of patterns, giving us a richer understanding of the software we produce and consume. Our community has produced a breadth of design patterns, but what we lack is depth. That is, we have a broad understanding of wide areas but only a weak ability to stitch them together into a comprehensive whole. It reminds me of the historical transition from alchemy to modern chemistry—until the periodic table came along, the collective wisdom of many intelligent researchers was precise but not strongly correlated. Arguably, the biggest impact of Dmitri Mendeleev's original periodic table was not so much that it provided a way for chemists to identify patterns between the building blocks of matter but that it provided a way to use those patterns to predict properties of then-undiscovered elements. Gallium and germanium were the first examples of this, with Mendeleev accurately describing their chemical and physical properties well before their discovery. The periodic table advanced chemistry from descriptive discipline to predictive science.

The emergence of design patterns within the software engineering community began with the publication of the seminal *Design Patterns: Elements of Reusable Object-Oriented Software* in 1995. The Gang of Four (or GoF), Erich Gamma, Richard Helm, Ralph Johnson, and John Vlissides, gathered the various collected wisdoms that had been percolating in the research and academic communities following Gamma's 1991 PhD dissertation. That work drew heavily from Christopher Alexander's earlier work in the 1960s. Alexander was a civil engineer and architect, and his work focused on finding patterns of solutions to particular sets of forces within particular contexts. His primary insight was that there are two types of design that occur within architecture, what he named *unselfconscious* and *selfconscious*.

Unselfconscious design is most often seen in so-called primitive cultures: a house design is copied faithfully, every time, and apprenticeships are used to ensure fidelity and faithfulness to that particular design. This design changes rarely, and adherence to a given form is considered the goal, primarily because the particular design is the distillation of centuries or millennia of trial and error—it works, and if it ain't broke, don't fix it. While the problem of providing people with housing is universal, the various contexts in which that problem occurs, such as rain, desert, ice, swamp, and forest, give rise to an amazing array of styles and designs, but within a particular context, a single design may be considered "the only solution," and it is frequently incredibly effective given its specific environmental needs. The design, however, is applied without much, if any, individual discretion or decision making.

Selfconscious design is a more modern invention; the designer is free to make conscious decisions at almost every turn involving style, aesthetics, and materials. This architectural freedom can be seen in the wide array of modern architecture within a given locale, city, or neighborhood. Even on your own street, you are likely to see a plethora of styles and distinctive flourishes, each the result of many conscious decisions on the part of the architect. The modern designer has a wide palette of styles to choose from, and generally speaking, the only problem is balancing the owner's aesthetics and wallet. Sure, the houses meet the basic criteria of putting a roof over the occupants' heads, but that's a pretty low bar to set when there are so many other axes on which a design can be examined. When a designer is freed to do anything, it becomes even harder to pick the effective solutions out of the nearly infinite set of inappropriate or just plain bad ones. Building codes are one way we try to limit the bad choices in housing design, but even given those as a starting point, the task is daunting. Merely reading building codes and adhering to them is not going to produce an effective work of architecture. Building codes are generic, but good architecture takes into consideration the environment at every level of detail, from global latitude and regional weather patterns to local soil grades and site-specific terrain or foliage.

You can see the results of this selfconscious design in almost any town or city. One house may be Georgian, one pseudo-Victorian, another a modern glass and steel box, or perhaps a split-level, a ranch, or any other number of styles, kinds, and types of construction, materials, and architectures. We have to ask ourselves, however, whether these designs work as optimal, or even just effective, solutions for that particular environment, for that particular context. Austin, Texas, for example, may not be the best place to build an unshaded glass-faced edifice because the sun is so intense in the summer, creating an added expense from the large increase in cooling costs. Upstate New York may not be an appropriate place for a flat roof because the weight of many feet of snow in the dead of winter adds a significant load to the room beams. The environmental context, the set of forces that create the situation in which the general problem of designing appropriate housing must be solved, is frequently ignored, and the solutions are generally only minimally satisfying or give rise to new problems that must be addressed.

It should be apparent how this applies to software engineering: we are capable of doing nearly anything that pops into our heads, even more so than the architects of physical buildings. This is the amazing strength of programming—and its Achilles heel. We can do just about anything, and usually manage to do so, but unfortunately, the subset of good things out of the set of anything is quite small, and our projects are often late, over budget, and frequently fail in ways spectacular and quiet. Rarely do we walk away from projects with a feeling of accomplishment— more often, we feel we dodged a bullet. Again. Why is this? Why, when we have decades of collective experience, and quite possibly millions of tallied person-years in the field, are we still thrashing in the weeds every time we approach a problem? Some designers and developers seem to be phenomenally able to sidestep the complexity and find the kernel of effectiveness in a design. The rest of us seem to be perpetually stuck between the unselfconsciousness of "because I was told to" and the paralysis of selfconscious design.

Alexander's work was an attempt to alleviate this problem for architects of buildings, to bring to light the disparity between the effectiveness of the primitive cultures at design and the nearly spastic try-anything approach of modern architecture. Somewhere in between is a balance to be struck. We need to find the underlying principles and general solutions that exist in unselfconscious architecture and describe them in a way that makes them applicable in a wide variety of contexts selfconsciously and with deliberate intent. The wisdom of the various attempts at solutions, hard-earned through trial and error, need to be distilled into a body of concepts that can be learned by anyone, applied in numerous places, and used as a guide for thinking about design.

This is what design patterns are—the distillation of expertise by an exuberant and robust community. This is crowdsourcing at its best. The patterns community that has grown over the decade-plus since the original GoF work is large and energetic, and our output is voluminous. Grady Booch and Celso Gonzalez have been collecting every pattern they can find in industry and academia at their website [11]. So far, they have over 2,000 of them. The quantity of output in this community is huge, and although there are some discussions about the quality, the more pressing problem is one of scale.

Even with a fully indexed, well-curated collection of quality design patterns, there is simply too much information for a nonscholar to sift through accurately and quickly. Worse, it is incredibly difficult for a student wishing to learn the principles behind good design to do so solely from examples of good design. It is a bit like trying to learn the mathematics of aeronautical flow from inspecting aircraft on a runway. For experienced patterns practitioners who believe they have uncovered a new design pattern, there's no ready way to compare a new pattern against existing patterns to see how it relates to the established literature, and there's no way to create tooling to support this need.

What the software development community needs is a more thorough understanding of what it has at its disposal, a methodology that explains how to more precisely describe the existing design patterns and does so using components and well-defined principles that are accessible to the student or new developer. What we need is a guide to the underlying basic principles of our design patterns literature so that we can better comprehend, teach, and learn our identified best practices. This book is a foundation for that guide.

1.1 Tribal Musings

The efficiencies we gain from documenting and passing along known best practices are important, but the reason we must do so has been largely ignored in our community. To put it bluntly, we are mortal, and our young field is aging. Already we have lost a number of luminaries who established the groundwork for our industry, and many more will be gone soon. It is just a fact of life, one that we are poorly prepared to deal with as a discipline.

Worse still, software has a peculiar trait of living long past its expected lifetime. COBOL is still a force to be reckoned with in business systems around the globe. Fortran still performs much of the computation in the world's scientific modeling software. Currently shipping major high-performance computer systems have code embedded deep in their firmware that was first created three decades or more ago, in assembler or C. You can be almost certain that somewhere in the millions of lines of implementation that came with your latest personal computer acquisition lies a piece of source code that no person currently understands.

We know we should document our software; we know we should keep it up to date; we know we should commit to pen or screen the whys, the hows, and the reasons; but we also know it is a pain. It really is, so we don't do it. What we have instead is a body of knowledge that is locked within the heads of developers, that is passed along in fits and spurts, when prompted and only where necessary, frequently without any comprehensive framework of common understanding among stakeholders.

Grady Booch has popularized the phrase "tribal knowledge" for such information [10], and it fits all too well. It also has some rather unsettling corollaries.

Cultures that rely solely on oral tradition for the passing of knowledge are limited in both bandwidth and accuracy, and that's assuming they have a *strong* tradition of passing along the information. Cultures with a weak discipline for veracity and precision in information transfer leave themselves open to more rapid corruption. A strong oral tradition, however, can result in a very different outcome.

The development community has what is ultimately an oral tradition of information transfer. Although we may write down bits and pieces of what we understand, we frequently do not write down the entirety of our comprehension, and we do not keep such documentation in sync with the evolution of our systems. This document rot is pervasive, and only by asking around for further information can we hope to fill in the gaps to find out why a particular system is how it is.

This isn't always seen as a bad thing, to be honest. Agile software development methodologies prefer working code over documented code, and it's hard to argue with this viewpoint. Until it matters, of course. Agile systems have a funny way of becoming legacy systems, of growing into mature codebases with larger teams that must work in concert. Eventually, code that started as an agile effort, if it is successful, will face many of the same challenges as traditionally developed systems. Developers leave. Documentation rots. Knowledge is lost.

Software as it currently stands is not what anyone could accurately call self-documenting, and extracting the salient reasons why a thing was done in a particular way, directly from the source code, has been considered nearly impossible for an automated system. This is unfortunate, because we would like to have our cake and eat it too. We want up-to-date documentation when and where we need it, but we don't want to be burdened with it otherwise. We'd like our code to be much more self-documenting, or at least automatically documentable, but most of us don't have that luxury. So we punt and hope for the best. Meanwhile, our collective understanding of the system degrades. In the end, what we have is best described as a very weak oral tradition.

The result is that the collected tribal knowledge degrades into "tribal mythology." "Why?" is not a question that can be answered any longer, except to say, "Because we've always done it that way." I have a sneaking suspicion that if you have ever been the new hire on a development team, you're nodding in horror right now. You've had that discussion in real life, probably more times than you care to recall.

Tribal mythology is action without comprehension. It is rote without any foundation on which to state why. Other indications that tribal mythology is active in a group include the following: "Because that's how I was taught it." "I'm not really sure, but Joe says that's how its done." "Jane could have told you, but she retired last year, so just copy what's there." "Oh no, don't change that! It'll break and we won't be able to fix it." These comments exhibit a failure to comprehend the reasons behind an action, or at least an unwillingness or inability to pass the comprehension along to the listener. Over time, this lack of understanding breeds a great deal of uncertainty and fear of change. Unfortunately, it is at some level the status quo on most projects, which is ironic given that our industry is driven by innovation, change, and advancement of the state of the art.

Tribal wisdom, however, is the virtuous flip side of this tribal mythology. It is prescribed action *with* understanding, *how* accompanied by *why*, and is adaptable to new environments, new situations, and new problems. It transcends rote copying, and provides illumination through a comprehensive discussion of the reasons behind the action. At some point in the past, for almost every action or decision in a system, someone knew why it was done that way. Carrying those decisions forward, even the small ones, can be critical. Small decisions accrete into large systems, and small designs build into large designs. By ensuring that we have a strong tradition of knowledge retention that facilitates understanding, we build a tradition of tribal wisdom.

Tribal wisdom is what design patterns were intended to collect. Sadly, they are frequently (mis)treated as tribal mythology, by applying the *how* without a clear comprehension of the *why*.

If you haven't yet had the pleasure of running into this situation in your career, let me offer another example that may be illuminating. Recently my wife and I bought our first house, and with it, our first yard. The region we live in is renowned for its rain and consequently its moss. Now, I like moss. It's green, it takes about zero maintenance, and it makes a nice soft ground cover. It satisfies all the usual requirements for a yard, with less work than grass requires, but we had an odd situation. Part of the yard is heavily shaded and rarely, if ever, sees sun. This area is basically solid moss, with no grass or any other vegetation. Even shade-tolerant grasses can't get enough light to thrive.

Twenty feet on either side of the heavily shaded portion, however, sunlight is available on most days when the sun is actually out. Moss grows in patches through this section, but in my initial assessment, I thought it was fine. The moss and grass were coexisting nicely, and the moss wasn't choking out the grass, merely filling in the places where the grass wasn't quite so thick. In the sunniest areas, there was almost no moss but lots of grass. In the shadiest areas, there was solid moss but no grass. In the transitional regions, the two coexisted. What could be better?

Unfortunately, long-time residents who saw this situation were horrified. "You have to get rid of all the moss!" When I asked why, I was met with answers such as "Because it's not grass." "Because it's what you *do*." "Because it's bad for the lawn." No one could tell me, to my satisfaction, *why* I should get rid of the moss. It seemed to me that if I removed *all* of the moss, in all areas, regardless of the local micro-environment, I would have a bare spot where grass wouldn't grow in the shade. This was less than optimal.

To make matters worse, as is the case in many software projects, I had inherited a situation in which I had no idea what the previous residents had done for maintenance in the yard or why. There was no documentation to indicate what I should do for my lawn or why the yard had been left in this configuration. So I ran a couple of experiments. In the shadiest areas, I pulled up a small section of moss and seeded it with grass. In the rest of the yard, I let the moss go to see what would happen.

The grass seed in the shadiest area never thrived. Some sprouted, but it could never get established well. Applying the tribal mythology would have resulted in bare dirt in a good section of my yard, and frankly, I prefer the moss to that. It is green and lush, and it thrives in that area without maintenance. For that specific area, moss is a good ground cover solution.

In the rest of the yard with little or no shade, it turns out that moss and grass *do* play well together, more or less. The grass grows nicely, and the moss can't overcome it directly. Unfortunately, the moss has a side effect. In the sunniest areas, the moss acts as a protective layer for weeds to sprout underneath, safe from birds and mice who would eat the seeds or shoots, and properly moist. The moss won't choke out the grass, but the weeds definitely will. By letting the moss exist in the sunny areas, I was giving weeds a nursery to get established, and when they penetrated the moss, they thrived in the sunlight and spread rapidly. The moss also provided a protective moist layer for the roots of weeds to travel along, offering them an unhindered growth channel.

In the shadiest areas, this wasn't a problem, because there simply isn't enough sun for grass *or* weeds to grow well, but in the sunny areas, it was horrible. Within a couple of months, I was fighting a literal turf war with the weeds. The moss was never a problem by itself, but it set the scene for a much larger one.

And now I know the *why* behind removing moss from a lawn. It's not so much the moss that is the issue, it is that the moss creates a secondary microclimate that sets up a serious situation. Essentially, the moss creates a new set of forces at play that form a new *context*. Within that new context, that new environment, new problems arise—like weeds. Now the advice to remove the moss makes sense, at least for areas where weeds are an issue, such as the sunny areas of my yard.

Because I know the why, I can now alter my application of this knowledge according to the environmental forces. In the sunny areas, I must remove and prevent the moss so that weeds are not a later problem. In the shady areas, I choose not to because doing so would create another problem for me, leaving me with bare dirt where I'd struggle to get grass to grow well.

As it is, because I know the reasons behind the advice, I can custom fit the solution I was given—"Remove the moss"—based on the context—sunny vs. shady—and not only solve my initial problem but prevent new ones from being created. What was initially tribal mythology is now tribal wisdom that can be shared, adjusted, and applied when and where appropriate. In essence, it is the beginning of a pattern.

1.2 Art or Science?

There is no doubt that patterns are a thriving meme, and one with great utility. Entire academic conferences are now dedicated to patterns, Ackerman and Gonzalez's patterns-based engineering is becoming a defined discipline in its own right [2], and industry consultants are now expected to have them under their belt and be able to whip out Unified Modeling Language (UML) diagrams of them on the spot. Tools exist to produce, display, generate, and extract patterns. Patterns, as a collective whole, are an assumed component of the software engineering landscape. We're just not quite sure how they fit into that landscape or how they fit with each other. Two issues prevent a more comprehensive approach to patterns, and unfortunately they are ubiquitous in the industry. The first is treating patterns as frozen elements to be blindly copied, the second is confusing language-specific pattern implementations with variants of the patterns themselves.

1.2.1 Viewing Patterns as Rote

Ask a dozen developers to define design patterns, and you'll likely get a dozen answers. Among the more traditional "a solution to a recurring problem within a particular context" answers, you're also likely to hear phrases such as "a recipe" or "an example structure" or "some sample code," betraying a rather narrow view of what patterns provide. Patterns are intended to be mutated, to be warped and molded, to meet the needs of the particular forces at play in the context of the problem, but all too often, a developer simply copies and pastes the sample code from a patterns text or site and declares the result a successful application of the pattern. This is usually a recipe for failure instead of a recipe for producing a good design.

Pure rote copying of the structure of the pattern "because this authority says so" is a reversion to Alexander's concept of unselfconscious design. We undermine the entire purpose of design patterns when we do that. We need to be able to describe the whys behind a pattern as well as the hows. Without the understanding of the reasons that led to the description of that pattern, rote application often results in misapplication. At best, the result is a broken pattern that simply does not match the intended outcome. At worst, it injects an *iatrogenic* pattern into the system—one that is intended and thought to be of benefit but instead produces a malignant result that may take years to uncover. It doesn't just fail to provide the expected enhancement, it actively creates a new problem that may be worse than the original one. This is patterns as tribal mythology—action without understanding.

The traditional design pattern form, as defined in *Design Patterns* [21], explains the whys behind a pattern—motivations, applicability, and consequences—but it is up to the reader to tease out the underlying concepts that form a pattern. To some degree, these subconcepts are described in the Participants (what are the pieces) and Collaborations (how do they relate) sections for each patterns, but again, these are frequently treated by developers as checklists of pieces of the solution for rote implementation instead of as a description of the underlying concepts and abstractions that comprise a solution.

1.2.2 Language-Dependent Views

Ask a developer how important patterns are to his or her work, and frequently the answer will be based on the implementation language the developer is using. This isn't surprising. Different languages offer different strengths centered around the concepts they support and how they express them. How those concepts happen to be expressed is more often the start of flame wars between language fans, but ignoring the underlying concepts leads to much argument over nothing of particular consequence in most cases. Whether blocks are delineated by curly braces, as in the C family, or by whitespace, as with Python, isn't nearly as important as having the concept of blocks in the first place.

What this means is simply that some patterns are easier to implement in some languages than in others. In fact, some languages can make the concepts behind certain patterns so simple to implement that they're known as language features. The *Visitor* pattern is a good example.[1] *Visitor*'s Implementation section [21, pg. 338] says, "*Visitor* achieves [its goal] by using a technique called double-dispatch. It's a well-known technique. In fact, some programming languages support it directly (CLOS, for example)." What does this mean? It means that mentioning the *Visitor* design pattern to CLOS (Common LISP Object System) developers will leave them scratching their heads. "A pattern? For a language feature? Why?" In CLOS, *Visitor* is essentially built in. You don't need a pattern to tell you how to best express the concept—it's already there in the language as a basic feature. In most other languages, however, Visitor provides a clean way of expressing the same programming concept of double dispatch.

This illustrates an important point. If you mention double dispatch instead of the *Visitor* pattern to the same CLOS developers, they would know what you mean, how to use double dispatch, and when not to use it. Terminology, particularly shared common terminology, matters a great deal.

---

1. You don't need to know what the *Visitor* pattern is right now. I selected it only because the discussion of *Visitor* explicitly addresses the point I'm making.

This is true for all languages and all patterns: some languages make certain patterns easier or trivial to implement and other patterns more difficult to realize. No language can really be considered superior to another in this case, however. One common myth is that design patterns make up for flaws in programming languages, but that isn't the case. Design patterns describe useful concepts, regardless of the language used to implement them. Whether a specific concept is baked into the feature set of a language or must be implemented from scratch is irrelevant. The concept is still being expressed in the implementation, and that is the critical observation that lets us talk about software design independently of software implementation. Design is concepts; how those concepts are made concrete in a given language is implementation.

When you get down to it, there's no reason you couldn't implement every pattern in the GoF text in plain C—but it would be extremely tedious. You'd have to build up best practices for binding data and functions into meaningful semantic units, encapsulating that data, ensuring that data is ready to use at first accessibility, and so on. This sounds like a lot of work, but these were concepts considered *so* important that they launched a revolution in language features to make them easier to work with. That revolution was object-oriented programming.

In object-oriented languages, those concepts are included as primary language features called classes, visibility, and constructors. Again, we can refer to the GoF: "If we assumed procedural languages, we might have included design patterns called 'Inheritance,' 'Encapsulation,' and 'Polymorphism.'" The authors felt that this statement was important enough that it appears in Section 1.1 in the Introduction. And yet again, this is a fundamental point that seems lost on most developers, so let me restate it.

Patterns are language-independent concepts; they take form and become concrete solutions only when you implement them within a particular language with a given set of language features and constructs.

This means that it is a bit strange to talk about "Java design patterns," "C++ design patterns," "WebSphere design patterns," and so on, even though we all do it. It's a mildly lazy form of shorthand for what we really mean, or should mean: design patterns as implemented in Java, C++, WebSphere, and so on, regardless of language or API.[2]

Unfortunately, if you're like many developers who have encountered one of the multitude of books on design patterns, you may have been trained, or at least have been erroneously led to believe, that there is some ephemeral yet fundamental

---

2. Some design patterns are unique to specific languages, and only those languages, but those patterns are often called *language idioms*. In this text when we use the term *design patterns*, we are specifically talking about concepts that are language independent.

difference between patterns as expressed in Java and those expressed in another language such as Smalltalk. There really isn't. The concepts are the same; only the manner in which they are expressed and the ease with which a programmer can implement them in that specific language differ.

We need to focus on these when investigating design patterns, and these abstractions must be the crux of understanding patterns. Unless we make the effort to look at patterns as language-independent concepts, we are merely learning rote recipes again and losing much of what makes them so useful.

1.2.3 From Myth to Science

The issues described previously belie an underlying problem with design patterns as they are often conveyed, used, and understood today. All too often, we still don't know why we do what we do, even when we use design patterns in our code. By using design patterns so inflexibly, we've simply better documented a body of unselfconscious snippets without the comprehension that comes from a methodical analysis of the snippets.

We have an art. What we need is a science. After all, we throw around the terms *computer science and software engineering* with abandon. Treating patterns as sample code misses the point of design patterns. Design patterns enable us as an industry to experiment with those concepts and share, discuss, and refine our findings.

Patterns as rote recipes are tribal mythology.

Patterns as concepts are the foundations of a science.

Elemental Design Patterns are the building blocks of that science.

Elemental Design Patterns

T he Elemental Design Patterns, or EDPs, are, at their core, a catalog of the basic concepts of object-oriented programming. Two traits make them unique: First, they are written in the style of the design patterns literature. Each is treated as a standalone concept with a specific name by which it can be discussed and mulled over until it is understood. This book presents each EDP along with a problem that it is suited for and discusses when the pattern should and should not be applied. You will find example implementations, comments on possible consequences of using the patterns, and related patterns that you should look at as well. This human-oriented definition of each EDP provides you with a common term you can use to clearly and precisely converse with other students or developers about the concept.

Second, design patterns are descriptions of solutions to common problems that were found through the examination of existing software systems. EDPs are also solutions to common problems, and once you know what to look for, you will find them *everywhere*. They are in fact so common that, until now, they have not been considered worth writing up in any comprehensive way. EDPs were originally identified as a comprehensive body of interrelated design concepts not in software but in a formal description of software. EDPs arise from the mathematical foundations of object-oriented languages, but rest assured, with the exception of an appendix safely tucked in the back, this text is mathematics free. (I do hope you get curious and read the appendix, though—it's rather interesting.) The solid yet simple ideas underlying the EDPs provide a strong framework on which to revisit these basic concepts, give them new life, and repurpose them for new applications. This foundation also gives you a compelling ability to use them as tiny building blocks, almost like atoms, to describe other design patterns in solid and direct ways. And, like atoms, you can build worlds with them.

This book gives you some background on EDPs, where they came from originally, and how they fit into the larger context of design patterns in programming. It also gives you just enough of a taste of object-oriented theory to understand how the patterns all relate to one another, but no equations, I promise. We discuss some of the ideas underlying the basics of object-oriented programming, much of which you may already be familiar with. Finally, you learn how that basic theory gives rise to a veritable stable of concepts that you can use in your everyday programming. Later chapters explain how you can use EDPs to make your designs better.

2.1 Background

The identification of EDPs had its beginnings in the System for Pattern Query and Recognition (SPQR) project at the University of North Carolina at Chapel Hill [35]. SPQR is a research project for identifying instances of known design patterns within an existing body of source code. It can find design patterns independent of the original source code language and can easily find various implementations of the same design pattern from a single pattern definition. If you're interested in the inner workings of SPQR, further information is available [35, 37, 38], but a basic understanding provides enough context for our discussion of what EDPs are and how they are defined.

I was inspired to create SPQR while working as a professional software engineer. I was on a team responsible for one of three libraries used in a real-time commercial and military flight simulation system. In one of our joint all-library development meetings with the application team, they thanked us profusely for a feature we had just added, stating that it was exactly what they needed. We said they were quite welcome, that's what we were there for, and so on.

After the meeting, the three library teams looked at each other and asked if the others knew what the application team had been talking about. None of us had *designed* the feature they were describing, we weren't even sure how it had come about, or that it was possible. We decided to get to the bottom of it, thinking that certainly it couldn't take much time.

Nearly 200 developer hours later, we had our answer. We had an instance of a *Decorator* pattern, one of the Gang of Four (GoF) patterns, embedded and hidden within the system. What was unique was that it didn't live in any *one* library. Pieces of it were scattered across the three libraries, and the application team had stumbled onto their integration as a whole. We were stunned. A rather heated debate ensued: Was this really a design pattern? After all, it hadn't been *designed*, it had just sort of *grown*.

Well, most software does just that. It grows organically, and often in unexpected ways. In managing software projects, we can only manage what we know, and knowing that there was this useful design element provided us an opportunity to enhance, streamline, and document its existence for developers to use effectively. Finding it—that was the problem. Remember, we had written the software in question, we were the experts, and it still took us an inordinate amount of time to deduce what was going on. Automation of the process was the obvious answer. As I mentioned in Chapter 1, what we really want is self-documenting code, or at least a system to extract that documentation. SPQR is such a system.

Creating SPQR necessitated solving a fundamental problem: I had to teach the computer how to identify design patterns. Patterns are not rote recipes; they are soft and amorphous things we humans call concepts. Most research and industry systems that attempt to find instances of patterns in source code do so by looking at patterns as constructs—as rigid forms that look like implementations—rather than as abstract concepts. This is a reasonable approach, and it treats patterns as many developers do: "This class has that field, and that subclass accesses it through a method named X," and so on. The thing is, this approach once more reduces the design patterns to specific implementations. Every variation of a possible implementation requires a new definition. It's the cut-and-paste methodology again [25, 30]. I don't mean that this work is of low quality—far from it. These tools are stellar examples of the approach and are worth your investigation. They do their job well, and they add value if you happen to meet their requirements.

The problem with this approach is that defining a pattern for queries as a construct is highly fragile. What if the particular method you define wasn't named X, but Y? What if the subclass wasn't a direct subclass, but there was another class between the two in the inheritance hierarchy? Or what if the subclass wasn't a true inherited subclass at all but used the superclass as a delegate object instead? None of these conditions would be found by a construct-oriented approach to design patterns, and they would require new pattern definitions. And that's assuming you're still working within one implementation language. Remember, patterns are implementation-language independent—the scope of the issue is much larger.

It seemed obvious that a different tactic was needed with SPQR. Diving into the background and history of design patterns yielded the necessary clue. The more I studied the GoF material and worked back through the inspirations that spawned it, the more I focussed on Alexander's original work. As I read his first and, at least within the software engineering community, least-cited treatise on design patterns, *Notes on the Synthesis of Form* [4], I realized something important had been lost: patterns are concepts, not constructs.

This simple truth fundamentally alters what I was trying to teach the computer to recognize. Teaching a computer system to look for language constructs bolted together in rigid structures will never give us the flexibility we desire with the accuracy we need. Instead, we should be teaching a system to look for programming concepts because that's what patterns really are.

Unfortunately for this particular task, the established design patterns literature is primarily geared toward describing high-level, abstract concepts, which is part of what makes them so powerful—they lift the discussion of a design to a higher level of abstraction. Programmers generally have a good working handle on lower-level abstractions, so establishing them as patterns has never seemed necessary. The design patterns community is rightly focused on documenting those lessons that are not already ingrained and well understood. These design patterns described by the software community tend to be at the larger end of the spectrum. Computers, on the other hand, are fundamentally only as knowledgable as the foundation we can teach them. For SPQR, we had to establish a chain of concepts from the ground up so it could help us deal with the concepts of programming. We had to fill in the gap between the highly rigid pieces of an implementation and the sometimes fluid concepts that they represent.

In doing so, it became apparent that the EDPs were just that—design patterns that form a fundamental basis from which to describe software design not just for automated analysis but for humans as well. This book is a partial catalog of the EDPs written for human, not machine, consumption. It is intended to be used by developers, students, and designers to help fill in the gaps in our understanding and our language when discussing software design. As expected with design patterns, each EDP has an informal write-up, or *pattern specification*, to use an accepted term, and also has an origin as a mathematical construct. This latter trait makes the EDP catalog unique. Each EDP is an abstraction of programming that lets us talk about even very small issues of software design independent of precisely how they are implemented.

This brings us to two ways of describing EDPs: their basis in theory and their genesis in pragmatism. The following section intertwines the two while keeping the formalisms to a minimum. You don't need to precisely understand the formal foundation at a mathematical level to continue in this book, but you may find it illuminating if you wish to move in that direction. If you find yourself wondering about the underlying mechanics and want a stronger understanding of how design patterns and programming language theory intersect, you can start in the appendix, which describes the ρ-calculus that forms the foundation of this body of work.

2.2 The Where, the Why, the How

Teaching a computer to look for the large-scale abstractions and concepts called design patterns, as they exist in the common literature, is a difficult task. What do we do when faced with a large and gnarly task in computer science? We break it down.

Deconstructing the design patterns literature is not a simple thing. A few attempts have been made over the years [12, 17, 32, 40, 41, 43], but they have been partial deconstructions, seen as oddities or curiosities by most developers and researchers outside the immediate field. After all, these smaller deconstructed pieces and concepts are *obvious*, right? They are basic concepts, basic things we deal with every day, so why bother describing what we already feel we know?

Well, if they're so obvious, how come they're not already documented?

The basic concepts of software design are as "obvious" as the "correct" way to build a domicile: it depends entirely on your context, your experience, and what you were taught. Someone who was trained in functional programming in ML understands recursion very differently from someone whose primary background is C. The two developers will have different assumptions about recursion, where it is useful, and how it should be applied, even though the basic underlying problem that it is solving is the same. Given the discussion of housing styles in Chapter 1, this idea should start to sound familiar.

I said earlier in this chapter that the lower-level concepts of programming have not been a primary target of the design patterns community because the literature is aimed at documenting concepts that are neither ingrained nor well understood. Simple concepts are seen as ingrained and therefore outside of that scope, but that doesn't mean they're actually well understood.

The low-level concepts we use in programming are unselfconscious, as Alexander defined it. We learn them more or less by rote in class and in the field, and we apply them because "that's the way it works," without having to make conscious decisions to do so. Most of us never study the principles underlying those concepts, but they exist and are well understood at a mathematical level.

Those concepts just haven't been properly exposed at a *human* level, and that's what EDPs are. In a nutshell, EDPs are the underlying core concepts of programming and software design that have remained mostly undescribed. Those that have been described have not been related to one another in a meaningful and well-founded manner until now. Each EDP is a selfconscious description of a core concept. The EDP catalog as a whole relates the EDPs to one another to form a conceptual framework that the student or developer can use to understand other patterns. It provides a taxonomy and lexicon for describing higher-level abstractions, homogenizing the language and abstractions such that when any two developers reference, for example, the EDP *Extend Method*, they both have a precise understanding of a common definition.

EDPs provide a language with which to reason about, describe, and discuss software, from the most fundamental levels on up. Mainstream design patterns have done an amazing job of providing this knowledge base for the seasoned pro, but until now, no one has aimed that same tool at the novice or student in a comprehensive way.

So how far can we deconstruct these concepts from the design patterns literature? As an example, let's look at *Decorator*.

2.2.1 Decomposition of *Decorator*

A quick note on naming conventions before we go any further: pattern names in this text are italicized and capitalized—for example, *Extend Method*. Types and classes in examples are capitalized and set in monotype font. Fields and methods are set in intercaps, or "camelcase" and in monotype font, as in `thisIsAMethod()`. Code examples use the same system.

The canonical example Unified Modeling Language (UML) for *Decorator*, as provided in the GoF's *Design Patterns* [21], is shown in Figure 2.1. For now, you don't need to understand what *Decorator* is; a visual inspection of the UML diagrams should suffice. In general, *Decorator* is a popular and commonly used design pattern that provides a mechanism for behavior to be extended dynamically at runtime. You can think of it as an internal plug-in or extension system, like you would find in a web browser.

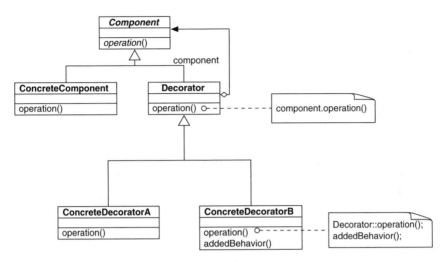

Figure 2.1 *Decorator*'s usual example UML.

Suppose you want to decompose *Decorator* to better understand it. It is, after all, a rather high-level abstraction. If you can absorb smaller pieces individually, you can almost certainly have an easier time understanding the pattern. Better still, you should be able to use those smaller pieces to help you understand other design patterns you may encounter, as long as they're described in similar terms.

It's not unlike trying to understand how a complex piece of machinery such as a race car works. You can buy one, put it in your garage, break out the tools, and disassemble the whole car, or you can learn about the pieces individually. You can study the internal combustion engine, for instance, or the hydraulic braking system. Those systems can be further broken down into parts that you can investigate one by one to make the larger study task easier.

In the end, if you know how a gasoline engine works, you not only have the facility to comprehend that portion of the race car as a unit, as an encapsulated abstraction, but you can apply that knowledge to other vehicles, or even lawnmowers, generators, and any other gasoline-engine-driven machine. Decomposing design patterns serves a similar purpose: identifying the smaller pieces that you can treat on their own merits, learn thoroughly in more digestible chunks, and apply in novel situations.

After an exhaustive search of the existing literature on design patterns (and remember, there are thousands), you might notice that *Decorator* shares similarities with two other patterns.

One is *Objectifier*, first described by Walter Zimmer in 1995 [43], shown in Figure 2.2. *Objectifier* describes a way for a single *object interface* to represent multiple

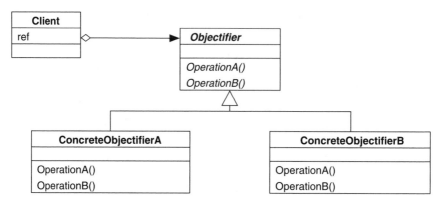

Figure 2.2 *Objectifier* as UML.

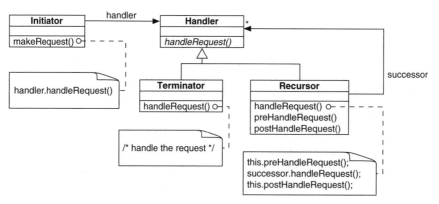

Figure 2.3 *Object Recursion* as UML.

concrete implementations in a way that is opaque to a client. When a client requests
a method to be invoked through the *Objectifier* interface, it does not know which
of the two (or more) concrete method bodies is executed.

The other is *Object Recursion*, outlined by Bobby Woolf in 1998 [41], shown
in Figure 2.3. *Object Recursion* chains together two objects with related types.

Looking at the UML diagrams in Figures 2.2 and 2.3, you can see that *Objectifier and Object Recursion* look quite a bit like pieces of the *Decorator* pattern.
Although they are not exactly the same, certain features in their structure of the
UML are similar enough that we can describe parts of *Decorator* in terms of these
other patterns—we can say that *Decorator* is composed of these patterns.

A closer look shows that *Objectifier* can be considered a part of *Object Recursion*. *Object Recursion* uses *Objectifier* as the backbone of its form, but it adds a
link between one of the concrete implementations and the interface, and it does

so for the same method. In other words, when the `Initiator` class calls `han-dleRequest()`, by the intent of *Objectifier*, either the `Terminator` or `Recur-sor` class might handle it. If `Terminator` handles it, the request is complete. If `Recursor` handles it, an additional call is made through the interface for another `handleRequest()`, and the process starts over again. This chain continues until `Terminator` is the handler, at which point the chain, unsurprisingly, terminates.

Given this series of actions, we can say, "A *Decorator* uses *Object Recursion* to traverse a chain of objects, presumably at least two in length, and perform the same method call on each." That seems rather vague, though, and it also misses a lot of the detail in *Decorator*. We should have a better decomposition to work with, but at least we know that patterns *can* be described in terms of smaller patterns.

2.2.2 Down the Rabbit Hole

We've established that we can build *Decorator* from some smaller pieces, but are these pieces as small as they can be? What is the smallest deconstructed pattern we can make that is still a pattern?

To answer that question, we need to ask again, What is a pattern? We know it is a concept, we know it is an element of design, and we know has certain critical components. Let's set aside the question of what a concept is and address the other two portions. Design is the manner in which parts of a whole interact with and relate to one another, as illustrated in the outline of a design pattern written in the accepted canonical format popularly described in the GoF text. GoF's outline shows that participants and collaborations are core pieces of a design, and that they highlight both the parts of the design and how they interact with and relate to each other.

Consider a common definition of *design pattern:* "A common solution to a common problem within a particular context." Most of the pieces of a canonical format design pattern specification can easily be placed into those three categories: solution (or implementation), problem (or description), and context (or environment), as in Table 2.1. The structure, implementation, and sample code are unmistakably the solution. The intent, motivation, and known uses describe the problem space. The context, the environment in which the problem occurs, guides applicability, frames the discussion of possible consequences, and often indicates if the current pattern isn't exactly right and which of the related patterns is a better choice.

After sorting these elements we have two parts left that don't easily fit into one of those three categories: participants and collaborations. They're obviously part solution in that together they form much of the solution. But they're also part

Table 2.1 Pattern pieces sorted into three categories of a pattern definition

Solution	Structure
	Implementation
	Sample code
Problem	Intent
	Motivation
	Known uses
Context	Applicability
	Consequences
	Related patterns

problem description because they almost always directly reflect how the problem is phrased. Finally, they're part context in that they are created in response to the needs of the environment in which they are placed. They describe the parts and their relationships that lie at the intersection of the three arms of a design pattern.

Relationships form the core of design. The design of a car is more than a pile of pieces: it is also a blueprint for how they fit together. A house is more than a stack of lumber, a case of nails, and some copper piping; it has a form, or plan, that fights entropy and, we could say, keeps the structure at a higher energy level than just a rubble pile. The parts list ensures that you have everything you need to begin building, but the relationships in the design tell you how to make them work in concert.

Let's flip the question around a bit: What is the smallest relationship we can define? Well, that one is easy. A single relationship between two things is simplest. Now we can apply this insight to the deconstruction of design patterns.

This gives us a clear goal. With each subsequent smaller design pattern, we can look at it with a critical eye and ask, "Does this embody more than one relationship?" If not, then we've definitely reached our goal. If so, it's still possible that we've done so.

Why would we already "possibly" be done if there is more than one relationship involved? Well, not all relationships are created equal. Some are quite important when discussing design, and some are there to provide a context. The primary contextual relationship is that of *scoping*, and it appears in many forms.

Whenever you declare a variable, define a method, or describe a class, whatever that new item "lives" in is called its *scope*. The scope is how that element is made unique from all others in the system. If you have two classes, each named Menu, but one is defined in a package named GraphicalUIElements and the other is defined in a package named `RestaurantNecessities`, you can be pretty sure that they're not the same thing. Their scope indicates that they are distinct classes, never to be confused. This principle applies any time there is an enclosing *something* that has a name and within which you define something new.

Classes are scopes for the methods and fields they define. Namespaces and packages are scopes for anything inside of them. Methods and functions are scopes for the local variables declared within them. Over and over again we see the same mechanism at work in many different language features. To access a specific element, we state precisely which one we want by providing the scopes from the top down. Unfortunately, it isn't always this simple. Sometimes these scopes are implicit, and we can leave them off, such as when referring to a local variable within a method or to another member within a class. Furthermore, despite their common behavior, these scopes can have different syntaxes through which they are accessed. For instance, in C++, to access the `Menu` class within the `GraphicalUIElements` namespace, we would state it as `GraphicalUIElements::Menu`, using a double colon. Given an instance of that class, however, we would access its list of menu items as `aMenu.theItems`, using a dot operator. Both of these techniques specify which element we wish to select from a scoping element, but they do so in different ways. This text defines a single way in which we can treat *all* scoping, regardless of how it is implemented for specific language features within specific languages.

Consider class A that has a method f, and class B that has a method g, as shown in UML in Figure 2.4 and in code in Listing 2.1. A has a field b of type B. In the `main()` body, an instance a of type A is instantiated, and then `a.f()` is invoked. The method `f()` is scoped by the object a. In object-oriented languages, functions and methods are always enclosed by some scope, even if the scope is implicit.

Even in C++ global functions and fields can be considered as though they reside inside an invisible and implicit object representing a global namespace, which is how the runtime effectively treats them. Check Clause 3.3.6 [basic.scope.namespace], paragraph 3, of the 2011 C++ ISO Standard Working Draft [6] for confirmation. Further, the use of file-scoped elements in C++, those declared global and static, is now discouraged by the conventional wisdom in favor

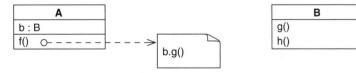

Figure 2.4 A simple method call as UML.

Listing 2.1 A simple method call as pseudocode.

```
 1  class A {
        B b;
 3      f() {
            b.g();
 5      };
    };
 7
    class B {
 9      g() {};
        h() {};
11  };

13  main() {
        A a;
15      a.f();
    };
```

of *unnamed namespaces*, which perform the same function more explicitly. In other words, each translation unit gets its own object for scoping, and the fact that the scope has no name means it can't be used outside that translation unit. Again, objects are being used to scope and wrap elements that have previously been considered as freely roaming.

Getting back to the code example, a.f() in turn calls b.g(), and a relationship exits between those two methods. The relationship between a and f, one of enclosure or scoping, is contextual. It helps specify which method we are talking about. A similar relationship exists between b and g. The call from a.f() to b.g(), however, is not just contextual, it is the *primary* relationship between those two methods. In other words, this is the relationship we're interested in, but we have to use scoping to get there.

Scoping relationships help us refine our view to a particular design element. We need exactly two such design elements to form the single relationship described in an EDP. There may be a number of scoping relationships that set up the final single relationship we are interested in, but we are not immediately concerned with them. They are part of the description of the elements of programming that comprise the endpoints of the relationship we wish to work with. Returning to our earlier metaphor of housing styles and design, the scoping elements are a bit like stating that a piece of wood is a two-by-four or a half-inch-thick sheet of bias-grain plywood. That information doesn't tell us how to orient one to the other or where to drive the nails. Scoping provides a context to help define *what* an element is, but it doesn't do much to explain how that element relates to others in the system.

We can now tweak our question of whether we've reached our decomposition goal to, Does this embody more than one relationship of interest?, which gets us closer to our goal. Now we just have to determine what a relationship of interest is. So far, we've described scoping relationships, which include class ownership of methods and fields, as well as namespaces, packages, and all the other grouping techniques available in programming, and we stated that we're not interested in them at the moment. Let's consider instead what remains that we could form relationships between.

What remains are classes, their fields and methods, and little else. One item seems to be missing from the list: objects. It *is* object-oriented programming, after all! We'll add objects to the list for completeness, and later we'll show how they're central to this approach. (For a formal explanation, see the appendix.) For now, we have these four kinds of programmatic entities on our list: objects, methods, fields, and classes, or types. This may seem like an odd thing to do, but it actually makes solid sense.

We don't call them classes, because not every object-oriented language has classes, but every object-oriented language has types. Remember that we're looking to describe design patterns in a way that can cross language borders, so we're going to be looking for features that are common to, and a requirement for, each and every object-oriented language. So how do we make the transition from classes, which most people are familiar with, to a more classically "pure" object-oriented approach? It's not that complex, really: it simply involves splitting a class into its constituent parts.

A class is an interesting beast in that it is so common in most object-oriented languages that many students and developers consider it a primary and necessary element. The reality, from a strictly object-oriented viewpoint, is that it is not. Some languages, such as Self and Lua, don't even have the concept of a class. Instead, they rely on prototyping, cloning, and other actions on objects to perform the same functions. It's not just esoteric languages that exhibit this use of objects in places where most languages use classes, as a variety of this usage can be seen in JavaScript. Even Smalltalk, arguably the progenitor of most object-oriented languages, has a quite different implementation and understanding of a class even though the same term is used.

In general, a class in current common object-oriented languages such as C++ and Java performs two duties. First, it describes the elements that will be in instantiated objects of that class, the *member* methods and fields. Most of us expect a class to be used in this way. Second, it describes elements that are common across all instantiated objects of that class, the *class* methods and fields. This is what happens when, in C++ or Java, we declare a method or field to be `static`. The first use case corresponds directly to a type in the formal sense, and the second use case can

Listing 2.2 Fields within classes, instances, and namespaces, as defined and used in C++.

```
   namespace MyNamespace {
2      int aField;
   };

4
   class MyClass {
6  public:
       static int sharedField;
8      int instanceField;
   };

10
   main() {
12     MyClass mc;
       mc.instanceField = 0;
14     MyClass::sharedField = 1;
       MyNamespace::aField = 2;
16 };
```

be re-created using a special-purpose object. Consider a field declared static in a class in C++ and how it is accessed, as in Listing 2.2.

Notice that in `main` the use of the class field `sharedField` is prefaced by the class name `MyClass`. This is exactly the same notation used to access `aField` in the defined `myNamespace`. We can think of the entity that holds the class-shared elements of a class as a "live" object, and we can think of a namespace in the same way. We provide the name of the object and the piece we want selected out of it, just like any object that was instantiated from a class in the normal way. When the language provides a namespace, a package, or a class, it is providing a way of instantiating these objects automatically.

Still not convinced? In Smalltalk, the class is represented by an object. Literally, it is named the *class object*. To instantiate an object of that class, we send the class object a message—the Smalltalk equivalent for "call a method of the object"—to return an instance of that class. Class methods and fields live in that class object. It is almost exactly the scenario we are describing here.

Or, look at Java. In Java the class object is a special object that is available for inspection through reflection and is associated with a class that a developer defines. Unlike in Smalltalk, it is not directly accessed by the developer in "normal" use but is usually reserved for more complex reflection actions. The same basic principle applies as in Smalltalk, except that the new `MyClass` construct borrowed from C++ hides the process under a bit of syntactic sugar.

Listing 2.3 shows a Java snippet in the top half and one possible decomposition of the class in the bottom half. If you think of the usual new `MyClass` as being a synonym for `MyClass_Object.new()` in this case, and then access to the static members being done through the `MyClass_Object` instead, as in

Listing 2.3 A Java class, and one possible equivalent object and type.

```
   class MyClass {
 2 public:
       static int sharedData;
 4     int instanceData;
       static void sharedMethod() { ... };
 6     void instanceMethod() { ... };
   };
 8


10
   MyClass:
12     int instanceData;
       void instanceMethod();

14
   MyClass_Object:
16     int sharedData;
       void sharedMethod();
18     MyClass new();
```

`MyClass_Object.sharedData` or `MyClass_Object.sharedMethod()`, then it's not that different than what you may be used to in Java already. Similar mechanisms are available for C++, where no reflection option exists.

Although the details of how it is handled will differ from language to language, in every case a class can be emulated using a type and an object. While this may sound a bit foreign to you at first, it quickly becomes second nature in practice. Just remember that a class with no static members (using the C++ and Java terminology) is just a type. Any defined class members would be moved into a corresponding class object, as in Smalltalk, or into the reflection-accessed Java class object.

We needed types in order to satisfy basic properties of typed languages, and objects are the core of object-oriented languages regardless of their class features. By using these two in conjunction, we can emulate classes from class-based object-oriented languages. This allows us to simplify our set of items needed to define design patterns to just our four previously mentioned items: objects, methods, fields, and types.

In what ways can the items on this short list interact? Table 2.2 is a complete list of possible ways in which the entities in the left column can interact with the entities on the top row. Objects and types can contain, and therefore define, any of the four elements, but we're going to eliminate those "contains" relationships from consideration under the scoping mechanism. Methods can, in some languages, similarly define, or scope, inner methods or types, and of course we can define local variables or fields. Methods can also call other methods, use nonlocal fields, and have a return type. Fields are simpler in that they can be assigned the return value of a method or of another field. And, of course, they have a type. Finally, types can

Table 2.2 All interactions between entities of object-oriented programming

	Object	Method	Field	Type
Object	Defines	Defines	Defines	Defines *or* is of type
Method	N/A	Defines *or* method call	Defines *or* field use	Defines *or* returns of type
Field	N/A	State change	Cohesion	Is of type
Type	Defines	Defines	Defines	Defines *or* subtyping

Table 2.3 Nonscoping interactions between entities of object-oriented programming

	Object	Method	Field	Type
Object				Is of type
Method		Method call	Field use	Returns of type
Field		State change	Cohesion	Is of type
Type				Subtyping

define through scope any of the four entity kinds, and types can rely on other types through subtyping.

Not that many interactions are possible now, which means that we can start enumerating them into a finite and, better yet, quite small set of possibilities. Table 2.3 shows the interactions that don't include defining another entity.

A field has a type on which it relies; this is simply the type of the field. The same holds for objects. Similarly, methods have return types. They are used to define what a piece of data *is*, whether it is a field or another object such as a parameter or a return value from a method. Much like scoping, defining data has the feel of describing the object or field itself, not providing a relationship between two entities.

For instance, look at the code snippet in Listing 2.4. The data member `pos` is defined as being an instance of the type `Position`. This tells us what `pos` *is*, and its scoping within `Glyph` tells us some of how to interpret it, but it doesn't tell us how `pos` interacts with other elements in the system. Similarly, the types of the parameters to the `scaleCopy` method only tell us what those parameters are, not how they relate to anything else.

On the other hand, other relationships, such as a type relying on another type, provide more information than just a description of one element. Type reliance on

Listing 2.4 Typing as context.

```
   class Glyph {
2      Position pos;
       Glyph scaleCopy( float x, float y );
4  }
```

other types, which is most often seen as inheritance, is rather well documented. We might even say it is ingrained and understood.

For the purpose of defining the EDPs, there are only the four basic relationships left in the center of Table 2.3, where either a method or a field relies on another method or field for its value, to get its job done, and so on. Those relationships are a method call (method relies on method), a field use by a method (method relies on a field), a field being set by a method (field relies on method for a state change), and a field relying on another field, such as a = b + 1. As shown in the preceding tables, we can call these a method call, a field use, a state change, and cohesion. Believe it or not, nearly this entire book concentrates on just the first one, a method call reliance. Yes, there is a lot to be said about a simple method call reliance when looked at in the right light.

It has probably occurred to you that a method call looks an awful lot like a structural entity, not a conceptual one. This is true, and that's why I started sneaking in the word *reliance* earlier. A reliance by one element on another doesn't require a direct connection. Consider a method f that calls method g in its body. We say that f relies on g. Now assume that g in turn calls another method h, as in Listing 2.5. We say that g relies on h. It should be self-evident that this relationship is transitive—if f relies on g, and g relies on h, then f also relies on h. It's not a direct reliance, but that doesn't really matter: f still relies on h to complete its work so that f can do its work.

Let's turn this around a bit. If we want f to rely on h, does it matter if it is a direct method call or if method g is in the middle? It does not. As long as f relies on h by some path, our requirement holds true. We just made the leap from a structural connection, that of a method call, to a conceptual connection, that of a method call *reliance*. This frees us from having to discuss low-level programming concepts of design in a structural manner and enables us to describe them in the conceptual way outlined earlier as necessary for working with and finding design pattern instances with SPQR. We discuss this in more detail and show how it forms a critical portion of working with EDPs in Chapter 4, Section 4.1.1.

In the process of teaching SPQR about programming concepts, we made the transition away from rigid structures of programming and instead gained a

Listing 2.5 A method call chain as pseudocode.

```
   function f() {
2      g();
   };

4
   function g() {
6      h();
   };

8
   function h() {};
10
   function main {
12     f();
   };
```

flexible and forgiving way to describe the relationships that form software design. By using these same techniques ourselves, we provide developers and designers with the same flexible thinking and ability to abstract design from implementation in a methodical yet understandable manner. We get double duty out of the same approach.

So let's recap. We have reduced our list of interesting elements of programming to just four: objects, methods, fields, and types (which, depending on your implementation language, you may think of as classes). Other programmatic entities, such as namespaces, packages, and so on, help us describe which element we're looking at, but they don't create the kind of relationships we're focused on when inspecting nontrivial design. Of those four elements, there are really four relationships, or reliances, that we're most concerned with: method–method, method–field, field–method, and field–field. We concentrate almost exclusively on the method–method reliance in this book.

Can this one reliance, based solely on method calls, really do anything useful to help us describe the larger design pattern literature? Given the right context, anything is possible.

2.2.3 Context

The previous section was all about finding the right relationships for our discussion. We focused on primary reliances such as those between methods and fields, bypassing other kinds of relationships, such as type–type reliances or inheritance. Now it's time to bring these contextual relationships back into the discussion.

For a given method call reliance, there are three other pieces of information we can work with to help us figure out what the purpose of that reliance is in a particular design. These are obvious if you look at a method call, as shown in

o	.	*f()*	calls	*p*	.	*g()*
enclosing object		calling method		enclosing object		called method

Figure 2.5 The parts of a method call.

Listing 2.6 Simple method call for Figure 2.5.

```
1  class Class2 {
       void g() {};
3  };

5  class Class1 {
       void f() {
7          Class2 p;
           p.g();
9      }
   };
11
   void main() {
13     Class1 o;
       o.f();
15 };
```

Figure 2.5. In object-oriented theory, there's really no such thing as a plain method or function. This isn't that unusual. In hybrid object-oriented programming languages such as C++, you can put functions in the global space. In more pure languages such as Java, you cannot; each method must be in an object, either as an instantiation of a class or as a static class-level method, which is equivalent to placing the method with the class-object for that class. Let's assume that every method must be embedded within an object. For any given method call reliance, then, there are four pieces: the calling method, the called method, and the object (class-object or instance) each resides in. Listing 2.6 sets up the classes and objects for such a method call in C++. Figure 2.5 illustrates the four pieces of the method *o.f()* calling the method *p.g()*. These pieces are present in every method call.

The three pieces of information hiding in plain sight are:

1. The similarity between the enclosing objects
2. The similarity between the types of the enclosing objects The
3. similarity between the calling method and the called method

I've introduced a new word here: *similarity*. Colloquially, it means what you think—a resemblance between two things. But what does it mean in the context of method call reliance?

Object similarity is the extent to which one object is like another. Is it the same object? Is it an alias to the second object through a pointer? Is it completely unrelated?

We can also discuss the similarity of relationship between the types of the objects. Are they the same type? Is one a subtype of the other? Or maybe one is a sibling type of the other, with a common supertype ancestor?

Method similarity is a bit trickier. We need to determine whether two methods are trying to do a similar task. We could look at many aspects: we could map keywords in comments, perhaps, or do a full analysis of the method bodies to determine what they computationally accomplish. There is a much easier way, however, if we take a page from social engineering and look at the method names and, to a lesser extent, the method signatures.

No, really. Think about it for a moment. What's the primary means by which a developer conveys the intent of a method? The name. This is even ensconced in Kent Beck's [5] *Intention Revealing Selector* pattern (emphasis mine): "You have two options in naming methods. The first is to name the method after how it accomplishes its task. … The most important argument against this style of naming is that it doesn't communicate well. … The second option is to *name a method after what it is supposed to accomplish* and leave "how" to the various method bodies. This is hard work, especially when you only have a single implementation. Your mind is filled with how you are about to accomplish the task, so it's natural that the name follow how. The effort of moving the names of method from "how" to "what" is worth it, both long term and short term. The resulting code will be easier to read and more flexible." Beck sums this up as, "Name methods after what they accomplish."

Robert Martin's *Clean Code* [27] spends an entire chapter on naming alone, because it's so important. Perhaps this can be best encapsulated using that text's invocation of the old adage "Say what you mean. Mean what you say." This is just good practice, and although not every developer group will follow it religiously, it is common enough that it can be leveraged to save us a tremendous amount of hard work. At worst, we can fall back on synonym lookups and word reordering for realizing that `makeAString` and `stringCreator` are close in intent, but it's rather shocking how often a simple lexicographic comparison will do in most cases.

Overloaded methods, those with the same name but different argument lists, offer a small hiccup, but again, we can look to how human developers reason about similarity for clues. A method is more similar to one with the same name but a different argument list than it is to a method with a completely different name. A perfect match is one with the same name and the same argument list. For the purposes of this text, however, we can set aside this detail.

This algorithm is what SPQR uses with stunningly good results. I originally selected the algorithm solely because it was the simplest to implement, and I never expected it to actually work. It was to be only a placeholder until an appropriate approach could be selected after initial testing. Once SPQR started producing data and it became obvious that this method was sufficient for most cases, the reason why had to be worked out. It's obvious in retrospect, but then, unexpected discoveries usually are clearer in hindsight.

We shouldn't have been surprised that this approach worked. When a developer reads code to try to ascertain its purpose, the first thing he or she does is look at the names of things as clues to what they do. This is Beck's naming principle at work– we *expect* things to be named appropriately, and more to the point, consistently. We expect things that perform similar functions to have similar names. All we're doing here is leveraging that expectation. SPQR was simply taught to do the same thing we all do when reading code: to try to ascertain how things relate to each other. In turn, that experience guided the formation of the EDP catalog by providing a better understanding of how humans perform that task and offering a simple and natural way to describe our third similarity.

For any method call, we can therefore look at the objects involved, the types of those objects, and the similarity of the methods through some fairly simple analysis, whether automated or manual. What does this give us?

It gives us three independent axes of context in which to place and describe any method call. We can think of these three axes as defining a three-dimensional space that we can start to explore. Any method call will, depending on the similarity assessments for our three contexts, sit in exactly one spot within this space. In other words, all method call reliances that share the same space have a similar form, and we can describe those forms independently of who wrote them, how they were written, the software system they appear in, or even the language used to implement them.

We can describe the reliances on the basis of what they do for us and what we intend when we use them. We can discuss when they're best used, how they relate to other reliances around them in that three-dimensional space, and how to transform from one method-call reliance to another.

This gives us the first group of the EDPs.

2.2.4 The Design Space

Sticking with our method call reliance, let's explore what this three-axis-defined space might look like. We have three orthogonal and independent ways of

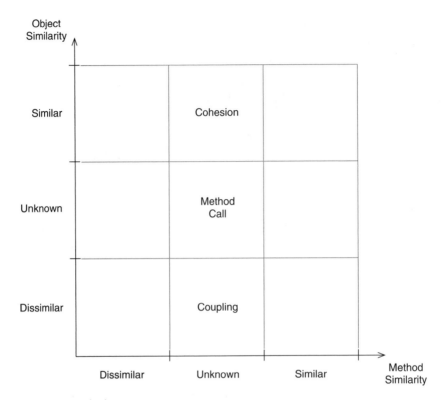

Figure 2.6 A simple design space.

describing a single method call based on three relationships: the objects that enclose the methods, the types of those objects, and the methods themselves.

This may seem like a lot to remember, but it's easy enough to visualize. For simplicity, we can start with method calls in which we ignore the object type relationship, instead concentrating on the object and method similarities, as in Figure 2.6.

We have a three-by-three grid and, along each axis, positions for *similar, unknown,* and *dissimilar*. *Unknown* is included for reasons that will be explained shortly. It should be pretty obvious that the center square is just a plain, vanilla method call. We don't know anything about the objects or the methods involved. Surprisingly, this is where most software analysis and research lives. When someone talks about method calls without indicating a relationship between the methods, their enclosing objects, or the types of those objects, then *all* of those method calls live in that one square. All of them.

In the top center square, we have method calls with object similarity. For the purposes of this discussion, let's just call that similarity object *equivalence*. These are method calls within a single object, known as an object's *cohesion*, or how tightly it is bound with its own methods [42].

In the bottom center square, where we have dissimilar objects, or for this discussion, different object instances, method calls form the basis for *coupling*, a measure of the binding *between* objects [15].

The top and bottom center squares together represent the core of a wide body of research [7–9, 13, 16, 22, 23, 31, 34], which, along with the original center square, form just one-third of the space we've defined. What is in the other two-thirds? The most interesting slots are those in the four corners, where we have knowledge of both the objects and the methods.

Figure 2.7 fills out these four corners with the names of the programming concepts associated with them. For instance, a method call from an object to itself, to the same method, is what we all know as *Recursion*. We can write this as in Listing 2.7, with recursion occurring within `countDown()`. That one's easy and obvious, but what about the other three?

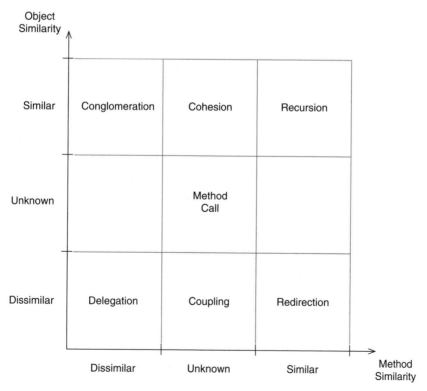

Figure 2.7 A simple design space with EDPs.

Listing 2.7 Example of a *Recursion* method call in Java.

```
1 class Timer {
      public void countDown(int counter) {
3         if (counter > 0) {
              this.countDown(counter--);
5         } else {
              // Ignore this branch for now
7         }
      };
9 };
```

Listing 2.8 Example of a *Delegation* method call in C++.

```
1 class VicePresidentOfSales {
  public:
3     void increaseQuarterlySales();
  };
5
  class CEO {
7     VicePresidentOfSales vpOfSales;
      void increaseProfits() {
9         vpOfSales.increaseQuarterlySales();
      };
11 };
```

In the opposite corner, we see *Delegation*, which is a catch-all word used in a number of ways in software design. Here we give it a precise definition to mean a method call between two distinct objects and between dissimilar methods. An example is shown in Listing 2.8. Why use the word *delegation*? Because the calling method is delegating part of its work to another method in another object. It's saying, "Go do this so I can get my work done." It's doling out a portion of its work that is part of, but unlike, its own intended task. Think about the CEO of a company delegating to the vice presidents in charge of various departments. The CEO has a job described as "run the company," but each VP has a job described in different ways: "manage HR," "ensure financial fidelity," "investigate and deploy technologies in IT." The CEO is asking each VP to do a task that looks nothing like his own, but each is critical to the CEO successfully completing his job.

Contrast this with the bottom right corner, labeled *Redirection*. The calling method is now asking another object to do some work, but it is asking for the *same* work to be done that the method itself is supposed to do. It is *redirecting* part of its workload to another object, but that part looks a lot like its own overall task. An example is shown in Listing 2.9. This is a bit like an assembly line branching out to work on multiple units in parallel during a particular task, then bringing the results back together onto one main line to continue to the next station. Imagine

Listing 2.9 Example of a *Redirection* method call in Objective-C.

```
 1 @interface Painter {}
       -(void) paintCar: (Car) theCar;
 3 @end

 5 @interface PaintShopManager {
       Painter subpainter;
 7 }
       -(void) paintCar: (Car) theCar;
 9 @end

11 @implementation PaintShopManager
       -(void) paintCar: (Car) theCar {
13         [subpainter paintCar:theCar];
       }
15 @end
```

that your company is building cars, and you're in charge of painting them. The long drying time, however, means that you would be holding up everyone else if you did them yourself in sequence. Instead of doing them all yourself, one at a time, you hire several teams and set up paint stations for each of them. Now you're in charge of routing the cars to each one as they complete the previous one. Your job is to ensure the cars are painted. Their jobs are to ensure the cars are painted. Their job is a subset of yours that looks awfully similar. You've taken on a routing responsibility, but that's only as part of completing your primary task: ensure the cars are painted. The routing is an implementation detail, the similarity in work between you and your subordinates is what makes this type of parceling out of work redirecting as opposed to delegating. Together, *Redirection* and *Delegation* form the basics of how objects can be coupled.

This leaves just the top left corner, the one marked *Conglomeration*. This is the flip side of *Recursion,* and together they define the backbone of cohesion. *Conglomeration* is the act of bringing together disparate elements into a whole—in this case, pulling together subtasks that look little like the main task (as in *Delegation*), but here just one object does the work. There are no other objects to delegate or redirect work to because this is a one-object task, but it is broken down into smaller portions that are handled by different methods within the one object. This may be done for readability, flexibility, or, as is often the case, marshaling together atomic behaviors into a more complex one some time after the atomic ones were defined. In any case, it involves one object and disparate methods, as shown in Listing 2.10, which revisits our `Timer` example from Listing 2.7.

These four basic concepts, *Recursion, Delegation, Redirection,* and *Conglomeration,* are four EDPs. Yes, they're simple. Yes, they're patterns that programmers

Listing 2.10 Example of a *Conglomeration* method call in Java.

```
 1  class Timer {
        void goDing();

 3
    public void countDown(int counter) {
 5      if (counter > 0) {
            // Ignore this branch this time
 7      } else {
            this.goDing();
 9      }
    };
11  };
```

use every day by reflex, but that's rather the point, isn't it? The uses are reflexive, not premeditated, and each has consequences for later implementation and design issues. If you're new to programming, these concepts are not reflexive, not yet ingrained, and you may have questions about them. "When do I use them?" "What are they good for?" "What other concepts are related?" This is exactly the type of tribal wisdom that design patterns were created to express and pass along. Look ahead to the EDP entries in the catalog following this chapter for more detailed discussions of these four EDPs. Do so even if you're a seasoned pro—there's more there than you may first think.

What about the final two entries in the grid where the object similarity is unknown but the method similarity is? Well, no one's quite sure at this point. If you can think of what programming concept or design issue is addressed by those two spaces, there's an opportunity for you to add to the EDP collection. This isn't without precedent, after all. As developers stumble on new ways of using established pieces, some ways will be seen as useful and will develop semantics. These new techniques, if useful enough, inevitably end up in the next generation of languages as primary language features. You might be the person who helps define them. In the meantime, let's remove the center column, where existing research sits, and the center row, which we're really not sure what to do with yet. This leaves us with four entries in a two-by-two grid, as in Figure 2.8.

What's interesting is that we derived these simple concepts from basic principles of programming theory. Once we start playing with the object types as well, the concepts become much more complex even though the theory remains just as simple. Let's see what happens when we add that third axis.

Figure 2.9 shows the three axes. Where before we were not concerned at all with the object type, we can now work with the four entries we defined earlier for the object type similarity axis. The unknown entry has as little utility here, as it did in the previous grid, so let's again remove it. For now we'll concentrate on just

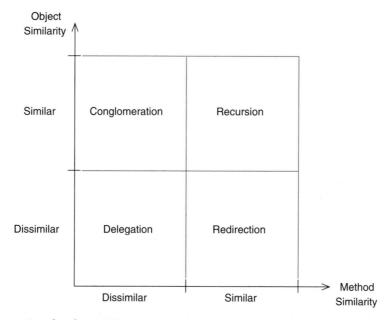

Figure 2.8 Our first four EDPs.

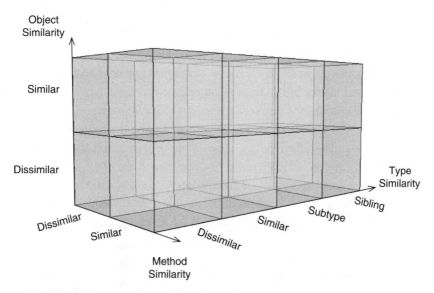

Figure 2.9 The design space extended to three dimensions.

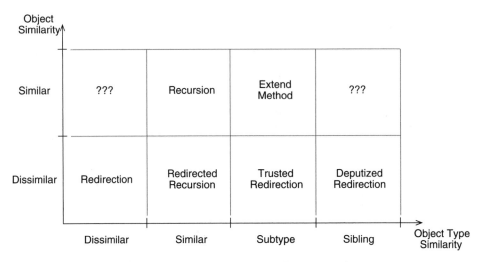

Figure 2.10 The design space with method similarity fixed to similar.

the right-hand slice defined by fixing our method similarity to similar, as shown in Figure 2.10. The remainder of this space is more fully discussed in Chapter 5.

We can place *Recursion* on this grid by recognizing that the type of the object can't be *completely* dissimilar for the object to be similar and calling a similar method.[1] The definition of *Recursion*, however, is that the exact same method implementation is being called by itself, which does require both object and type similarity.

Likewise, we can place *Redirection* on the grid by realizing that it is best described as a dissimilar object and a dissimilar type. This is the most general form of *Redirection*. What happens when we make an incremental change, though, and we retain object dissimilarity but make the objects of the *same* type? This common design trait, where an object hands off a request to another object of the same type, forms a chain of like objects parceling out a task among themselves. Because this combines aspects of both *Redirection* (a dissimilar object) and *Recursion* (the same type), we use the extremely clever name of *Redirected Recursion*.[2]

Let's continue this exploration of *Redirection* and change the type relationship a bit. If we redirect a method task to another object that is not of the same type, but a supertype of the current object, we can let an entire family of types handle

---

1. Does it have to be exactly the same? No! We'll get to that in a moment.
2. We could have gone with *Recursive Redirection*, but in early feedback, that term implied to most people a loop between two objects, while this one did not, for some reason. Also, there's a formal reason given if you care to dive in to the appendix.

the call polymorphically. You'll notice that this is the first time polymorphism has explicitly popped up in our discussion. Until now, we talked about calls between similar (same) types and dissimilar (different) types, but we hadn't refined the latter category. Now we have, and suddenly a whole new level of object-oriented design comes to light.[3] This type relationship we simply call Subtype.[4]

We can add one more subdivision of the dissimilar type bin, and that is the Sibling type relationship. A sibling relationship occurs when the types of the objects involved share a common ancestor supertype, but neither is a supertype of the other. We tossed the method call up our type hierarchy and then limited it back down to a trusted subset of that tree. We call this variation *Deputized Redirection*.

Let's go back to *Recursion*, and then slide one square to the right, where the object instance is the same, but the type relationship is a subtype. Read that again. It actually does make sense to talk about having the same object, and a method call from that object to itself, but with two object types involved in that method call. In fact, to do so is super.

Specifically, *super* lets you access a supertype's implementation of a method from within a subtype. In Java, it is done with the `super` keyword. In C++, an explicit type-scoping mechanism is used as in `Supertype::`. Other languages have a variety of mechanisms, but they all do the same thing—they give an object access to a supertype's implementation of a method. How is this useful? Well, consider a case where you want to extend the functionality of a method, not completely replace it with new functionality. You would subclass the type, override the method, and then wrap a call to the original method in your bit of extra code. As you might expect, this EDP is simply called *Extend Method*.

Notice that in the preceding discussion, we took an existing, familar concept and moved just one space away from it at each stage, tweaking one detail or another at a time. The result of this simple progression is a surprisingly broad collection of concepts and design elements from programming. Look at the variety of the UML diagrams for the preceding eight EDPs if you're not convinced that we've covered a lot of conceptual ground. Consider just the ideas involving *Recursion* and *Deputized Redirection*, shown in Figures 2.11 and 2.12. They look nothing alike, yet they sit just three steps from each other in the design space for a single method call.

Again, two mystery boxes remain. Let's not ignore them this time but instead discuss what they *could* mean conceptually. In the first slot on the left, we have the

---

3. If you're unfamiliar with the term polymorphism, start with the *Inheritance* EDP. That will give you a good overview of the concept.
4. Recall that reliances go from the calling method to the method that is called; in this case the calling method is defined within a subtype of the type enclosing the method being called.

Figure 2.11 *Recursion* Example UML.

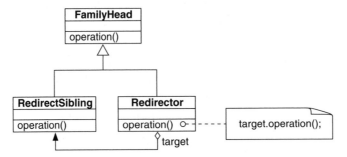

Figure 2.12 *Deputized Redirection* example UML.

same (or similar) object but utterly dissimilar typing on each side of the method call reliance. How can this be? Well, I'm not sure. Although some rather esoteric typing relationships exist out there, this one doesn't make a lot of sense. For now, it is unknown territory, but perhaps a language will find a reasonable use for this context combination in the future. The BETA language [26], for example, has a unique *inner* construct that is the mirror image of super, creating a Supertype similarity instead of a Subtype similarity. This is exceedingly rare, however, and not used in our object similarity axis for that reason. It may be added later if it proves to be an interesting and viable design element.

An analogous situation occurs for the slot on the far right. Again, we have the same (or similar) object, but now a Sibling type similarity, and again, no language that I am aware of offers this possibility. These open slots are ripe for interpretation and thought experiment. Best of all, we can predict some properties for these unde-scribed entries in the design space, much like elements in a periodic table.

That's just over half the method call EDPs that will be presented in full later in the reference section. It's remarkable how many concepts can be expressed with a single method call, isn't it? One method call. That's all we've been discussing, and yet we have a wide range of design components to play with.

2.3 Core EDPs

To this point, we've discussed just method calls, but recall that we said there are three other forms of reliances that we can play with: field usage, state changes, and cohesion. What about those? Well, they are still being explored at the moment, fleshed out, and written up. Method calls were approached first because they're the smallest, simplest design space to work with. The others are quite a bit larger. There are a few basic concepts that should be addressed, however, to fill out this first group, and they form the core of object-oriented programming from both formal and pragmatic points of view.

To begin with, there's the entire "making objects" idea. It is one of the distinguishing characteristics of object-oriented programming, after all, or the entire paradigm probably would have been named something else. Look at the *Create Object* EDP for guidance here. At this vantage point, three decades or so into object-oriented programming, it seems odd that there was ever objection to it as a programming approach, but it had large hurdles to overcome. One objection was that anything that can be implemented in object-oriented programming can be implemented in procedural programming. While technically true—anything doable in any higher-level system is doable in procedural, in assembler, or in raw binary; otherwise it wouldn't *run*—object-oriented programming allowed the easy enforcement of certain principles. *Create Object* outlines one of the major ones, creating a relationship between a single object and a single type at the same time.

Once we create objects, how do we get them talking to one another? Well, by using method calls, obviously. Okay, but how do we get them to *find* one another in the first place? We could statically create all the connections between the objects, but that's rather limiting because it means the system cannot react to runtime input. The programmer must anticipate all possible uses of the system, including details such as maximal memory use for all possible data needs, regardless of the actual amount used. To get around this problem, we have to allow objects to gain access to other objects during execution. The *Retrieve* EDP does this, dynamically creating runtime connections between objects.

To instantiate an object, we need a type from which to do so. Often the types available to us are almost, but not quite, correct. Instead of rewriting a proper type from scratch every time, though, we'd like to leverage what we already have as a starting point. The ability to reuse types is made possible through *Inheritance,* another core EDP. *Inheritance* is a type reliance, which we mentioned earlier by one of its aliases, subtyping. It forms a connection between a base type and a type that relies on it for much of its basic functionality (methods) and state (fields). It allows a new type to reuse large chunks of logic and data in a well-formed way.

Another type-related EDP is *Abstract Interface*. It forms a reliance between two types that is a bit different in that only one end of the relationship is known ahead of time. It uses a method as a bridge between the two types. If a type declares a method to be abstract, it doesn't have to—and in the strictest sense isn't *allowed* to—give a method body implementation. This EDP creates a promise that at some point another type will inherit from this one and give the method a proper implementation. What that type is isn't yet known, but it has to happen for this type to be usable. Until then, this type is incomplete.

These four EDPs, *Create Object*, *Retrieve*, *Inheritance*, and *Abstract Interface*, allow us to create objects with enforcement of certain guarantees, relate them to one another at runtime, define object types in terms of other types, and declare promises for future, unspecified types. Together, they form much of the basis for object-oriented programming. Along with the method call EDPs such as *Delegation* and *Recursion*, they provide a solid start to treating design as a reproducible discipline, one that uses well-formed building blocks connected in methodical and precise ways. Why don't we see what we can do with just a handful of them?

2.4 Conclusion

This chapter introduced you to the Elemental Design Patterns. It gave a brief synopsis of the driving problem they helped solve and some background on how they came about. You saw how patterns such as *Decorator* can be described in terms of smaller patterns. This led to the conclusion that to better describe the more abstract design patterns in the standard literature, finer-grained patterns are necessary.

You were introduced to a minimalist form of object-oriented programming theory and shown how it gives rise to a small number of possible relationships, or reliances, that can occur in programming. These reliances form the basis for the smallest patterns we can define. One of these reliances, the method-call reliance, forms the core of this book. You saw that every method call has a context, defined by three simple pieces of information—the object, type, and method similarities—and that these create a design space in which well-known programming concepts live. The other three reliances—field use, state change, and cohesion—give rise to their own design spaces that are in the process of being defined.

The method-call design space was explored lightly. Code examples were given for many of the EDPs, and you saw how they relate to one another. Finally, you learned a set of the core EDPs, which define many of the basic concepts that underlie object-oriented programming.

You now have a solid footing to understand the importance and utility of the EDPs and are ready to start learning how to work with them. In Chapter 3, you'll learn a valuable way to graphically depict pattern instances to help you visualize their interactions.

Pattern Instance Notation

Before we explore the impact of what we can do with Elemental Design Patterns (EDPs), I want to take a bit of a side jaunt and introduce a new graphical notation, the Pattern Instance Notation, or PIN. PIN is used from here out to help you visualize some of the concepts we discuss.

This chapter provides an informal description of PIN and how it is used in this book. If you're interested in further information or in how PIN can be used in tool support for software design, PIN is fully described in "The Pattern Instance Notation: A Simple Hierarchical Visual Notation for the Dynamic Visualization and Comprehension of Software Patterns" [36].

3.1 Basics

PIN is a visual representation of the concepts and ideas that comprise patterns. It is intended as a quick and easy way to document and describe design patterns and their interactions. The name PIN was chosen because it also is useful in showing instances of patterns or concepts in other diagramming notations, such as UML. This was the original use case.

In Chapter 2, Section 2.2.2, I mentioned the Participants section of a design pattern specification. Participants are the parts of a design pattern that must exist for an instance of the design pattern to occur. Another name for them are the *roles* of the design pattern, because each participant has a particular role to play in bringing together the pattern. In other words, each participant fulfills a role of the pattern. When we say "the participant named `ConcreteDecorator` of the *Decorator* pattern," what we really mean is "the class of the implementation that fulfills the ConcreteDecorator role of the *Decorator* pattern." The roles are abstractions as well, because they provide a name for, and constraints on, the implementation or design features that will act as participants.

It's not unlike a play, such as Hamlet. Hamlet is a role, as are Ophelia, Rosencrantz, and Guildenstern. They describe a part and provide guidelines for the kind of actor who will be cast in each role. The actor is a participant in the stage production, and all the actors collaborate to form it.

The play is analogous to a design pattern, and the particular stage production is an instance of the pattern. The script is like the design pattern specification: it describes roles, and it describes how they communicate and interact. The actors who are cast in those roles are the participants.

UML has a graphical feature, the collaboration element, to describe such situations. An example using *Decorator* is shown in Figure 3.1. This isn't a bad notation by any means, and it is very flexible, but it suffers from a couple of problems for our needs. For one thing, it is a bit messy in practical use at anything other than in trivial diagrams. It only adds information to a UML diagram. The more you use it, the more complex the diagram becomes. Abstractions such as design patterns are intended to *reduce* complexity and detail by letting us operate at a higher level of abstraction. A sticking point of UML collaborations is that they aren't capable of reducing the complexity in a UML diagram. They can't reduce the amount of exposed information as a higher level of abstraction should. A collaboration element also requires a complete UML diagram to be placed in, in the first place. This may seem like an odd complaint when we're discussing a UML feature, but it turns out that there are plenty of situations where we may want to discuss how patterns interact without having to create a diagram for all the pieces necessary to implement them.

Another common notation for design patterns is the pattern:role notation introduced by the Gang of Four (GoF) [21]. It is also an annotation to be used on top of UML, and it uses an external flag that is named with the pattern and the role. This annotation can be applied to a class, package, field, or method as needed, as shown in Figure 3.2. It's very flexible and obvious, but it isn't without issues.

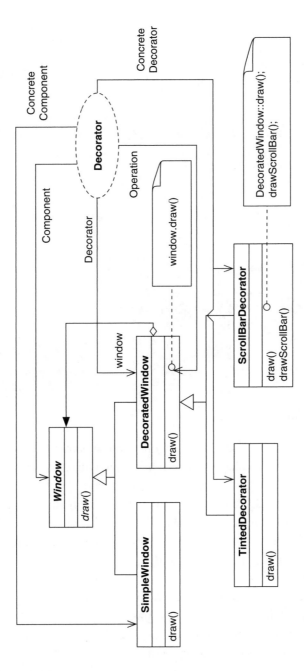

Figure 3.1 UML collaboration diagram.

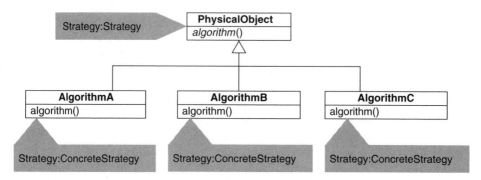

Figure 3.2 *Strategy* as pattern:role tags in UML.

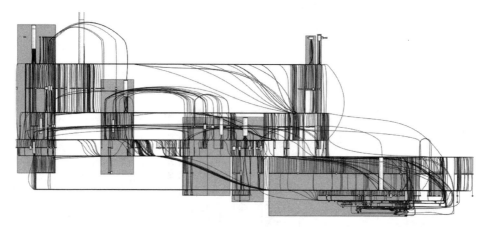

Figure 3.3 Huge UML of a not-so-huge system.

This approach isn't so bad when only one pattern is involved and displayed, but what happens when you have a pattern hidden in a diagram with hundreds or even thousands of pieces? Say, something like in Figure 3.3?

Figure 3.3 is an actual UML diagram from an actual project. It's unreadable at this scale, but practically speaking, it's almost unreadable at any scale. If you were to print it at actual dimensions, such that the type was 10-point size, it would be 86 by 32 *feet*. That's a lot of paper: 3,290 standard U.S. letter-size sheets. At this size, it's too small to be read, but at the full size, it's too large to be searched visually. Frustratingly, a wealth of patterns are recorded in the diagram, ready to be found and learned from to help document the system.

As a more concrete example, consider a UML diagram such as in Figure 3.4. There are two instances of the *Strategy* pattern in Figure 3.4, but using the pattern:role notation, we can't tell which pieces go with which pattern instance, even in this small example.

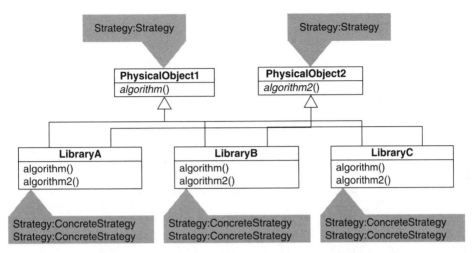

Figure 3.4 Multiple instances of *Strategy* as pattern:role tags in UML.

This was the initial reason for the PIN: to be able to clearly express multiple instances of patterns in a single diagram as first-class entities. Hence the name, Pattern Instance Notation. Other goals are that the notation be simple, flexible, and usable in conjunction with other notations such as UML without being reliant on them.

3.2 The PINbox

The core notation in PIN is the PINbox. It represents a single pattern instance and lets you choose the level of granularity you want to expose. We start with a PINbox in its simplest form and work our way up into more interesting variants.

3.2.1 Collapsed PINbox

The collapsed PINbox is just a name label with a thick double border, as in Figure 3.5. The interior border stroke is a rectangle, the external border stroke has curved corners. If possible, the border is shaded gray. The label on the box is the name of the pattern.

That's it. That's the simplest form of a PINbox. Don't worry, there's more to come. Even here, though, we have something useful to work with. We can use this as an annotation onto a UML or other diagram by just drawing an arrow from the PINbox to whatever element in the diagram is most closely associated with it, as in Figure 3.6. When it comes to graphical notations, experience shows that boxes and lines are about as simple as it gets.

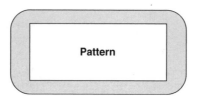

Figure 3.5 Collapsed PINbox.

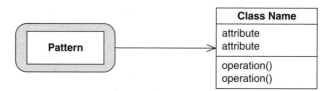

Figure 3.6 Collapsed PINbox as annotation.

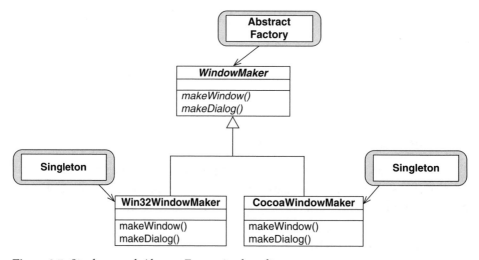

Figure 3.7 *Singleton* and *Abstract Factory* in class diagram.

For some examples of how this might work in real life, consider Figures 3.7 and 3.8. The example using *Singleton* and *Abstract Factory* shows PIN being used with a class diagram, while *Template Method* indicates a pattern in a sequence diagram.

The collapsed PINbox is best used when you need a mnemonic, a quick reminder that a pattern exists in a system, and the pattern is one that has a single, defining feature you can point to. This is an informal notation but one that has utility, particularly when sketching out a new design.

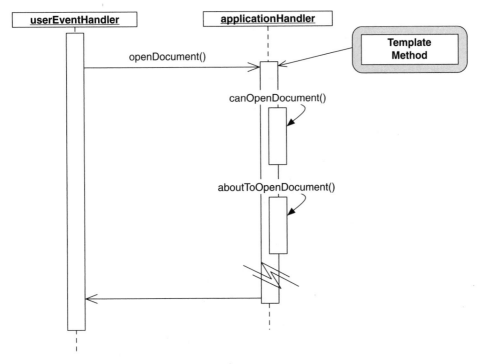

Figure 3.8 *Template Method* in sequence diagram.

Figure 3.9 Standard PINbox.

3.2.2 Standard PINbox

Taking things up a level, we have the standard PINbox. We expand the thick gray border of the collapsed form so that we can add text to it. Specifically, we add the roles that make up the pattern listed in the middle, as in Figure 3.9. The roles are named using the same conventions outlined in Chapter 2, Section 2.2.1. Adding the roles lets us express some significantly finer-grained connections. For instance, because each pattern has a well-formed and distinct set of these roles, we can connect each role to the elements of a UML class or sequence diagram, as in Figures 3.10 and 3.11.

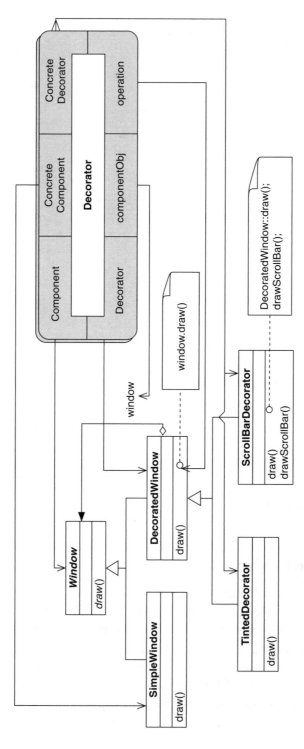

Figure 3.10 PIN used with UML class diagram.

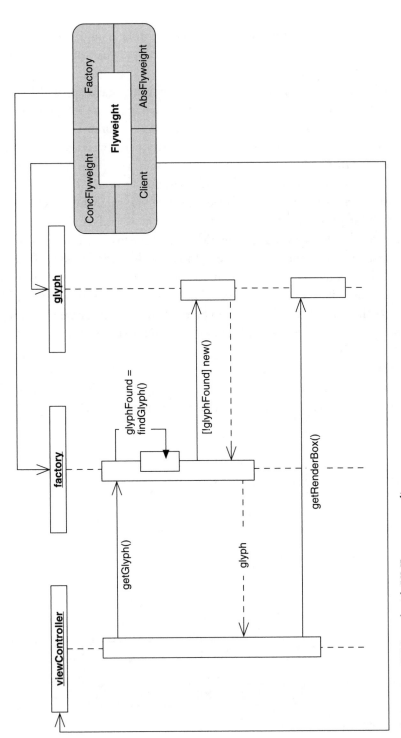

Figure 3.11 PIN used with UML sequence diagram.

The arrangement of the role names around the border is up to you; however it looks best on the final diagram is fine. Whatever ordering makes the final diagram easiest to read is preferred.

This looks an awful lot like a UML collaboration from Figure 3.1, but PINboxes can do some things that collaborations can't. Note that in Figure 3.11, the instance of *Flyweight* has the AbsFlyweight role not attached to anything. This is fine in this case because we're just trying to depict the interactions between the other three roles. If we tried this with a collaboration element and wanted to retain all of the information about the roles of the *Flyweight* pattern, we'd either have to have a dangling arrow with the unused role name or, worse, *not show it at all*. Neither is optimal. With the PINbox, we don't lose the information, and we don't clutter up our diagram needlessly. For another example, say we have two pattern instances in a software design and we want to indicate that the same class that fulfills a role in one fulfills a role in another, tying the two pattern instances into a combined structure. We could do this as in Figure 3.12. Notice that this diagram doesn't use any UML; it only shows the connection between two patterns in a particular way. Things get much more interesting when we connect multiple PINboxes together.

There is no UML.

There is no code.

There are no classes, methods, fields, no anything, just a relationship between two patterns, two *concepts*, and that relationship ties them together in a particular

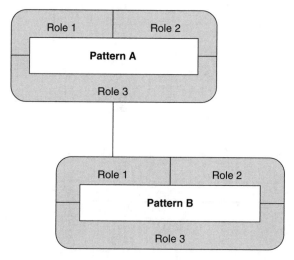

Figure 3.12 Standard PIN role connections.

way. We use this capability to show how patterns can be combined into new concepts in the next chapter.

We can do still more, though.

3.2.3 Expanded PINbox

If we make a small tweak to the PINbox, it becomes much more flexible and powerful. Let's start by expanding the box in the center, the one that currently just holds the pattern name. We end up with something that looks like Figure 3.13. Now we can use this new blank area to draw additional PINboxes. Why would we want to do this? Well, look at Figure 3.14. Here we've filled in the canvas. What this shows is that *Pattern* has five roles and can be decomposed into two smaller subpatterns: Subpattern A and Subpattern B. Further, it shows exactly how the roles on the outside ring map to the roles of the inner subpatterns. If we have Subpattern A and Subpattern B, such that Role 3 in Subpattern A is fulfilled by the same entity in a system as Role 1 from Subpattern B, then we could replace those two instances with a single instance of *Pattern*. In other words, we could raise the level of abstraction a bit. Instead of having to keep track of two things, we only have to manage one pattern instance.

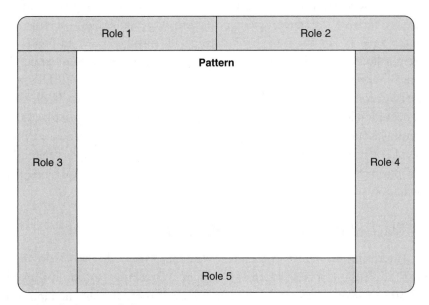

Figure 3.13 Blank expanded PIN instance.

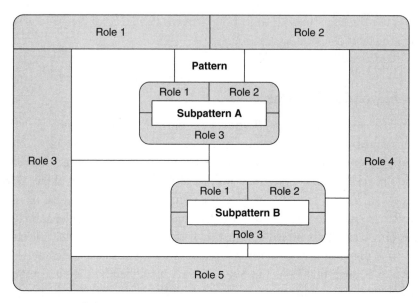

Figure 3.14 Expanded PIN instance.

On the other hand, if we had an instance of *Pattern*, it's clear that we also have an instance of each of the subpatterns. They may be buried a bit, but we know they *have* to be there.

The expanded PINbox lets us reveal the hierarchical nature of patterns to whatever degree we wish. We can leave a single pattern at the highest level of abstraction, or we can keep expanding it to show more detail. Also, as shown in Figure 3.15, we are not limited to using just the PIN on this canvas. We can integrate UML or some other notation to illustrate a particular point. In the case of EDPs, which cannot be decomposed into smaller subpatterns, the ability to display UML offers a direct definition instead. Alternatively, we may want to place the UML diagram that demonstrates one implementation of, say, the *Decorator* pattern, inside the PINbox. This could be used as a reference illustration for a student or as a quick reminder in a design support tool. Flexibility is what makes PIN so uniquely useful for depicting the definition and composition of patterns.

3.2.4 Stacked PINboxes and Multiplicity

Many patterns have a multiplicity to their elements. Generally, more than one participant fulfills the Concrete Decorator role in a *Decorator* pattern, for instance, and *Abstract Factory* loses much of its usefulness if there is only one kind of factory. Using a strict interpretation of the PINbox definition, we'd have to use one

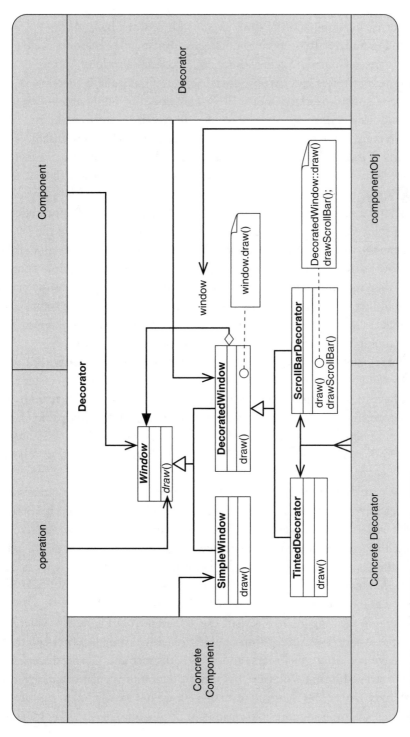

Figure 3.15 Expanded PIN instance using UML.

PINbox for each combination of the elements. Look at the basic *Abstract Factory* diagram in Figure 3.16. To properly annotate it with standard PINboxes, we'd need four: one for each Concrete Factory times each Concrete Product. And we're only discussing two factories and two products right now. Imagine if there were, say, four factories and 10 products. Forty PINboxes would be impossible to navigate and horrendously confusing. And we would but we also want to make sure that someone looking at the diagram knows that these individual pattern instances are simply parts of the same pattern instance at a higher level, that they are fundamentally connected. We can show the relationships by using a stacked PINbox, as in Figure 3.17.

We added a second outline "behind" the PINbox to give the appearance of PINboxes stacked like a deck of cards. Also, notice that we changed the arrows coming from the Concrete Factory, Concrete Product, and Abstract Product roles. The tail now has a forked appearance to indicate that there are multiple connections, and then the line splits to point to each of the entities that previously would have been indicated by a unique PINbox. To help illustrate where the splits occur, a small circle is added at the junction points. Junction points that lack this indicator are where multiple roles are satisfied by the same element, as before.

In general, multiplicity connections should be used with care with PINboxes. Remember our goal is simplicity, and if two roles have multiplicities associated with them, we have to be extremely clear that the relationship is properly defined by the abstraction we are denoting. In this case, having three roles with multiplicity makes sense. Each Concrete Factory must handle each of the Concrete Products, and the Abstract Products are clearly linked with their corresponding concrete subclasses. It's hard to get confused in this case.

If, however, there were multiple *Abstract Factory* entities, each would necessitate the creation of a new stacked PINbox instance. Think of it this way: if a pattern lends itself well to use as a collapsed PINbox, then it likely will be useful as a stacked PINbox with several multiplicities, *if and only if* the role that makes it useful in the collapsed form is *not* associated in a multiplicity. In other words, if there is one role that is so prominent that it can be used in the collapsed form successfully, then it can be used as the linchpin role for a stacked PINbox.

Building on this, Figure 3.18 revisits the situation from Figure 3.4, where we had multiple instances of *Strategy* but couldn't reliably distinguish between them. Now we have two *Strategy* clusters, and each is distinct and clearly discernable. We use the stacked form to indicate that there are multiple concrete strategies for each pattern instance. This is useful, certainly, but what if we wanted to capture the very idea that we are using multiple clusters of *Strategy* in concert?—not a single

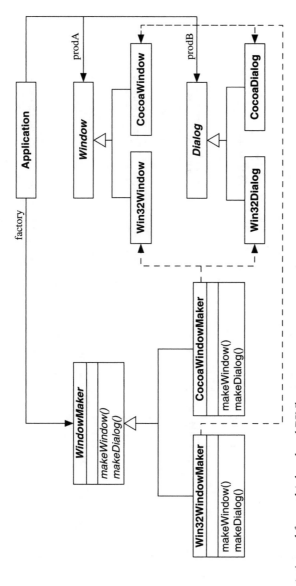

Figure 3.16 A need for multiple related PINboxes.

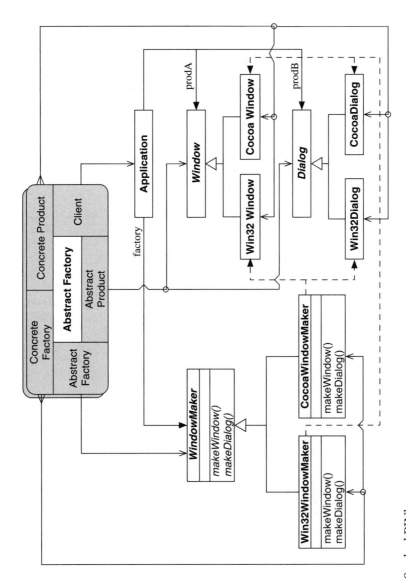

Figure 3.17 Stacked PINbox.

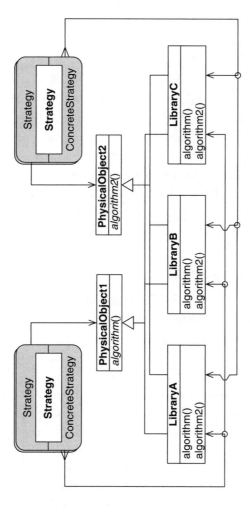

Figure 3.18 Multiple *Strategy* instances as PINboxes.

Figure 3.19 Showing the interaction between multiple *Strategy* PINboxes.

Strategy, but more than one, acting together. In other words, what if we decided that this multiple *Strategy* situation was common enough that we wanted to tell someone else about it, clearly and cleanly. In such a case, we might use Figure 3.19 to explain it. We stripped out the UML, the portion that corresponds most closely to our implementation, and we abstracted out the connection between the *Strategy* clusters into something simple and precise. This diagram is much simpler than our original in Figure 3.4 and provides a mechanism for faster sharing and clearer communication of what we are trying to get across: "There is more than one *Strategy* at work here, and the same classes are acting as concrete strategies for each." This could even be the seed of a new design pattern writeup.

3.2.5 Peeling and Coalescing

There's one last trick of the expanded PINbox that is useful to know about, even though we don't use it extensively in this book. Recall that in the discussion of the UML collaboration notation, I mentioned that it can only add, not subtract, information in a diagram and that it fails to be useful as an abstraction mechanism at large scales because of that limitation.

Imagine that we're looking at a system such as in Figure 3.17. We've accurately identified the stacked PINbox for the multiple instances of the *Abstract Factory* design pattern, but we haven't made the diagram any *simpler*. This is only moderately useful.

Imagine that the UML snippet in Figure 3.17 is instead part of a much larger diagram. Let's add some connections to it but leave them ambiguous, as in Figure 3.20. It's difficult to see what was added, isn't it? Now, let's place the UML portion from Figure 3.17 *inside* an expanded form of the PINbox, as in Figure 3.21. The same information is still in place, but we're now using the PINbox as a proxy mechanism. Anything attached to the outside edge of a role connects to what is attached to the inside edge of a role. You can think of the gray role border as a pass-through layer.

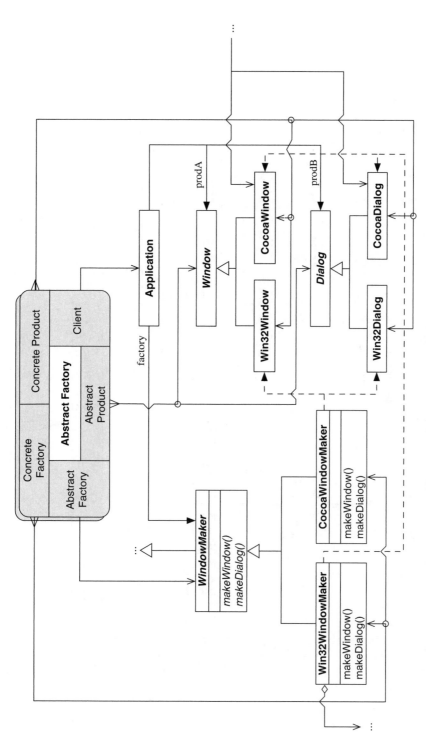

Figure 3.20 *Abstract Factory* as part of a larger UML diagram.

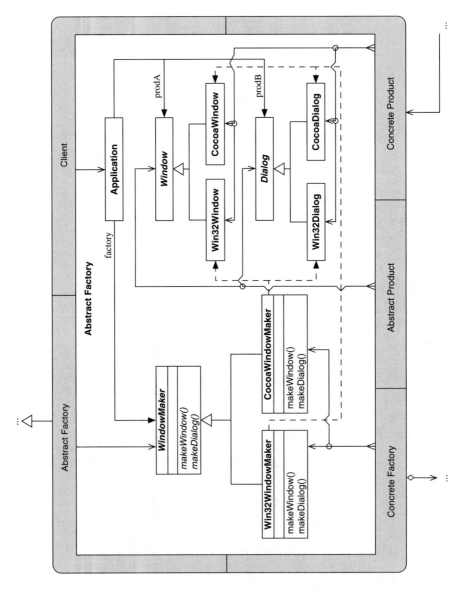

Figure 3.21 *Abstract Factory* subsumed within the expanded PINbox.

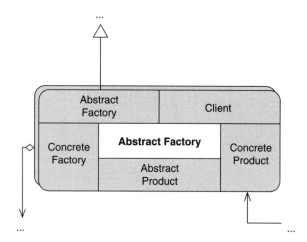

Figure 3.22 Coalesced PINbox.

Now collapse the PINbox to the standard form, as in Figure 3.22. The diagram just got a lot simpler, didn't it? Now you can see precisely what the new connections are. All the details of the design pattern instance have been replaced by a single PINbox. The PINbox now acts as an abstraction should, by subsuming the details that the abstraction represents and by making the situation *easier* to comprehend, not harder. See the discussion of *Abstract Factory* in Chapter 7, Section 7.1.1, for a use of an expanded PINbox to show the internal structure of the pattern.

In this case, if you wanted to reveal the details, you could expand the PINbox again. The act of removing the PINbox entirely and reconnecting the internals to the externals is called *peeling*. The journal article [36] mentioned at the beginning of this chapter expands on these ideas.

3.3 Conclusion

PIN is designed to be a simple and flexible way of visually describing design elements in software. It can be used by annotating other software design notations such as UML or as a standalone notation for showing the relationships between design elements such as design patterns independent of implementation needs. It offers the user nearly unlimited choice in degree of granularity of what can be exposed at a particular point in time, based on specific needs.

Working with EDPs

Until now we've talked about Elemental Design Patterns (EDPs) using a number of metaphors, including building blocks, and comparisons to the periodic table of chemistry. Those metaphors and comparisons were selected because they are used in domains where composition of fundamental pieces into larger, more useful constructs is critical. This applies for us as well and leads to an assumption that EDPs can be joined into meaningful larger pieces. In Chapter 3, you were introduced to Pattern Instance Notation (PIN), and part of that discussion showed how PINboxes can be joined in a diagram, illustrating how multiple instances of design patterns such as EDPs can interact.

In this chapter, we put all of this information together and demonstrate that EDPs are not just small individual concepts. EDPs form the basis for much larger abstractions and design patterns and can be used effectively in a multitude of situations, including designing, implementing, and rewriting a system.

4.1 Composition of Patterns

Let's revisit our discussion and deconstruction of *Decorator* in Chapter 2, Section 2.2.1. We identified that *Object Recursion* was being used and that *Objectifier* was a part of *Object Recursion*. The deconstruction process required deep knowledge of the existing design patterns literature, yet the end result was vague and did not give us a comprehensive understanding of *Decorator*. We'll use EDPs to give a more complete picture.

Let's start with one of the basic object-oriented programming EDPs we just described, *Abstract Interface*. We stated that it promises that a future subclass will provide an implementation for the specified method. Let's go ahead and mock up the pieces of this pattern with UML. We know we have *Abstract Interface*, and we know we need *Inheritance* because we talk about a subclass. We can show these as in Figure 4.1.

Now let's connect these two EDPs in a very specific way. We know that *Abstract Interface* talks about an "unspecified subclass" of the `Abstractor` class, suggesting that the class fulfilling the Abstractor role is a superclass. Let's show that by having the Superclass role in *Inheritance* point also to the Abstractor class. This merges the two UML diagrams into one, as in Figure 4.2. We applied what we first saw in Chapter 3, Section 3.2.2, connecting the two EDP instances, and created a larger design. We added one more piece of information to this diagram: the Subclass role of *Inheritance* provides the concrete definition of the operator role from *Abstract Interface*. This is new and appears in neither EDP.

This new definition fulfills the contract that is the *conceptual* essence of *Abstract Interface*, that a subclass would provide an implementation for the abstract method, and gives rise to the name for this new design pattern: *Fulfill Method*. This is a concept you haven't seen yet in this book, although I'm sure you've seen it if you've ever programmed in an object-oriented language. We alluded to the composition

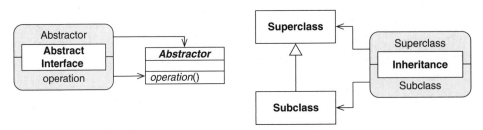

Figure 4.1 *Abstract Interface* and *Inheritance* EDPs as UML.

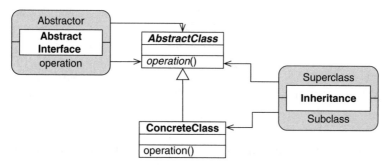

Figure 4.2 Internal definition of *Fulfill Method* as UML.

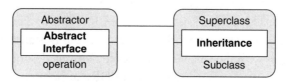

Figure 4.3 *Fulfill Method* as simple connected PINboxes.

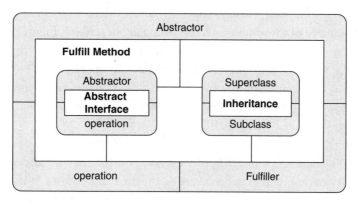

Figure 4.4 *Fulfill Method* as expanded PINbox.

of patterns at the end of Section 3.2.2, and showed this in Figure 3.12, but it wasn't fleshed out. Let's do that now.

Let's redraw Figure 4.2 but without the UML, as we talked about in our PIN discussion. In Figure 4.3, the implementation details are removed, and the figure shows *only* the relationship between the two EDPs. It cleanly abstracts out the relationships that are contained within each EDP. A simple diagram remains, showing more clearly what the connection is between these two concepts. We can then wrap this new simplified diagram with the *Fulfill Method* PINbox, as in Figure 4.4.

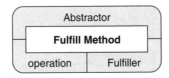

Figure 4.5 *Fulfill Method* as standard PINbox.

The real payoff for this style of notation is illustrated in Figure 4.5, when we collapse the expanded PINbox and move to a higher level of abstraction. This is equivalent to each of the preceding figures but is a simple, single PINbox that can be used to annotate a UML diagram or, as we'll see later, as a part of yet larger design pattern definitions. This almost fractal nature of PINboxes and design patterns will come up over and over again in working with patterns. Design patterns are made of smaller patterns, with the smallest, indivisible patterns described by the EDPs. In turn, all design patterns, starting with the EDPs, are usable as building blocks for larger patterns. At every level of granularity, PINboxes can be used to concisely depict the concepts under consideration.

If you were following closely, you may have noticed that along the way we dropped one piece of information. When originally describing Figure 4.2, I stated that "we add one more piece of information to this diagram: the Subclass role of *Inheritance* provides the concrete definition of the operator role from *Abstract Interface*. This is new and appears in neither EDP." The concrete definition of the operation, however—the entire defining feature of *Fulfill Method*—was not carried forward from Figure 4.2 to Figure 4.3.

This highlights two important points that you must keep in mind when studying patterns and using PIN. First, PIN is not a notation for the formal description of patterns. It is not designed to define every tiny feature of a pattern. It is designed to let you work with pattern instances quickly and easily and, where possible, *assist* in the depiction of pattern definitions. If you are looking for a mathematically precise formalization of design patterns, I can only point you once again to the appendix as a starting point. PIN is an approximation of that formalism, intended for human consumption.

Second, and much more important, you must never forget that when it comes to any design pattern, it is the write-up or pattern specification—the prose description of a design pattern—that is the essence and heart of the pattern. Mathematical notations can describe what a pattern looks like, they can list and name the pieces and how they are hooked together, but they can never tell you the most critical thing about patterns. They cannot tell you the *why*. They cannot tell you the *when* or *where*. At best, they can tell you the *what*. *What* is good, but *what* is not wisdom. Wisdom, the knowledge that patterns are intended to impart, is everything else surrounding the what. If at any time you are confused about a pattern, about how it is being applied, about its applicability or its critical concepts, consult the canonical document for that pattern. Refer to the specification. In your studies and application of patterns, notations such as PIN or even formal calculi will never be a complete substitute for the write-up, only a mnemonic assistance.

The preceding example may not seem like much, but it's a critical step in understanding EDPs and how they form larger patterns. We took two EDPs, each of which define one relationship between two entities, and stitched them together to form a slightly larger pattern. What you just saw is the essential action of good design—taking small, understandable pieces that are appropriate to the problem at hand and putting them together in meaningful ways. What's more, there is no end to this process. Every time we add a new relationship to a program, we alter the design in some way. The trick is recognizing which alterations are helpful and which ones lead to trouble.

In such a small case as constructing *Fulfill Method*, this may seem painfully obvious. "Well of course," you might say, "how else would you put those two EDPs together?" Well, we *could* try to connect them as in Figure 4.6. These are the same two EDPs, but we reversed which class is the subclass. Now we *can't* add that method definition like we wanted to![1] To make this easier to see, let's redraw this connection with just the PINboxes, as in Figure 4.7. This is simply not the same graph as Figure 4.3.

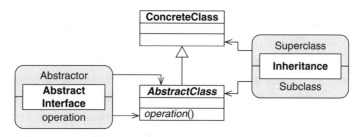

Figure 4.6 Flipping our EDPs in *Fulfill Method*—oops.

---

1. This isn't strictly true: some languages do allow for such removal of methods via later abstraction, but we won't get into them here because that's an advanced theoretical trick well beyond the scope of this book. Besides, such a removal would be a very different concept, wouldn't it? We wouldn't be fulfilling a prior promised method implementation, we'd be *erasing* access to prior method implementations.

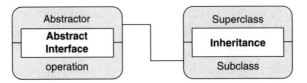

Figure 4.7 Flipped EDPs as PINboxes.

Only one specific combination of concepts will get us to where we wish to be. This is the magic behind design patterns: through trial and error, we can find the best-practice solutions to problems we keep running into. We can write down these solutions as a combination of smaller concepts that can be reused and sculpted into new forms while retaining the wisdom of the original conceptual connections. EDPs allow us to build our best-practice solutions out of primary blocks instead of through trial and error.

Another point to be made is that Figure 4.2 shows the absolute *minimum* UML that satisfies the EDPs in the PINboxes, not the *exact* solution. This is not *the* implementation; this is *one* implementation. Recall that we're giving ourselves a way of talking about design issues such as patterns without limiting ourselves to a highly specific and rigidly defined implementation. We can return to the individual EDPs that comprise *Fulfill Method* and look at how they can differ in their implementations yet still be the EDPs we wish them to be.

4.1.1 Isotopes

Any given design pattern, whether one as small as an EDP or as large as a full-blown pattern such as *Decorator*, can be implemented in a vast number of ways and still embody the concept being described. This flexibility is a hallmark strength of design patterns. We call these differing implementations *isotopes* of the pattern. The name is intended to be congruent with the term *elemental*. In chemistry, an isotope is a variation of an atom of a particular element. Atoms have three components: electrons, protons, and neutrons. The protons and neutrons form the nucleus of the atom, and the electrons orbit the nucleus. The number of protons in the nucleus determine what element the atom is, and the electrons determine how that atom connects and interacts with other atoms. An isotope of an element has the same proton count as other atoms of that element, and it has the same electron shell structure. Because of these two traits, it behaves chemically the same as other isotopes of that element. It connects to other atoms in the same way, forms the same bonds, and for most intents and purposes can be considered the same as any other isotopic atom of that element.

Internally, however, an atom of an isotope has a different number of neutrons in the nucleus. From the outside, it looks and acts the same chemically, but the internal differences can cause small, insignificant side effects, like, oh, nuclear fission. This tends to be rather disruptive.

In software, we call this unexpected nuclear fission a crash.

An isotope of a design pattern in software is defined similarly. It is an implementation of a design pattern in which the core concepts of the pattern—what define that design pattern to be different from all other design patterns—and the external interface remain the same.

In other words, the roles that must be fulfilled do not differ from the expected design pattern description.[2] This is analogous to the electron shells in the atom metaphor and is made explicit in the PINbox notation. All that an external entity, such as another pattern instance or code element, will see are the roles surrounding the "nucleus" of the definition.

The proton count in an atom is what distinguishes it from all other elements and places it in a specific position in the periodic table. We have a similar situation with design patterns, where the problem, solution, and context are unique. What the design pattern does, what it solves, and so on, is its discriminator. It is what makes it unique from all other design patterns. Change the problem, and we have a different design pattern. Change the context and, again, the design pattern must adapt and change into something else. If it's a small change, and the resulting new pattern looks a lot like the original, then we have a variant; if it's a large change, then we may have something wholly new.

With EDPs, the analogy to atoms and the periodic table is even stronger, because the axes of design context defined in Section 2.2.4 create a well-defined space within which we can uniquely place each EDP. This is directly comparable to chemistry's periodic table, which creates a well-defined space in which the elements can be placed and the properties of those elements can be predicted.

The position of an EDP within the method-reliance EDP design space—as defined by the object-, type-, and method-similarity axes in Section 2.2.4—is absolute. Alter the value of any one of these three axes and the position within that space changes. The original EDP has mutated to another one, and you can predict what the properties of the new EDP will be. Change anything *else* about the EDP,

---

2. If the roles do differ, it indicates a fundamental change to the design pattern. This change is called a *variant* of the pattern and is a clue that something very substantial has changed, such as the problem being solved or the context in which it is occurring.

however, such as how it is expressed in a particular instance, and the EDP stays the same while the implementation shifts—different implementation but the same properties.

With an isotope, either chemical or in design patterns, what differs is the internal structure. In the atom, it is the neutron count that changes. In the instance of a design pattern, it is the *how* that instance was implemented. These can have far-ranging effects, even if they are not immediately identifiable from the outside. At any moment, an unstable atom can split depending on its neutron count, and at any moment, a poorly implemented instance of a design pattern may cause a crash, even though from the outside it looks fine.

The idea of separating the implementation from the external interface is not new to object-oriented programming, it is quite natural and embedded. The new concept introduced in isotopes is separating the implementation and interface of a *concept* in the same manner. Remember that each design pattern has a series of roles—noted in the participants section—that must be fulfilled by portions of an implementation. These roles are the external interface through which the design pattern interacts with other concepts and patterns.

The collaborations section describes how these roles interact internally at the conceptual level, but these interactions can be described and discussed independently of the implementation. This is where the formalisms from the appendix come into play and provide a tremendous amount of flexibility, but the concept can be shown here with a code example. We hinted at this back in Section 2.2.2 with a simple example of transitivity between methods, but now we can go into it in more detail.

Start with the left side of the following code examples, where an object f has a method `foo` calling method `bar` of object b. We say that `f.foo` relies on `b.bar`. The object, type, and method similarities between those two endpoints is well defined and specifies the EDP between them. If the implementation is changed, for instance, by injecting a new object in a method-calling chain, the construct is altered, but the relationship between the *endpoints* remains unchanged, as in the right-hand side of the code example. The original reliance is intact, and the three similarities remain intact. New reliances have surely been created, but the original ones necessary for the design pattern remain. The new implementation is an isotope of the original EDP: it looks the same and acts the same when viewed as a concept from the outside, even if it looks different internally.

More important, it allows developers to talk about the design of the system without having to be concerned with every tiny implementation detail. We can discuss the design at a higher level of abstraction.

```
1 class F {
    B b;
3   void foo() {
      b.bar();
5   };
  };
7 F f;
  f.foo();
```

```
  class F {
2   G g;
    void foo() {
4     g.goo();
    };
6 };
  class G {
8   B b;
    void goo() {
10    b.bar();
    };
12 };
  F f;
14 f.foo();
```

f.foo() relies on b.bar()   f.foo() **still** relies on b.bar()

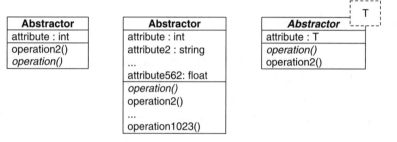

Figure 4.8 shows alternative Abstractor classes.

Abstractor
attribute : int
operation2()
operation()

Abstractor
attribute : int
attribute2 : string
...
attribute562: float
operation()
operation2()
...
operation1023()

Abstractor
attribute : T
operation()
operation2()

Figure 4.8 Alternative classes that can fulfill an *Abstract Interface* EDP.

As an example, let's revisit the construction of *Fulfill Method* and see how iso-topes can help provide flexibility with even this small example. At the end of that construction, I mentioned that the UML shown in Figure 4.2 was the minimal UML required, not an exact requirement. Had we defined *Fulfill Method* using that exact UML, then any alteration to how we implemented *Fulfill Method* would require a new definition for the pattern. Because the number of ways that *Fulfill Method* could appear in a system are many, this would lead to a large number of definitions for such a simple concept. This is suboptimal.

The class that fulfills the Abstractor role in *Abstract Interface* can have any num-ber of other fields and methods associated with it. It just has to have at least one method that is abstract. Figure 4.8 shows multiple UML classes, any one of which can have an *Abstract Interface* instance associated with it. Any one of these can be used to show the existence of an instance of *Abstract Interface*. It doesn't matter how many attributes or fields a class has, how many other methods it may have, or whether it's a template or generic class. The class simply has to have one method that is abstract.

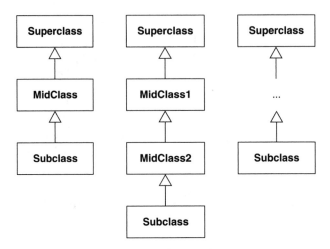

Figure 4.9 Alternative structures that can fulfill an *Inheritance* EDP.

Stated differently, the instance of *Abstract Interface* shown as a PINbox in the diagram for *Fulfill Method* in Figure 4.4 can stand in for any of these or for a nearly infinite number of other implementation possibilities. By using just the PINboxes, we don't have to deal with all the possible UML representations or code implementations.

Likewise, the two-class, minimalist version of *Inheritance* we saw in Figure 4.2 isn't the only way to satisfy that EDP. Any number of classes can be in the inheritance chain between the two classes we're interested in, as shown in Figure 4.9. The depth of the inheritance tree doesn't matter because a subclass is still a subclass.[3] Again, the instance of *Inheritance* depicted by the PINbox in Figure 4.4 is representative of any of these possible implementations.

We can take this isotope concept even a bit further. Recall that not every language has explicit classes. This was a component of the discussion for using the term *type* in Section 2.2.2. How does subclassing work in such languages? We revisit that in the specification for *Abstract Interface* in Chapter 5, but even that kind of significant language-based change can be encapsulated by an isotope. We do not want to have to *care* what the implementation language may be, remember, and this is what lets us do that. By working at the level of EDPs and PINboxes, we remove ourselves from even the semantics of the language that may be used for implementation. Being

---

3. This is another example of transitivity, and it is a core feature of the ρ-calculus described in the appendix, and what gives the EDPs their real power. See, I told you I was going to keep giving you nudges to go read the formal bits.

language-agnostic is extremely powerful. What we've accomplished here, more or less, is polymorphism of design concepts.

With so many possible implementations for any given design pattern, you may be wondering how we know what the correct definition is for a design pattern. After all, I just showed you that for any given design concept, a huge number of possible implementations can exist. The patterns community still selects and writes down one canonical form for sharing, so what's the criteria for selecting *that* one?

Simply put, what is transcribed is the simplest possible implementation and set of participants and collaborations. The final form provides nothing extraneous and gets to the essence of the concept being communicated. Anything beyond that simple core would obfuscate the central concepts and lesson. Isotopes almost always add additional items to the canonical description, yet in such a way that the concepts are still embodied.

Design patterns are created and edited in such a way as to get to the essence of the problem, the solution, and the context, to make teaching, learning, and using them as simple as possible. In the end, the simplest description is the best description. Let the isotopes handle the modifications of implementation.

4.2 Recreating *Decorator*

So far in this chapter, you've seen how very small concepts and design issues can be composed in well-formed and specific ways to form larger concepts. You've also seen how these concepts are an encapsulation of the implementation, so the design discussion can be simplified through abstraction. We're going to combine these elements to build up a much more satisfying and robust definition of *Decorator* than we started with in Chapter 2.

We start by revisiting our initial UML diagram for *Decorator* in Figure 4.10 and our UML version of *Fulfill Method* in Figure 4.11.

Looking again at *Decorator* (Figure 4.10), we can see where the structure from *Fulfill Method* is found, in two places, with the Component class acting as the Abstractor role in both. On second thought, this is looking quite like our *Objectifier* pattern from Figure 2.2, isn't it? Good eye. This is exactly what *Objectifier* is—the expansion of a single *Fulfill Method* across several concrete subclasses, as in Figure 4.12. Again, we're using the PIN for *Fulfill Method*, shown here in its stacked form (see Section 3.2.4) to indicate how the underlying concepts fit together. We just defined a design pattern that already existed in the literature, but from first principles, by building it out of smaller, well-understood pieces. In Figures 4.2 through 4.5, we wrapped *Fulfill Method* in a PINbox. We do the same wrapping of

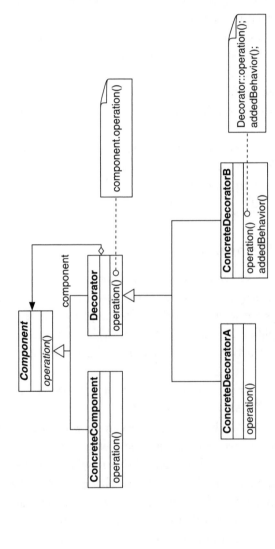

Figure 4.10 *Decorator's* usual example UML.

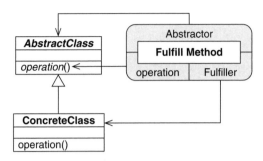

Figure 4.11 *Fulfill Method* definition as annotated UML.

Objectifier using Figure 4.12 as the internals but omitting the diagrams in between. This gives us a PINbox for *Objectifier*.

Taking this a step further, we can define *Object Recursion* as well. Recall that we said in Section 2.2.1 that *Objectifier* is a component of *Object Recursion*, but we did not address what the remaining part was. We can now identify it as the *Trusted Redirection* EDP. Figure 4.13 shows the two patterns as UML. In combining to form *Object Recursion*, FamilyHead and Objectifier will merge, as will ConcreteObjectifierB and Redirector.

Figure 4.14 shows *Object Recursion* in a slightly cleaner form than as introduced in the original Figure 2.3, now annotated with the PINboxes for *Objectifier* and *Trusted Redirection*. The Objectifier role from the *Objectifier* pattern and the Family Head role from *Trusted Redirection* are now being fulfilled by the same entity, the class named Handler. Likewise, ConcreteObjectifierB and Redirector have merged into Recursor. This is shown more succinctly by the PIN diagram in Figure 4.15.

We can now discuss *Object Recursion* in terms of smaller patterns and in a much more precise way than we could before. "*Object Recursion* uses polymorphism, through the *Objectifier* pattern, to determine at runtime which type in a related family of types will handle a specific call. By applying *Trusted Redirection* to at least one of the possible implementations, it also chains together two or more objects from that family such that they can handle that same call in turn and bring their own implementation to bear." This statement is precise, it is direct, and it avoids having to discuss the pattern in structural terms. Furthermore, if someone is unclear on the underlying concepts, he or she can study the full pattern specifications of each of the subpatterns. We can leverage those specifications and definitions from the patterns literature to make our descriptions of higher-level abstractions and patterns much easier to comprehend.

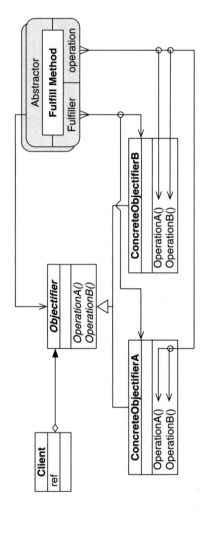

Figure 4.12 *Objectifier* UML annotated with PIN.

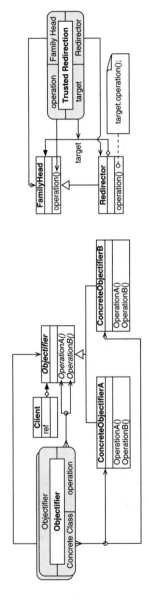

Figure 4.13 *Objectifier and Trusted Redirection.*

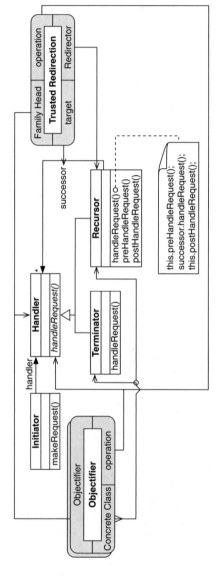

Figure 4.14 *Object Recursion* annotated with PIN.

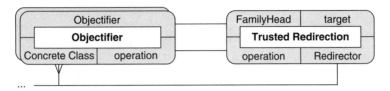

Figure 4.15 *Object Recursion* as just PIN.

We composed the top half of the *Decorator* pattern and have just one piece left to go to finish our definition. The remaining concept is *Extend Method*, which fills out the bottom of *Decorator* by extending *Trusted Redirection*, as shown in Figures 4.16 and 4.17. *Extend Method*'s original behavior and recursor from *Object Recursion* merge into *Decorator*, tying these two smaller patterns together.[4]

We can simplify this by reducing it again to just the PINboxes, as in Figure 4.18. Furthermore, we can always wrap and reduce this to a single PINbox indicating an instance of *Decorator*, as in Figure 4.19. The role names here are taken directly from the participants section of the *Decorator* specification in the Gang of Four (GoF) text [21], with two additions: operation and componentObj. These are implicitly discussed in the participants section, but we make them explicit here to clarify the pieces involved.

Now we have a simple, concise notation for the *Decorator* pattern. At this point, however, we can go the other way as well. We can use expanded PINboxes to increasingly expose finer granularity in *Decorator* by showing the underlying hierarchy of concepts. Figure 4.20 shows *Decorator* as an expanded PINbox, revealing its direct internal wiring. Figures 4.21 and 4.22 drill into *Object Recursion* and *Objectifier*, respectively, and finally Figure 4.23 expands *Fulfill Method* to the EDP level, at which point we can decompose no further. *Decorator* is now fully revealed. Each of these diagrams is equivalent to the others.

So that's *Decorator*, and we built it with just four EDPs: *Abstract Interface*, *Inheritance*, *Trusted Redirection*, and *Extend Method*. Each is a simple concept, but together, linked in a very specific combination, they describe a fairly high-level abstraction that is commonly found in software systems. What's more, we demonstrated that interim concepts can be studied and mastered to gain a more thorough understanding of *Decorator*.

---

4. `ConcreteDecoratorA` and `Decorator` form another leg of *Inheritance*, but we're leaving it out for clarity at the moment.

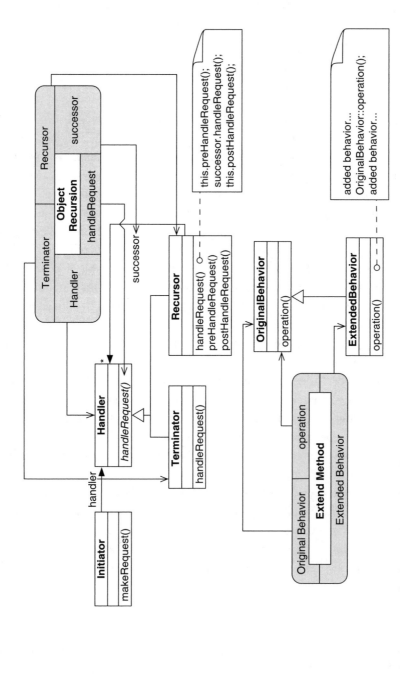

Figure 4.16 *Object Recursion and Extend Method.*

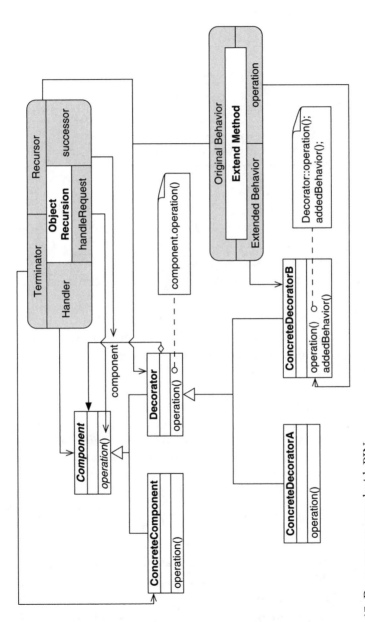

Figure 4.17 *Decorator* annotated with PIN.

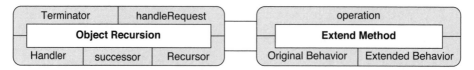

Figure 4.18 *Decorator* as PIN.

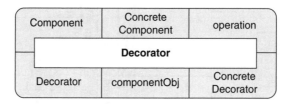

Figure 4.19 *Decorator* instance as a PINbox.

Most important, we never once discussed code. We didn't bring up classes, or methods, or fields. We talked about concepts and ideas only, yet we achieved a framework that provides guidance and precision.

In EDPs, we have the building blocks with which to form great software that we *understand*.

The final section of the GoF text [21, p. 358] uses a quote from Christopher Alexander to describe what is "good design." I can think of no more fitting description of their own design patterns when viewed as dovetailed and intertwined examples of the EDPs.

> It is possible to make buildings by stringing together patterns, in a rather loose way. A building made like this, is an assembly of patterns. Is it not dense. It is not profound. But it is also possible to put patterns together in such a way that many patterns overlap in the same physical space: the building is very dense; it has many meanings captured in a small space; and through this density, it becomes profound. [3, p. xli]

The design patterns literature is full of profundity through the composition of smaller concepts in dense and precise ways. EDPs let us view that density with clarity and insight.

One more comment. Do you recall the example from the beginning of Chapter 2 about the hidden *Decorator* pattern in industrial code that inspired SPQR? SPQR, using the EDPs, composition technique, and formalisms described here, was able to identify its existence in just a couple of seconds without being given any hints. Compared to almost 200 hours, that's a lot of coffee breaks that could be taken instead.

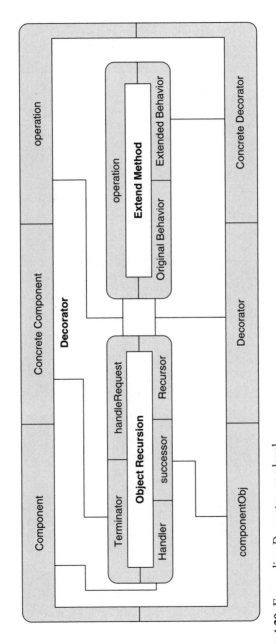

Figure 4.20 Expanding *Decorator*: one level.

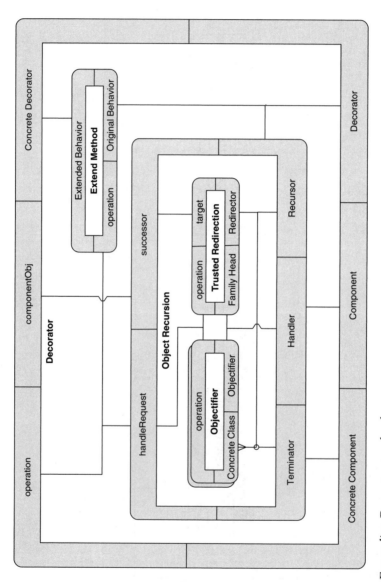

Figure 4.21 Expanding *Decorator*: two levels.

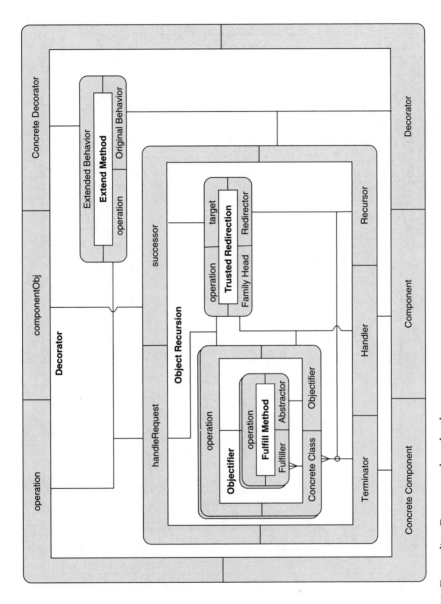

Figure 4.22 Expanding *Decorator*: three levels.

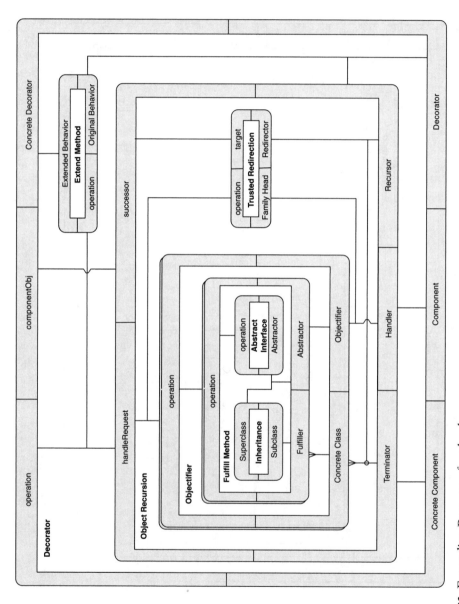

Figure 4.23 Expanding *Decorator*: four levels.

4.3 Refactoring

In discussing isotopes in Section 4.1.1, I stated that a pattern isotope instance might look the same as another instance of that pattern from the outside but have a buggy implementation that causes problems later. Worse than a single poorly implemented design pattern, however, is having multiple interacting design patterns that all bring well-meaning and rational implementation choices to the system but form a problem when combined. Recall that the initial driving problem for SPQR, described in Section 2.1, was that a design pattern arose organically and unintentionally. Malignant designs can form just as easily, and because the number of ways to produce poor code is greater than the number of good designs, they tend to arise much more readily.

When it comes to design patterns, we can classify some of the "bad design" issues that can appear.

First are the *anti-patterns*, which you may have heard of [14]. These are patterns that should be avoided whenever possible. They express common poor practices, not best practices. If they exist in your system, you should work to remove them and find a proper design pattern to address the use case instead.

Next up are proper design patterns that are misapplied. Perhaps they simply weren't implemented correctly and are missing critical pieces. Perhaps they weren't understood by the designer or implementer and aren't quite fully formed. These *partial* design patterns often are just one or two small tweaks away from expressing the original pattern.

Malignant patterns, on the other hand, are patterns that grew, but grew poorly. Where they may once have been applied and implemented correctly, code modifications over time have broken or mutated them into forms that no longer fulfill their original purpose. The worst side effect in this case is that documentation, if it exists, will frequently still refer to them and thereby mislead developers.

Finally, *iatrogenic* patterns are design patterns that were implemented correctly to solve an existing problem, as it was understood when the solution was selected. Unfortunately, larger design issues brought to bear forces and constraints that were ignored or unknown. The pattern solved the original problem but, by interacting with these other context forces, inadvertently created a new situation that may be worse than the original.

All of these problems can be solved by properly *refactoring* the code, which mainly requires moving functionality from one location to another to better streamline a design. The features and executable functionality of the system are not appreciably altered, but the ways the pieces hook together are. You're not directly altering what the code is *doing*, but you may be enhancing what the code *could* do. By improving the design of the system, you're improving the readability of the system, which means that it is easier for a developer to understand and modify the code. Adding new features, fixing bugs, and many other desirable actions are simpler and faster to undertake and complete.

Refactoring of code is well established in our field, and two sources in particular are worth pointing out. Martin Fowler's *Refactoring* [19] and Joshua Kerievsky's *Refactoring to Patterns* [24] form a dovetailed set of recipes for converting code from one configuration to another. Both are well worth your time to check out. If you've ever used an integrated development environment (IDE) such as Eclipse, Visual Studio, or Xcode, you have probably used refactorings via the capabilities provided in those tools. They automate the process of performing simple, useful tasks, and *Refactoring* was the starting point for much of this functionality. If you want a solid understanding of how best to use the automated tools, you can't go wrong with these books.

Fowler's text lays the groundwork for a catalog of small, discrete refactoring actions that you can take to improve your code design. For instance, he starts with "bad smells," which are situations in which you know something is not quite right with the code even though it may perform correctly. He describes these gut feelings as possible indications of a subconscious uneasiness with the code design, with how understandable or cleanly expressed it is. The more experience you have with programming and the more exposure to good design principles, the more you'll learn to trust your instincts in these cases.

For each bad smell, Fowler provides a series of actions to alleviate the problem. These actions are wide ranging and varied, but I focus on only three here.

Extract Method, for example, is a refactoring action that can be used to solve a smell involving a method that's too darned long and difficult to understand. In its simplest form, it directs you to extract a self-contained portion of the long method into its own method and call it. Great significance is given to the naming of the new method, which shouldn't surprise you by this point.

This significance is exemplified in *Rename Method*, used to clarify intent when a method's usefulness or applicability may be obfuscated.

Similarly, *Move Method* is used to clarify which methods belong together. Clarification is needed when, as Fowler states, "a method is, or will be, using or used by more features of another class than the class on which it is defined." In other words, use *Move Method* when, for some reason, the method is in the wrong class.

Now, these may seem trivial, but each one has implementation subtleties that make Fowler's contribution necessary and rightfully a classic in our field. More to the point, Fowler uses these tiny, well-formed actions as building blocks for larger refactorings that are more complex. Kerievsky takes this concept and runs with it, using Fowler's catalog as the seed for even richer refactorings that show how to methodically and precisely migrate toward implementations of the more common design patterns. Sound familiar?

An interesting parallel is at work here. We can continue it by considering the *Extract Method* refactoring. The effect of this refactoring is to create a new method and a new call to that method. The method that the chunk of code is extracted from is the calling site, and the new method is the callee. Obviously, the two methods can't be the same,[5] so we assume at this point that the methods are dissimilar. Also, because the new method is being formed in the same class/type—according to the refactoring definition—we have the same type and also the same object. Well, we know what this is from our discussion in Section 2.2.4. The EDP with the same object, same type, but dissimilar method is *Conglomeration*.

Next, let's ponder *Rename Method* and what it might mean for an EDP that the renamed method is involved in. Remember, method similarity is (partially) determined by the name of the method. If we alter the name, we could be moving from a method-similar EDP to its method-dissimilar equivalent. For example, consider an instance of *Delegation*, as in Figure 4.24. If the target method `called()` is renamed to `caller()`, it now is similar to the calling site, and *Delegation* has become *Redirection*, as in Figure 4.25. Of course, the rename could be to anything, and this EDP transformation only holds if the new name is a similarity match. So now we can say that *Delegation* + *Rename Method* (to similarity) = *Redirection*. Going the other way, *Redirection* + *Rename Method* = *Delegation*.

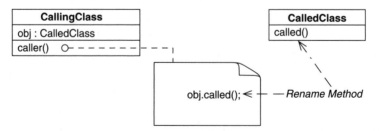

Figure 4.24 *Delegation* before *Rename Method* refactoring.

---

5. Once again, we're ignoring overloading for now. Assume that similarity is based not only on the name but on the entire method signature.

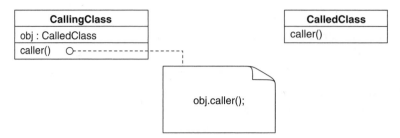

Figure 4.25 *Delegation* after *Rename Method* refactoring—*Redirection*.

With each change in the design, no matter how small, we alter the EDPs that are components of it. The EDPs will in turn affect the design patterns that are formed from them, and so on up the compositional hierarchy. By knowing precisely how alterations such as those enumerated in the refactoring literature will affect our design on multiple levels of granularity, and by knowing precisely how those refactorings will percolate changes throughout our system, we can better predict what the larger ramifications of a planned design change will be.

Large changes aren't required to substantially alter a design, however, or to trigger a ripple effect. We transformed *Delegation* to *Redirection* by applying *Rename Method* such that it created a method similarity where there wasn't one before. Let's reverse that similarity change but start with *Trusted Redirection*, which we used to help create *Decorator* back in Section 4.2. What do you think happens if we perform a *Rename Method* refactoring on the method used in *Trusted Redirection*?

Simple. The instance of *Decorator* ceases to exist.

By renaming the method, no matter how deeply nested in the implementation— which is possible because of isotopes—we remove *Trusted Redirection* and replace it with its method-dissimilar equivalent, *Trusted Delegation*. When we remove *Trusted Redirection*, we remove a central and necessary piece of *Decorator*. What have we turned it into? Good question. In some ways, the new design looks a bit like a *Strategy*, another design pattern from the GoF that shares some conceptual similarities with *Decorator*, but in any case, our *Decorator* is no more. If our documentation or expectations about the system include that instance being there, we now have a mismatch between our understanding of the system and how it actually exists in implementation. That is a recipe for mistakes.

For more fun, let's consider *Move Method* and what happens to the reliances between it and any method that calls it when it is moved. First, we have to recognize that moving the method means that it is going to be moved to a new class/type. Being in a new type means that any method that calls it may have to do some cleanup to

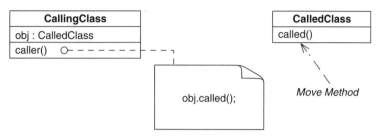

Figure 4.26 *Delegation* before *Move Method* refactoring.

continue using it after the move is accomplished. Let's start with a simple example using *Delegation* again, as shown in Figure 4.26. As a reminder, this is a method call between two dissimilar methods contained in two different objects of different and unrelated types. We know that applying *Rename Method* changes the method similarity. But how will this EDP change as we move the method around?

This refactoring has a number of possible effects, depending on how it is implemented. The range and impacts are numerous enough that now is a good time to briefly introduce the other half of the EDPs. Recall from *Section 2.2.4* the two-dimensional grid of method-similar EDPs in *Figure 2.10*. In Figure 4.27, you'll find their method-*dissimilar* counterparts. The object type axis is flipped to exactly mirror the first figure, because these are equivalent to the ones we discussed before, except for the method similarity.

In moving a method, the most general case is to move it to a related type, as in Figure 4.28. Such a move retains the *Delegation* instance, but it isn't very interesting. Consider instead what happens when we move the method into the same class type as the calling method, as in Figure 4.29. Of course, now calling `called()` on the `obj` object doesn't make much sense.

There are two possibilities for fixing the mismatch within the method `caller()`. First, the `caller()` can elect to change the type of the object `obj` to the destination type. In other words, `obj` becomes an instance field of the same type as the type it is defined in. Second, `caller()` can eliminate the object completely and call its own instance using `self`. Which path is taken depends on the data usage needs of `called()`. If `called()` works primarily on data that is passed to it via `caller()`, and that data is instance data in the object encapsulating `caller()`, then that data can be accessed by `called()` directly and no longer needs to be passed as parameters. In this case, the second choice is a good one. Otherwise, the former design is preferred.

But what EDPs represent these two cases?

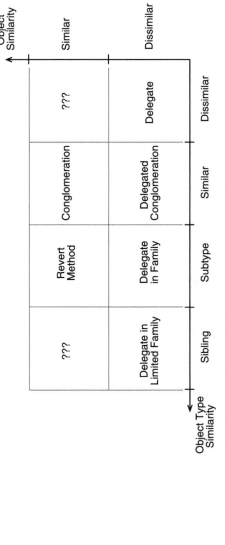

Figure 4.27 The design space with method similarity fixed to dissimilar.

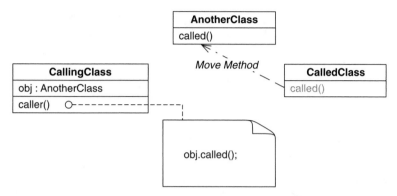

Figure 4.28 *Delegation* after *Move Method* refactoring: boring case.

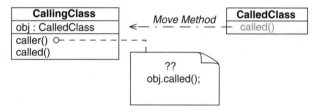

Figure 4.29 *Delegation* after *Move Method* refactoring: into same type.

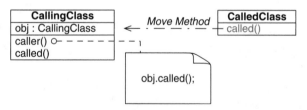

Figure 4.30 *Delegation* after *Move Method* refactoring: *Delegated Conglomeration*.

The first choice, changing the type of the object, results in a method-call EDP between differing methods of differing objects of the same type. By looking at Figure 4.27, as dissimilar object, similar type, we can see that this is an example of a *Delegated Conglomeration*. Much like *Redirected Recursion*, it involves two objects of the same type, working in concert. Unlike *Redirected Recursion*, however, in this case the two methods are dissimilar. Figure 4.30 illustrates this situation.

The alternative is to simply replace the called-upon object with `self`, eliminating the need for the field object, as shown in Figure 4.31, and resulting in the

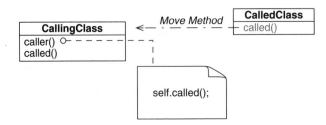

Figure 4.31 *Delegation* after *Move Method* refactoring: *Conglomeration*.

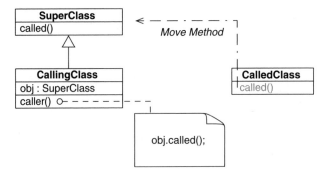

Figure 4.32 *Delegation* after *Move Method* refactoring: *Trusted Delegation*.

same dissimilar-method relationship as before, but now with a similar type, *and* a similar object. Figure 4.27 tells us that this is *Conglomeration*, which we discussed back in Section 2.2.4.

A similar duality occurs in other type-related decisions. If the method being moved is moved to a supertype of `CallingClass`, then we have either *Trusted Delegation* or *Revert Method*, depending on whether the called-on object is retained with the new type or eliminated in favor of *super*. Figures 4.32 and 4.33 demonstrate these outcomes. *Trusted Delegation* is extremely common and appears when the delegation is to be handed to a trusted group of related types and handled appropriately. This is easiest to do by using a polymorphic call on an object whose type is a superclass of the calling site. The superclass provides the trusted group of types, and the polymorphism means that it is handled appropriately.

Moving the method `called` to a sibling type of `CallingClass` results in a situation such as in Figure 4.34. As you might expect, it is an example of *Deputized Delegation*. Here, the trusted group of possible handling types is refined by restricting the polymorphic root to a sibling class of the calling site.

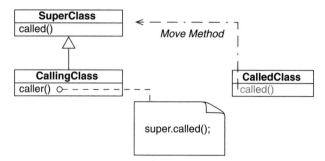

Figure 4.33 *Delegation* after *Move Method* refactoring: *Revert Method.*

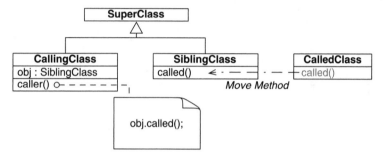

Figure 4.34 *Delegation* after *Move Method* refactoring: *Deputized Delegation.*

Finally, it should be noted that each of the transformations has a symmetric transformation that reverses it. We could just as easily go back to *Delegation* from any of the EDPs we transformed into and then on to any other endpoint EDP. In doing so, we traverse the entirety of Figure 4.27. With that one simple refactoring of *Move Method*, we routed between all six EDPs described.

As you can see, refactoring can have far-reaching effects in a design, even when the actions taken may seem trivial. It is important to keep in mind where your design is going to end up when undertaking refactoring efforts, and EDPs can help you plan ahead.

We can summarize the actions and resulting EDP transformations that we've discussed so far, as shown in Figure 4.35. You can see how applying *Move Method*, starting from *Delegation*, leads us to each of the other five EDPs on the left side of the diagram though the paths in bold. I've filled in the remaining possible transformations, including their mirror transformations. The use of the refactoring *Rename Method* to move left and right hints at a symmetry here, which we revisit in the next section.

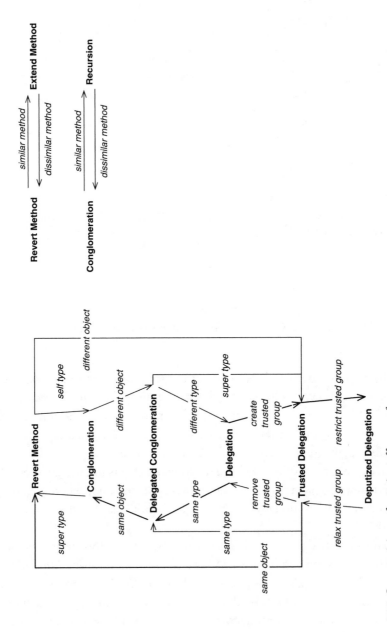

Figure 4.35 Summarizing refactoring effects so far.

4.4 The Big Picture

So far, this chapter has been a series of lessons on working with EDPs. You learned how to compose EDPs and other patterns into larger abstractions that have solid and workable definitions. You learned how to look for patterns that you already know of when reading about new patterns. We discussed isotopes, which allow design patterns and their implementations to be decoupled somewhat, allowing the encapsulation of design concepts and flexibility of expression in code. You even were introduced to the established libraries of refactoring approaches, saw how they work in concert with the EDPs, and saw how the well-defined relationships among the EDPs can facilitate refactoring planning.

We covered a wide range of topics, but now we can summarize them into some fairly simple charts and diagrams. The following figures provide a better sense of how the EDPs relate to one another. Some pattern names will be new to you. They haven't been discussed in detail, but you'll find them in the catalog chapters later in this book.

Figure 4.36 shows which EDPs are used by other EDPs and particularly which of the core EDPs are involved in the method-call EDPs. As you can see, there are some clear arrangements that form conceptual constellations. In some cases, the uses here are implicit, not explicit. *Redirection*, for instance, doesn't explicitly use *Retrieve*, but because *Redirection* operates between two objects, *Retrieve* must be involved at some point to make one object available to the other for calling a method on it. On the other hand, *Inheritance* explicitly appears in the six EDPs that use subclassing.

First, notice that *Retrieve* is used heavily in the top portion of the digram. The EDPs that use *Retrieve*, as you would expect, involve two objects. These are the dissimilar-object method-call EDPs. Below them are the four similar-object EDPs.

Second, *Inheritance* dominates the middle section of the diagram. Method-call EDPs involved with *Inheritance* are those whose object *types* are in a subclass or sibling class typing relationship.

Note also that there is a symmetry in the diagram from left to right in the method-call EDPs. On the left are the EDPs between *dissimilar* methods; those on the right are EDPs between *similar* methods.

Finally, the patterns outside the core and method-call EDP boxes are those composed of two or more EDPs. Our old friend *Fulfill Method* uses both *Abstract Interface* and *Inheritance*, for instance.

I showed you part of the design space for method-call EDPs in Section 2.2.4, and it is now further fleshed out graphically in Figures 4.37 and 4.38. Each shows

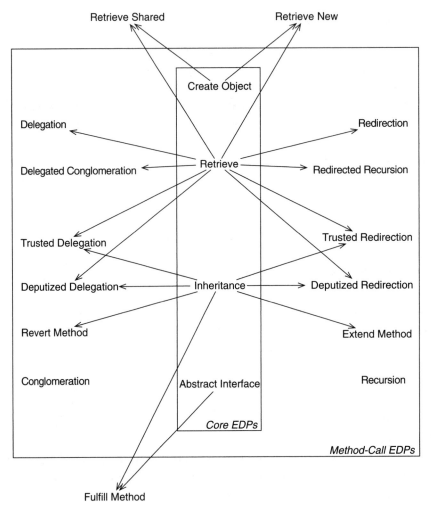

Figure 4.36 Implicit used-by relationships among the EDPs and selected other patterns.

one half of the design space. Using this as a conceptual map as you read the EDP descriptions will help you see how they relate to one another.

These two diagrams are aligned to match with the left and right sides of Figure 4.36. Figure 4.37 shows all method-call EDPs with *dissimilar* methods; it is the application of Figure 4.27, from our discussion in Section 4.3, onto the left long side of Figure 2.9. By turning this cuboid, we can look at the right long side, as in Figure 4.38, with the *similar*-method EDPs. Figure 4.38 is the application of Figure 2.10 onto the right long side of Figure 2.9. We discussed these EDPs in Section 2.2.4,

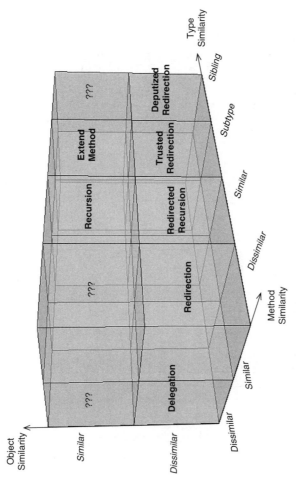

Figure 4.37 The full method-call EDP design space: dissimilar method.

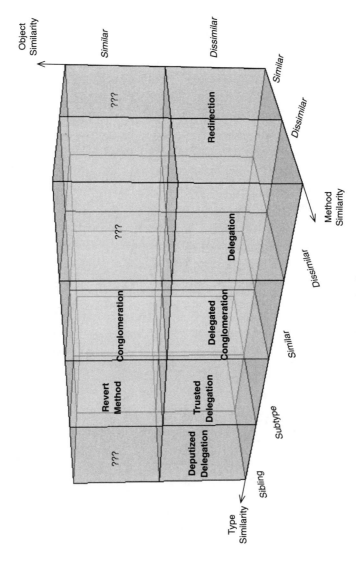

Figure 4.38 The full method-call EDP design space: similar method.

when we considered EDPs with similar methods. These two diagrams are just the left and right sides of the same constructed space. They show where each EDP sits in the design space defined by the three similarity axes we started with: method, object, and object type. Each EDP is related to the EDPs surrounding it by explicit changes along those axes.

Describing those changes gives us the view in Figure 4.39, by building on what we showed in Figure 4.35. This lists the change required to transform each method-call EDP into another one, a single step at a time, to provide the atomic refactorings introduced in the previous section. This diagram will be useful as the requirements of a system change. You can better predict what the resulting system will look like if you know where you will need to end up in this EDP space. The figure on the left corresponds to Figure 4.37, with the dissimilar methods, and the figure on the right matches up with Figure 4.38, with the similar methods. If the method similarity property of an EDP changes, you shift from the left to the right, or vice versa.

For instance, if you implemented an instance of *Recursion* but need to break up the task among multiple objects, the arrow labeled *different object* points you directly to *Redirected Recursion*. If instead you find that the *Recursion* needs to be broken up into distinct subtasks, then you will be introducing new methods, and you know that you will no longer retain the method similarity. In that case, the large arrow in the middle labeled *dissimilar method* indicates you should slide left to the corresponding location on that tree, and you end up at *Conglomeration*. Each decision point that you have at your disposal will lead you to the proper, related concept.

When applying other refactoring actions, such as those from Fowler [19] and Kerievsky [24], you will find those actions moving your design elements along these routes. By knowing ahead of time how the EDPs will change and shift, you can better predict where your design will end up and manage potential problems.

These four diagrams are the conceptual core for understanding how the individual EDPs relate to each other and how they provide possibilities for design alterations. As you read the following catalogs, you might want to refer back to these figures to keep the larger picture in mind. While each design pattern is a self-contained concept, distinct relationships exist between them that form a richer system for working with and reasoning about them as a group.

4.5 Why You May Want to Read the Appendix

Okay, so I'm cheating a bit. I said that you didn't have to understand any of the mathematics behind the EDPs to understand or use them. At this point, though, I'm going to offer a couple of claims based on the formalisms, and you can either

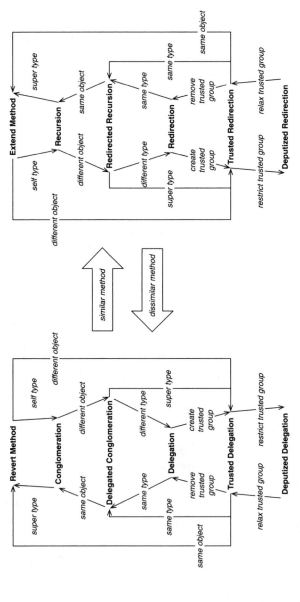

Figure 4.39 Method-call EDP refactoring relations.

take them on faith or you can go read the appendix to convince yourself of their validity. I hope you're skeptical and dive in.

First off, taken as a whole, the formal body of EDPs provides complete coverage of the possible designs of object-oriented programming. Remember, this book touches on only one-quarter, at best, of the possible EDPs that exist. It is simply impossible to write an object-oriented program without using the EDPs. Yes, I know that's a bold claim. Please read the formal tidbits for the full explanation. Hint: we established in Chapter 2 that binary relationships are the smallest relationships we can form. Given a finite number of things between which we can form relationships, there must be a finite number of possible relationships. Considering we're starting with only objects, methods, fields, and types, how small do you think this set can get? If your answer is "about the size of the Elemental Design Patterns," give yourself a cookie. That's precisely what the EDPs are: a project to describe all of the possible smallest relationships in object-oriented programming in human terms so that we can share, understand, and use them more effectively. This book is a start; I hope you join in for the remainder of the discussion.

Second, the formalisms defined by the ρ-calculus are fundamentally where the EDPs come from. Most design patterns are created by finding repeating solutions by inspecting existing software systems. This approach lets us describe what we've done before, which is critical, but EDPs are unique in that they are definable from first principles, not just after the fact. To be sure, they are ubiquitously present in existing systems, and those instances are what we use to discern the intent of and write the specification for the EDP, just as with any other design pattern. The EDP design spaces defined by our orthogonal axes of context, however, provide a framework for filling in gaps we didn't realize we had and for establishing exactly how the EDPs relate to one another.

The difference is akin to that between early mechanical engineers sharing blueprints for creations that they designed through trial and error and modern engineers able to simulate a complete design before ever fabricating a single part. The former is a description of what was tried; the latter prediction is based on formal reasoning and modeling. EDPs enable us to describe systems precisely and predict what impact even the smallest changes will have. Furthermore, as you saw with the reconstruction of *Decorator*, EDPs let us work with large abstractions at varying levels of granularity based on the needs of the moment. EDPs also enable us to describe new design patterns as they are found, composing their definitions in terms of existing abstractions. There's really no end to the possibilities.

These features mean that EDPs allow us to do two crucial things with software systems. First, we can define and describe a piece of object-oriented software, *any* piece of object-oriented software, in terms designed to be used and understood by humans, regardless of the implementation language. We can capture the concepts in the code and express them in a way that is appropriate for a human to reason about. We showed that these small concepts quickly build into larger, more interesting concepts that solve real-world problems using best practices, such as the GoF patterns. We can document our software at multiple levels of granularity and choose which level of abstraction to operate on, depending on our needs in the moment. Second, and more enticingly, because these concepts are each formalized, and the manner in which they can interact is likewise formalized, the process of extraction, detection, composition, and description can be *automated*. Not coincidentally, that is the problem that SPQR was designed to solve.

That's just the beginning.

4.6 Advanced Topics

This section introduces some advanced ideas that you might find intriguing. None of these are required for understanding the EDPs or reading the catalog. If you wish to skim (but hopefully not skip) this section, please feel free to do so.

4.6.1 Focused Documentation and Training

SPQR was originally intended to help document existing implementations of software, letting the concepts and abstractions described by the design pattern literature be found and documented directly from the implementation. The goal was that exposing these design pattern instances would give developers a better mental model of their systems, and they would have an easier path to produce that pesky documentation that we all hate doing as well as an easier time maintaining their codebases. Somewhere along the way, however, it became obvious that maybe we were looking at the wrong thing.

Design patterns are those concepts that we understand well. They are well documented, they are common, and they are a shared infrastructure among many systems. So if you find patterns in your software, great! You are using best practices to solve problems that others have already solved. Congratulations!

The entire documentation problem isn't solved, however. You still must explain how you implemented the patterns you chose and how they interact with the rest of the system. Beyond that, however, the problems that others have solved are almost certainly *not* what makes your software unique. They are simply the skeleton on which you hang the features and clever bits of code that make your system more compelling to your clients, those that make it stand out in the marketplace. Those unique sections are the portions of your software that you need to spend your time addressing in documentation. Your coworkers and those who inherit your code will thank you for doing so.

In other words, the portions of your system that are describable by design patterns are not necessarily the parts that are critical to document. There's still a documentation process to be performed. Delineating what portions of your system are covered by design patterns, however, tells you what you *don't* have to spend time documenting. It's the portion of the code that you *don't* have to spend excessive resources training new hires on, the portion you *don't* need to take hours to consider the impact of change to, the portion that you *don't* need to make sure stays precisely intact to satisfy your customers.

The portions that are describable in high-level design patterns are those that are your infrastructure, precisely because they are portions that other people have already broken ground to solve. By understanding where your added value begins and ends, you can reduce the scope of your costs and effort to the parts that really matter to your bottom line.

And of course and you get world-class documentation for the remainder, because other people have already written it. You just have to point to their work.

4.6.2 Metrics

In any engineering discipline, quantitative metrics are a must to provide feedback, to ensure fidelity with predicted results, and to give insight. Software engineering is no different, and EDPs and their underlying formalisms make possible new ways to measure what we do.

Clarity of Expression   We all have experienced software that is less readable than we would like. If we're lucky, we may have experienced software that is extremely easy to read. Why is this? What makes some software make sense, while another system that does the same thing is a nightmare to work on?

Readability is not just a matter of selecting the right names and using the correct whitespace formatting. A piece of software that clearly expresses the concepts that it implements is considered readable. When the cognitive load on the programmer tasked with understanding it is low, it is considered clear. If the software contains the proper concepts, but they are hidden in a tangle of other things, then the intent and the meaning of what the original developer was trying to do is difficult to find. This is a qualitative process. We know clear code when we see it.

So what's one way to ensure that the expression of a concept is clear and that the implementation is as readable as possible? Well, recall that we talked about isotopes. We can measure the relative clarity of the expression of the concept by how closely it matches the smallest, most direct, clearest expression of form. Usually, this is found in the canonical specification for a particular design pattern. If this canonical form was not already clear or not at its most reduced form, it is unlikely that it could have passed muster with the community. The specification of a design pattern is intended to be, above all else, clear.

For each additional step in a chain of reliances or each unnecessary piece in the implementation of an EDP, the developer has to work harder to see the relationship between the end points. It follows that we can measure the distance from optimal by counting the number of isotopic components that are unnecessary to expression of the concept but are present in the implementation. Basically, we count the extra pieces required to fulfill an individual pattern or concept instance.

Now, it may be (and probably is) true that those extra bits are necessary and useful for some other concept in the system, but their presence is obscuring that *particular* conceptual expression. We can use this as a measure of the clarity of a concept in the code. We can measure the conceptual readability, and we can do so automatically. Furthermore, we can provide guidance in clarifying these concepts by offering refactoring actions at the EDP-to-EDP level. It is up to the human engineers to decide which concepts are most important and need to be most clearly expressed, but at least this way they have a quantitative way to weigh the options and choose between refactoring plans.

Abstraction Density Using isotopes and EDPs to provide guidance for clarifying expression of intent works well for fine-grained precise measurement of specific concepts embodied in the code, but it is far from the whole picture. Another measure of code quality is to look at it in the aggregate and get a large-scale, 50,000-foot view of the system. Abstractions are a way for us to think about chunks of a system as a single concept, instead of having to deal with all details at all times. If you are told that a section of code is a for loop, that is much faster and cleaner than trying to describe the execution at the machine level, step by step. Likewise, each design pattern or concept is an abstraction that conveys a tremendous amount of information with minimal bandwidth. Further, as we showed that we can compose larger and higher-level abstractions from small ones, we can also describe quite large sections of a system at once if an appropriate abstraction can be found to encompass it.

It therefore follows that if we can describe 1,000 lines of code with one abstraction instead of 100 abstractions, we have less to manage in our heads at the same time. We can work with those thousand lines as a single whole and not have to worry about the internals. Larger sections of the system can be considered, mulled over, understood, and possibly refactored.

Overall, an implementation that can be described in a few high-level abstractions is preferable to one that must be described in many many small ones, all else being equal. We call this the *abstraction density* of the code, measured as the number of abstractions present in the code, weighted for their composition. In other words, an abstraction that encapsulates six smaller concepts is considered more important and preferable to the six small abstractions plus another small abstraction. In each case there are seven abstractions total, but in the former case, there's only one that is required to be carried forward by a developer for basic understanding; in the latter situation, seven pieces of information must be mentally juggled.

The key phrase in the preceding paragraph is "all else being equal." An abstraction may be formed from many pieces of information, but not all pieces of information will be part of a meaningful abstraction. We can measure the raw density in the code by measuring the number of context-free reliances it has. Remember, each reliance is a connection between two entities in the code; therefore each reliance is a connection that the developer must keep track of, but abstractions alleviate that burden. We call this raw number the *information density* of the code, presented as a number of reliances per line of code.

Taking the ratio of the two enables us to determine the number of abstractions per unit of raw information, the *relative abstraction density* (RAD). We can perform this analysis on a per-method, per-class, per-file, per-directory, or per-module granularity. It helps expose hot spots and potential trouble areas by alerting a project manager to the areas that are most likely to be problematic moving forward. Which isn't to say that such code is *wrong*.

The lower the RAD, the more we would expect that area of the code to be problematic to work with. It may be efficient, optimized, behave perfectly, and have no bugs. We just wouldn't consider it to be very maintainable when requirements change. Perhaps that's exactly what an engineer needs from that code in that case. Knowing where the potential problem spots are *before* they bite you, however, allows you and your team to plan accordingly.

On the other hand, you may have a module with a very high RAD but that you know is riddled with bugs. You may decide to go ahead and stomp the bugs there, because the high RAD gives you confidence that the code is more readable and should be easier to work with. Perhaps in that case, the training overhead is low enough that you can bring on a couple more people to help out. Again, it's a matter of getting the right information into the hands of the developers and project leads for decision making by humans.

4.6.3 Procedural Analysis

Throughout this discussion, there has been an underlying assumption that the implementation languages under consideration are object-oriented ones. After all, the formalisms are object oriented, UML diagrams are object oriented, and design patterns are object oriented, right? Well, no, not quite. Design patterns are just concepts like any other. Remember that some of them, such as *Create Object* and *Inheritance*, *can* be expressed in procedural languages with great fidelity. After all, that's where they were first found. Object-oriented programming arose because it enforced best practices that were used in procedural languages.

It turns out that, given the right set of assumptions, procedural code can be analyzed for design patterns just as easily as object-oriented code can be. Remember the discussion of how to model global entities in C++, back in Section 2.2.2? In C, everything is global, but the same technique applies. At IBM Research, we were able to successfully generate meaningful UML diagrams for systems with hundreds of thousands of lines of code, written exclusively in C. EDPs were the link. Creating a fine-grained enough set of formalized concepts allows for the fine-grained analysis required to match procedural idioms to object-oriented assumptions. Entirely new vistas for visualizing and considering legacy code start to appear.

4.7 Conclusion

I trust this quick introduction to EDP has been interesting. I hope it has also been illuminating. Software is one of our most critical modern conveniences, one that we have an extremely tenuous grasp on. Right now we are more alchemists than engineers, sharing nuggets of gold among ourselves without knowledge of a periodic table. The EDPs, and the research that spawned them, are a way of creating a basis for a more rigorous approach to software engineering that is also very *human*. Software is a collaboration between man and machine, between human and silicon, and attempting to optimize it for one inevitably causes issues for the other. I propose that we let the machines handle the constructs, that we handle the concepts, and that we use design patterns with EDPs at the foundation as the bridge between the two.

You're now ready to tackle the rest of this book, and I hope you find it as much of an eye-opener in the reading as I did in the writing. If we, as a community and an industry, can start thinking of software in terms of intent and focus on the concepts that form our designs instead of on the constructs that we use to explain them to a compiler, we can concentrate on what we do better than any machine.

We design. We collaborate. We communicate. We explain. We build.

We make the modern world run.

Let's take it to the next level.

EDP 5 Catalog

With the foundation we built in the previous chapters, you're ready to start investigating the first portion of the EDP Catalog presented in the remainder of this book. The first sixteen patterns presented are the four fundamental object-oriented programming patterns followed by the twelve method-call EDPs. You've been introduced to eleven of them so far, and there are five more for you to learn on your own from the included specifications.

The format used to write up a design pattern is fairly standardized. The first popular use was in the original Gang of Four (GoF) text [21], and I follow that form here. Each pattern is written in several sections, starting with the pattern's name, so that we have something canonical to refer to it by. The Intent section explains the pattern's purpose. Next, the Motivation section provides background on the problem this pattern solves, and then the Applicability section explains when it should (or should not) be used. A sample structure is provided next as both a UML diagram and, where appropriate, an expanded PINbox. This structure is not ever to be used as a rote recipe, remember, but only as an example. If you need to change the implementation and do so without altering the relationships you're concerned with, then do it. The concepts will still be there.

The Participants and Collaborations sections follow and address those concepts. The pattern specification continues with the Consequences and Implementation sections. Here, sample code is provided, but, again, it is to be taken only as a guideline. Your implementation language will almost certainly greatly impact how you choose to express a design pattern. Where appropriate, discussions of how these concepts are expressed in different languages are used to highlight just how varied different implementations may look, yet each still can provide the basis for consistent description of the underlying concepts as design patterns. A discussion of related patterns completes each specification.

The EDPs are organized into three main categories: Object Elements, Type Relation, and Method Invocation.

Object Elements are those elemental patterns that deal with the creation and definition of objects: *Create Object* and *Retrieve*. *Create Object* describes when, how, and why we instantiate objects, what makes them special over procedural systems, and why they are not merely syntactic sugar. *Retrieve* outlines how and why objects are used as data fields inside an enclosing object.

Type Relation contains two simple patterns: *Inheritance* provides a discussion of the primary method by which typing information and method body definitions are reused effectively in object-oriented systems, and *Abstract Interface* solves the problem of needing to defer implementations to type definitions that may be created at a later date.

The last group, Method Invocation, contains the final 12 patterns in this chapter, as described in Chapter 2.

The patterns in the collection, while small and precise, are important because of their ubiquity in object-oriented programming and because they are amenable to formalization, unlike most higher abstraction design patterns. Every programmer uses these patterns on a daily basis, usually without conscious effort. Because one purpose of patterns is to bring awareness to that which is subconscious and reflexively seen as useful, these specifications are intended to foster that awareness and facilitate discussion about the basic concepts of our field.

Additionally, the EDPs act as a foundation for better describing and discussing best-practice design patterns that may not be as readily understandable or memorable from the current literature. These EDPs are the building blocks of comprehension, empowering us to reshape our conversations about design patterns in a significant way.

Create Object	**Object Creation**

Intent

To ensure that newly allocated data structures conform to a set of assertions and preconditions before they are operated on by the rest of the system, and that they can only be operated on in predefined ways.

Also Known As

Instantiation

Motivation

In any executable run on a computer, data must have storage space to be placed in and functions or methods to act on that data. Data without behavior is incapable of action. Behavior without data is incapable of meaningful action. A fundamental talent for any programmer is knowing how to tie together data and functionality in ways that make conceptual sense and facilitate maintainability of the source code. Object instantiation solves two issues: establishing both a default valid state for data and a set of related defined behaviors on that data.

In procedural languages, data and behavior are distinct, with data structures defining the former and functions taking care of the latter. Data is more than just allocated memory: it is a set of assumptions about how to interpret, set, and work with the information in that memory space. In addition, those assumptions define a set of behaviors that are valid to operate on, or operate with, the data.

When data is needed, it requires a block of memory to occupy, which in many languages is simply allocated and handed back to the programmer for use. This data may be associated with a type, or it may be typeless and raw. In most cases, it is uninitialized, meaning that the memory has no default value. A developer must manually fill in the beginning values or risk that whatever random data happened to be in the memory location prior to allocation is still there. This process must be done every time, by every developer. Of course, a reasonable way of encapsulating this initialization behavior is to put it into a function to be called, but doing so only moves the requirement up a level, and now the developer must remember to call the initialization function. Failing to do so means that later functions that operate on that piece of data may be fed invalid or incorrect values, but this requirement is usually not automated or strictly enforced.

Listing 5.1 demonstrates this scenario in C. Assume you're writing a low-level GUI library for offering windows to an application. An initialization function has been supplied, but before it is called, as in lines 31 and 32, the values in the requested data are essentially random. I say "essentially" because some implementations of C do provide a default value of zero for integers, floats, and such, but this is only *some* implementations, on *some* hardware. On other systems, the values are simply whatever was in memory beforehand. Because Listing 5.1 is a complete program, you can run it on your system and see how your particular system behaves.

Listing 5.1 Uninitialized data.

```c
   #include <stdio.h>
 2 #include <string.h>
   #include <stdlib.h>
 4
   struct WindowData {
 6     int xPosition;
       int yPosition;
 8     int width;
       int height;
10     char* title;
   };
12
   void
14 initializeWindowData( struct WindowData* wd ) {
       wd->xPosition = 0;
16     wd->yPosition = 0;
       wd->width = 600;
18     wd->height = 800;
       // Allocate enough for the string
20     // (Plus 1 for terminating NULL)
       wd->title = (char*)malloc(
22         (strlen("Default_title") + 1) * sizeof(char));
       strcpy(wd->title, "Default_title");
24 };

26 int
   main(int argc, char** argv) {
28     struct WindowData wd;

30     // These usually print random data
       printf("width:_%d\n", wd.width);
32     printf("title:_%s\n", wd.title);

34     initializeWindowData(&wd);

36     // These *always* print 0 and "Default title"
       printf("width:_%d\n", wd.width);
38     printf("title:_%s\n", wd.title);
   };
```

This leads to the second issue involved with working with even well-formed data in well-formed ways: not only may the data be malformed in the beginning, but also there are few, if any, barriers to what functions may operate on it. Functions that were not designed to work on a particular piece of data may behave incorrectly due to a mismatch between assumptions of what is stored in the memory and what is actually there. In addition, a function's incorrect assumptions about the data may alter the underlying values in an invalid way. What was previously correctly formed data may now be invalid for the data type.

Often, data and a group of related functions are shipped as a library, but a library only provides them as a loosely defined group; nothing actively ties them together in a way that is enforced by the system. As an improvement, it is possible to bundle functions directly with the data they operate on in some procedural languages, provided you have access to some way of incorporating the functions into a data structure.

In C, this can be done with function pointers. A function pointer for each desired function to be associated with a struct is placed directly within that struct and then is carried along with the data.[1] This is a good way to indicate which behavior is associated with particular data, but it doesn't prevent a developer from simply stepping in and fiddling with the data directly.

To protect the data, we need *encapsulation*, which hides the data from view while providing a set of well-defined and limited ways to access and manipulate the data. Data hidden by encapsulation is said to be *private*. Encapsulation prevents a developer from directly manipulating the data and restricts the possible behaviors to the set bundled with the data. It is possible to perform data encapsulation in a procedural language, again, provided you have some lower-level access, such as through pointers. This technique is also called a *pointer-to-implementation (pimpl)*, *d-pointer*, *opaque pointer*, or *Cheshire cat*.

Combining the two techniques results in a decent way of protecting data and providing a consistent set of possible behaviors on that data. The behavior bundling and encapsulation are possible in only some procedural languages, however, and they are quite messy, error prone, and require

---

1. This is what early C++ systems looked like under the hood, when the `cfront` tool was the primary technique for compiling C++ code. If you're interested in the boundary between object-oriented and procedural languages, that is a good historical place to start.

Listing 5.2 Fixed default values.

```
1  struct WindowData {
       int xPosition = 0;
3      int yPosition = 0;
       int width = 600;
5      int height = 800;
       char title[] = "Default_title";
7  };
```

careful consideration and implementation. Worse yet, they still rely on these techniques being applied as a matter of policy, without automated enforcement by the compiler or language.

An object, on the other hand, is a language-enforced, single, indivisible unit composed of data and applicable methods that are conceptually related, as defined by an object type. The methods chosen to be part of the object type have been determined to have a meaningful association with each other and with the data. The data can easily be protected, we can ensure that this unit is in a specified coherent and well-defined state before we attempt to operate on the object, and we can ensure that only well-defined operations can be performed on the object.

In some procedural languages, while a developer can emulate an object reasonably well for encapsulation and bundled behaviors, they cannot absolutely ensure that the data is always coherent or that the operations on the state of that data are properly restricted. There is almost always *some* way to subvert the techniques described previously to address these issues.

Also, and critically, the practitioner cannot guarantee at the time of allocation of the record that the record's contents conform to *any* specific assertion they may choose to make. Building off of our earlier example, we could provide default values for the members of the WindowData struct, as in Listing 5.2.

Now we don't have to call initializeWindowData(). Whenever we define a new variable of the WindowData type, it comes prefilled with the appropriate values.

This approach works, provided these default values never need to change. Changing the values requires editing and recompiling the source code. Unfortunately, that's often not what we need. Consider what

Listing 5.3 Dynamic initialization

```
 1  void
    initializeWindowData( struct WindowData* wd ) {
 3      wd->xPosition = currentWindow()->xPosition + 10;
        wd->yPosition = currentWindow()->yPosition + 10;
 5      wd->width = currentWindow()->width;
        wd->height = currentWindow()->height;
 7      char * currTitle = currentWindow()->title;
        int counter = currentUntitledCounter();
 9      if (counter == 0) {
            // Set to "Untitled": 8 chars + 1 NULL
11          wd->title =
               (char*)malloc(9 * sizeof(char));
13          strcpy(wd->title, "Untitled");
        } else {
15          // Add enough chars for a ' ', and two digits
            // Limit of 100 Untitled windows at once
17          wd->title =
               (char*)malloc(12 * sizeof(char));
19          strcpy(wd->title, "Untitled ");
            char num[3];
21          snprintf(num, 3, "%d", counter + 1);
            strcat(wd->title, num);
23      }
    };
```

happens when you request a new document window in most modern GUI applications. A new window appears slightly to the right and below your current one, if one exists, and usually has the title "Untitled," but if one with that name already exists and has not been renamed, then the title appends a counter, such as "Untitled 1" and "Untitled 2." This sort of basic behavior should be offered by the library if possible, so it would be nice to have this information set automatically for when you request a new `Win-dowData`.

But we can't do that. The default settings just described rely on the existing state of the application and its documents, and we can't possibly know that when we're writing or compiling the code. We can, of course, put this sort of dynamic information gathering and assignment in a function, as in Listing 5.3, but then we're right back to requiring the developer to remember to call this function. Using default static values doesn't solve our problem as well as we'd like.

Having an initializer function would be an effective solution but not an enforceable one. Enforcement relies on policy, documentation, and engineer discipline, none of which have proven to be ultimately accurate or reliable. An engineer is therefore back to the original problem of not being able to guarantee that any given assertion holds true on the newly allocated data. A malicious, careless, or lazy programmer could allocate the structure, and then fail to call the proper initialization procedure, leading to potentially catastrophic consequences.

Object- and class-based systems provide an alternative. When an object is allocated by a runtime environment, it is initialized in a well-formed way that is dependent on the language and environment. All object-oriented environments provide some analogous mechanism as a fundamental part of their implementation. This mechanism is the attachment point at which the implementor can create a function (usually called the initializer or constructor) that performs the appropriate setup on the object. In this way *any* specific assertion, including those based on information only available at the time of object creation, can be imposed on the data before it is available for use by the rest of the system.[2]

There is no way for a user of the object to bypass this mechanism; it is enforced by the language and runtime environment. The hypothetical malicious, careless, or lazy programmer is thwarted, and a possible error is avoided. Because this type of missed-initialization error is generally extremely difficult to track down and identify, avoidance is preferred.

This enforcement of best practices in the procedural realm provides a strong policy-enforcement mechanism at the language level and promotes objects above mere syntactic sugar or convenience.

Applicability

Use *Create Object* when:

- You wish to provide a data representation and enforce that only certain operations can be performed on any particular instance.

- You wish to provide allocated instances of a data representation and ensure that a set of preconditions is met before use.

---

2. One popular language is a glaring exception to this rule: Objective-C does not enforce both allocation and initialization in one behavior, as most languages do. Instead, it has an alloc-init idiom intended to let developers handle the memory management and data initialization of objects as separate pieces. While it can offer optimization opportunities, as you might expect, it can also lead to developer error.

Structure

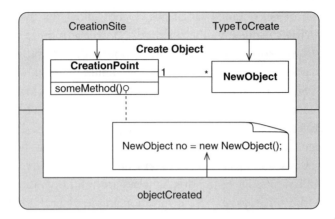

Participants

CreationSite
The object that requests the creation of a new object of type `objectCreated`.

objectCreated
The object to be created.

TypeToCreate
The type of `objectCreated`.

Collaborations

An instance of `CreationSite` requests that a new instance of object, `objectCreated`, of type `TypeToCreate`, be created. The exact mechanism for doing so varies among languages, but it generally consists of making the request "of" the object type itself. In reality, the request is given to the runtime environment, with the object type as an argument, but the syntax of most languages creates the appearance that the request is made directly to the object type. This is, as an astute reader will notice, a self-referential definition: you must have an object to be the `CreationSite` before making a new object. The initial object that kicks off this whole chain comes into play in the runtime mechanism of the language being used. For instance, in Java, the user tells the JVM (Java Virtual Machine) which class to find the `main()` method in to start the whole system. This is a static method, so it is in the class object for the class, but, still, it's a class object and satisfies our requirement.

Consequences

Most object-oriented languages do not allow for the creation of data structures using any other method, yet do not require the definition of a developer-supplied initialization routine. A default initialization routine is generally supplied that performs a minimum of setup.

Some languages, although object oriented, allow the creation of nonobject data structures. C++ and Objective-C are two examples, both derived from the imperative C language. Python, Perl 6, and other languages have similar historical reasons for allowing such behavior.

Once an object is created, only the set of methods that were supplied by the developer of the original class are valid operations on that object. See the *Inheritance* pattern for an example of how to alter this state of affairs.

Objects are disposed of at the end of their useful existence. This deallocation has an analogous function, the deallocator, or destructor, that is called before the storage space of the data is finally released. This function allows any postconditions to be imposed on the data and resources of the object. Although it is also a best practice to have a well-formed and definite deconstruction sequence for objects, it turns out that, from a computational standpoint, deconstruction is a matter of convenience only. With infinite resources at our disposal, objects could continue to exist, unused, for an indefinite amount of time, and we would never accidentally use an old one again. It is only because we have finite resources that destruction of objects is determined essential in most systems. The construction of objects, however, injects them into the working environment so they can be used in computation and is therefore a requirement, not a convenience. Conceptually, some object types may rely on the destruction of objects to enforce certain abstract notions (fixed elements of a set, etc.), but it is a matter for the class designer.

Implementation

In C++:

Listing 5.4 is a basic class showing encapsulation, bundled behaviors, and default state. For excellent advice on creating best practice C++ classes of your own, see Scott Meyers's *Effective C++* [28] and *More Effective C++* [29].

Listing 5.4 *Create Object* Implementation.

```
   class ThreadCount {
2  public:
       // Constructors
4      ThreadCount() {
            numThreads = getNumberOfRunningThreads();
6      };
       ThreadCount(int newData) {
8           numThreads = newData;
       };
10
       // Accessors
12     int    getNumThreads() {
           return numThreads;
14     };
       ThreadCount setNumThreads(int newData) {
16          if (newData > 1) numThreads = newData; };
       };
18 private:
       int numThreads;
20 };

22 int
   main(int argc, char** argv) {
24     // Instantiate an object
       ThreadCount mc;
26
       // Already set up and ready to go
28     // Will print out the number of running threads
       cout << mc.getPrivateData() << endl;
30
       // Won't change the data, value isn't good
32     mc.setPrivateData(-1);
34     // Will change the data, value okay
       mc.setPrivateData(100);
36
       // Prints out 100
38     cout << mc.getPrivateData() << endl;
   };
```

Related Patterns

Create Object is a core concept in object-oriented programming and as such is found everywhere. Any design pattern that concentrates mainly on the creation or distribution of objects builds off of this EDP. Examples include the *Retrieve New* and *Retrieve Shared* patterns in the next chapter and the Creational Patterns found in *GoF's Design Patterns: Abstract Factory, Builder, Factory Method, Prototype,* and *Singleton* [21].

Retrieve   **Object Structural**

Intent

To use an object from another nonlocal source in the local scope, thereby creating a relationship and a connection between the local scoping object and the nonlocal source.

Motivation

Objects are an established and well-understood mechanism for encapsulating common data and methods and enforcing policy, as shown in *Create Object*. Singular objects, however, are of extremely limited utility. In fact, if there were only one object in a system, and nothing external to it, it could be considered a procedural program—all data and methods are local and fully exposed to one another. Nonobject data types can be faked in any object-oriented system that supports the use of function objects and methodless classes. It is therefore critical that a well-formed methodology be put into place for transporting objects across object boundaries. There are two situations in which this methodology is necessary, and they differ only slightly. The simplest case is when an external object has an exposed field that is being accessed. The more complex case is when an external object has a method that is called, and the return value of that method is being used in the internal scope.

The simplest form is shown in Listing 5.5, using Java as the example language.

Listing 5.5 *Retrieve* with an update.

```
1 public class SoundSettings {
      public int volume;
3     // A player specific offset to adjust volume
      public int offset;
5 };

7 public class MusicPlayer {
      public void setVolume( SoundSettings ss ) {
9         // This is an instance of Retrieve
          this.settings.volume = ss.volume;
11    };
      private SoundSettings settings;
13 };
```

If the use of the external data is at the middle of a temporary expression, as in method `adjustVolume1` of Listing 5.6, then an equivalent can be considered, as in method `adjustVolume2`.

Listing 5.6 *Retrieve* in a temporary variable.

```
 1  public class MusicPlayer {
        public void adjustVolume1( SoundSettings ss ) {
 3          // This is also a Retrieve
            this.settings.volume =
 5              this.settings.offset + ss.volume;
        };
 7      public void adjustVolume2( SoundSettings ss ) {
            // Here the Retrieve is explicit
 9          int tempVar = ss.volume;
            this.settings.volume =
11              this.settings.offset + tempVar;
        };
13  };
```

Applicability

Use *Retrieve* when:

- A nonlocal object provides access to an object that is required for local computation and the required object is either:
    - provided by a method call's return value or
    - provided by an exposed field object.

Structure

Note that `selected` could be either a method or a public field.

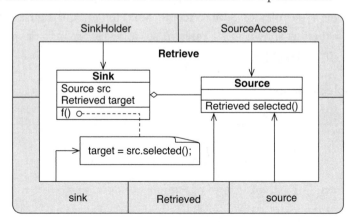

Participants

SourceAccess

The object (or class) type that contains `selected`.

SinkHolder

The object (or class) type that includes the item, `target`, to be given a new value.

Retrieved

The type of the value to be updated and the value that is returned.

sink

The field that is given a new value.

source

The method or field that produces the new value.

Collaborations

This simple relationship consists of two objects and two methods. The distinguishing factors are the transferral of a return value into the local object space and an update to a local field using that retrieved object. The local field may be a defined field, or it could be a temporary value in the middle of an expression.

Consequences

Tying two objects and/or types like this is an everyday occurrence, but it should not be done without thought. Any time you bind two objects in this manner, you are introducing a dependency: the target object now relies on the source object. Make sure it's what you need to do.

In languages with dynamic typing, such as Python, Ruby, or JavaScript, the type roles of SourceAccess, SinkHolder, and Retrieved may not be explicitly shown in all cases. Also, a developer may or may not provide strong typing.

Implementation

In C++:

```
1  class SourceAccess {
   public:
3      Retrieved source();
   };
5
   class SinkHolder {
7      Retrieved sink;
```

```
       SourceAccess srcobj;
9  public:
       void operation() { sink = srcobj.source(); }
11 };
```

In Java:

```
1  public class SourceAccess {
       public Retrieved source();
3  };

5  public class SinkHolder {
       private Retrieved sink;
7      private SourceAccess srcobj;
       public void operation() {
9          sink = srcobj.source();
       };
11 };
```

In Python (note dynamic typing):

```
1  class SourceAccess(object):
       def source(self):
3          pass // Return value here

5  class SinkHolder(object):
       def void operation(self):
7          self.sink = self.srcobj.source()
```

Related Patterns

Retrieve is a fundamental EDP and is found with any other pattern that involves two or more objects, where those objects are brought together at runtime. See the *Retrieve New* and *Retrieve Shared* patterns in Chapter 6 for variations on this EDP where object ownership and instantiation are involved.

Inheritance   Type Relation

Intent

To reuse another class's interface, implementation, and behavior with additions to or alterations of each.

Also Known As

IsA, Type Reuse

Motivation

Often, an existing class provides an excellent start for producing a new class type. The interface may be almost exactly what you are looking for, the existing methods may provide *almost* what you need for your new class, or, at the very least, the existing class may be conceptually close to what you wish to accomplish.

In such cases, it is useful and efficient to reuse the existing class instead of rewriting everything from scratch. One way of doing so is by copying and pasting the code into a new class. This technique is done quite often, but it has many drawbacks. If a bug is found in the original code, you now have two places to track and maintain the fix. If an enhancement is made to one copy of the code, anyone working on the other code location must be explicitly told that it exists. Copy and paste seems like a quick and easy approach in the beginning, but it doesn't just tie the copies of code together, it ties the *development teams* together. In addition, in many cases, you won't have the source code to copy at all, such as when using a vendor's development API.

A better way to accomplish this reuse is through the *Inheritance* pattern. Every object-oriented language supports this approach of code reuse, and it is usually a core primitive of such a language.

At its most basic level, this pattern offers a relationship between a *superclass* or *base class*, and a *subclass* or *derived class*. The superclass (let's call it `Superclass`) is an existing class in the system, one that provides at a minimum an interface of concepts for methods and/or data structures. A second class can be defined as being *derived* from `Superclass`; let's call it `Subclass`. The `Subclass` class *inherits* the interface and implementations of all methods and fields of `Superclass`, and this provides a starting point for a programmer to begin work on `Subclass`.

Assume that you are writing a library to display shapes in a graphical interface, such as might be at the core of a game engine. Every shape is going to have some basic information, regardless of what kind of shape it is. It will have a position on the screen, it will have a color, the line that draws its border will have a thickness, and so on. You could add this information, and implement the methods to work with the data, to each and every class that represents a shape. Or, you could use *Inheritance* as in Listing 5.7. The `Shape` class sets up the basic information for any shape in the system and provides a basic set of method implementations for working with that data.

You may notice that in the `Square` class we re-declared the instance method `setWidth:andHeight`. This is an example of *overriding* and

Listing 5.7 Basic inheritance example in Objective-C.

```
 1 @interface Shape
   {
 3     int xPos;
       int yPos;
 5     int lineWidth;
       Color* fillColor;
 7 }
   - (void) setPosWithX: (int) x andY: (int) y;
 9 - (void) setColor: (Color*) c;
   - (void) setLineWidth: (int) lw;
11 @end

13 @interface Circle : Shape
   {
15     int radius;
   }
17 - (void) setRadius: (int) r;
   @end
19
   @interface Rectangle : Shape
21 {
       int width;
23     int height;
   }
25 - (void) setWidth: (int) w andHeight: (int) h;
   @end
27
   @interface Square : Rectangle
29 {
   }
31 - (void) setWidth: (int)w andHeight: (int) h;
   - (void) setSize: (int) s;
33 @end
```

Listing 5.8 Overriding an implementation.

```
 1  @implementation Square
    - (void) setWidth: (int) w andHeight: (int) h
 3  {
        if (w == h) {
 5          [super setWidth: w andHeight: h];
        } else {
 7          printf("ERR:_Width_!=_height\n");
        }
 9  }
    - (void) setSize: (int) s
11  {
        [self setWidth: s andHeight: s];
13  }
    @end
```

is a behavior that commonly goes along with *Inheritance*. Overriding lets you customize certain methods from a base class by providing a new definition of the method. You can use it to change the behavior of an existing method, either by completely replacing it or by augmenting it in new ways. Listing 5.8 demonstrates overriding with Square. We'd like to let clients of both Square and Rectangle still use the setWidth:andHeight interface, since a square is just a special kind of rectangle, but now we have to make sure the sides are the same size. We add a check on the data, and then call the preexisting method from our superclass. There's no need to completely replace the implementation because we're just wrapping it in a validity check.[3]

Sometimes you need to keep intact the original behavior for code that relies on it, but you want to provide a fixed version moving forward for new code. You can do this by creating a new class that inherits from the original but overrides the broken method and provides a fixed version. Existing code can then continue to use the base class, complete with the bug that it may be working around, but new code can take advantage of the fixed version. As the old code is inspected and tested, it can be migrated to the new version as well.

For instance, assume you have a piece of Java code such as in Listing 5.9. This is a totally artificial example to demonstrate what is commonly called the *fencepost error*. If you have a fence that's 100 feet long, with

---

3. By the way, this calling of the superclass's version of the same method is an example of the *Extend Method* EDP. You can read that entry for a more thorough discussion.

Listing 5.9 Implementation assumption mismatch.

```
   public class Fence {
2      int[] fencepostHeights;
       public int getHeightOfPost( int post ) {
4          return fencepostHeights[post];
       };
6  };

8  ...

       Fence fence;
10     // Fence gets filled in at some point
       ...
12     Scanner scanner = new Scanner (System.in);
       System.out.println(
14         "Enter fence post to get height of:");
       int p = scanner.nextInt ();
16     System.out.format("Post #%d has height of: %d%n",
           p, fence.getHeightOfPost(p - 1));
18         // Workaround for error ^^^^
```

a fencepost every 10 feet, how many fenceposts are you going to need? If you said 10, you're in good company. Many people forget that there's an extra fencepost at the zero mark on the fence as well. It is a surprisingly common bug, also known as an off-by-one error. The implementation for fencepostHeights simply returns the height of the requested fencepost. The problem is, the array of heights is zero-based in Java. This means that the first element has an index of 0, the second element has an index of 1, and so on. The problem is that most people don't think of fences in this way. Assume that client code asks the user which fencepost he or she wants the height of, and then passes the entry to a fence, as in fence.getHeightOfPost(p). The client code must adjust the value of p by subtracting 1 before sending it in, or the result will be the height of the post *after* the one the user expects. The client code must work around this problem. By the way, it's easy to argue that an off-by-one error isn't a bug, that it is how Java arrays work. That much is true. It is also how C and C++ arrays work. The bug isn't in the code; it is in the miscommunication of intent between the class implementer and the developers who use the class. The developer who implemented the class did so with reasonable assumptions. The client using the class also has reasonable assumptions. They're just not the *same* set of assumptions.

Starting with Listing 5.9, what happens when someone realizes the mismatch and decides to fix fencepostHeights (Listing 5.10)?

Listing 5.10 Obvious fix—but likely not feasible.

```
   public class Fence {
2      int[] fencepostHeights;
       public int getHeightOfPost( int post ) {
4          return fencepostHeights[post - 1];
           // Bug fix for off-by-one ^^^^
6      };
   };
```

Listing 5.11 Fixing a bug while leaving old code in place.

```
1 public class MendedFence extends Fence {
      public int getHeightOfPost( int post ) {
3          return fencepostHeights[post - 1];
      };
5 };
```

This obvious, straightforward, and simple fix just broke every piece of client code that was adjusting the value sent in to `getHeightOfPost`. Now the client code will be using the height of the post to the *left* of the expected one. This is probably not as helpful a fix as was intended. If there is a large number of clients, or if they are on different schedules—which is almost *always* the case—then it's nearly impossible to coordinate all teams to incorporate the fix at once. The usual outcome in these cases is that the bug perpetuates, and the workaround must be incorporated into every client. This solution is fragile and prone to error.[4]

A better way to fix this is to provide a fixed version of the `Fence` class that can be used by new clients and to allow old clients to migrate to it on their own schedule. The fix is shown in Listing 5.11, based on the original `Fence` class in Listing 5.9. Newly developed code can use this version instead. It is cleaner and doesn't need to remember to adjust the post number. Old client code can continue using the old code until it has time to move to the new `MendedFence` class. Once all client code is using the new class, it and the old one can be merged into one class for everyone. Note that this fix can also work when the source code for `Fence` isn't available. This is common when you're using a library from another developer.

---

4. It also resulted in one of my favorite vanity plates. It was a mid-60s VW Beetle in Seattle with the license plate FEATURE. Because any bug, if left long enough, eventually becomes a feature that someone, somewhere, is relying on.

Applicability

Use *Inheritance* when:

- An existing class provides an interface, implementation, and data storage that is almost, but not quite, what is needed for a new class.

- Copying and pasting the code from the original class is either undesirable for maintenance reasons or not possible because the original source code is unavailable.

Structure

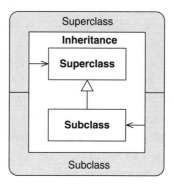

Participants

Superclass

An existing class in a system that is used as a basis for producing a further class.

Subclass

The secondary class that relies on the first for its basic interface and implementation.

Collaborations

The `Superclass` class creates a basic set of method interfaces with any accompanying optional method implementations. `Subclass` inherits all the interface elements of `Superclass`, and, by default, all of the implementations as well, which it may choose to override with new implementations.

Consequences

Inheritance is a powerful mechanism that has some interesting limitations and consequences. For one thing, due to a bit of subtlety at the heart of object-oriented programming theory, a subclass may not *remove* a method or data field. It can be stated informally, however, that inheritance creates what is called an IsA relationship between the subclass and the superclass. The subclass literally "Is A" specialized version of the superclass. The interface is what constitutes the definition of what the class *is*, so saying what the superclass is by defining an interface, and then turning around and removing portions of that interface in a subclass, means that the subclass no longer is everything the superclass is. Yes, it's all rather existential, but that's object-oriented theory for you. Best to stick with the simpler concept: If the subclass cannot be described without reservation *as* an instance of the superclass, then do not subclass.

Many languages offer *multiple inheritance*, allowing a subclass to have multiple superclasses. This effectively allows a subclass to be described as each of the superclasses in turn. For instance, milk is both a fluid and a foodstuff. If a class `Milk` were to inherit from `Fluid`, then it could be described by the properties of a `Fluid`, such as viscosity and freezing point. If `Milk` also inherited from `FoodItem`, then you could discuss its nutritional content or expiration date. There are issues to be considered in such situations, however, and many languages reject multiple inheritance in favor of the simpler single-inheritance model.

In some languages, a subclass may *hide* a method by making it private, but this is not universal. In all languages, a subclass may override a method and simply provide an empty implementation, effectively erasing the behavior while the interface remains the same.

It may seem that overriding is a waste of good code in the base class, and this is true in many cases. The *Extend Method* pattern solves this problem by overriding a method while still using it.

In some cases, you may not wish to inherit an entire existing class and its interface but instead to inherit only small pieces of functionality. You may lack confidence in the implementations of the method bodies if the original source code is unavailable, you may be reluctant to absorb the cost of integrating a large class into the current system when only a small segment of that class is needed, or you may have a variety of other reasons for using only part of the existing class.

Consider using the *Redirection* pattern when you wish to retain some, but not all, of an interface. An instance of the class you wish to reuse is placed in the new class using *Create Object*, and the portion of the interface you want to retain is replicated, as in Listing 5.12. Here, the `Square` class has effectively removed the `setWidth:andHeight` method that had to be worked around before. The downside is that you have to implement wrappers for *every* method you wish to retain, all the way back up the inheritance hierarchy. For instance, Listing 5.12 wraps methods from `Shape` in *Redirection* instances.[5] You are effectively erasing the unused methods of the original class, but you do not get to take advantage of polymorphism in statically typed languages when you do so. Dynamically typed languages, particularly those that allow for runtime determination of method availability, such as Objective-C and JavaScript, let you play with the typing a bit more loosely, having effective polymorphism among types not in a subclassing relationship. Languages based on prototyping, such as JavaScript, Self, and Lua, offer dynamic typing almost universally and allow ad hoc polymorphism without penalty.

Listing 5.12 Using *Redirection* to hide part of an interface.

```
1  @interface Square
   {
3     Rectangle rect;
   }
5  - (void) setPosWithX: (int) x andY: (int) y;
   - (void) setColor: (Color) c;
7  - (void) setLineWidth: (int) lw;
   - (void) setSize: (int) s;
9  @end

11 @implementation Square
   - (void) setPosWithX: (int) x andY: (int) y
13 {
      [rect setPosWithX: x andY: y];
15 }
   - (void) setColor: (Color) c
17 {
      [rect setColor: c];
19 }
   - (void) setLineWidth: (int) lw
21 {
      [rect setLineWidth: lw];
23 }
   - (void) setSize: (int) s
25 {
      [rect setWidth: s andHeight: s];
27 }
   @end
```

5. You can even say that, as far as the interface is concerned, *Inheritance* can be considered a gathering together of multiple *Redirection* pattern instances, with one `Redirect` object being shared among them.

Compare this situation with one in which you want to reuse the implementation and/or data storage of a class but are unsatisfied with the interface and wish to provide a new one. In this situation, you can use an object instance in the new class, much like was done in the *Redirection* example but access it via the *Delegation* EDP. Now you are erasing the original interface and providing a new one while still using the underlying data storage and implementation of behaviors. This feature is common in classes that are to be used as facades, those that adapt between interfaces or APIs.

These techniques to work around limitations of *Inheritance* using a combination of *Redirection* and *Delegation* are so common that some languages provide native support for the feature, such as with C#'s `delegate` keyword.

Implementation

The mechanism for creating an inheritance relationship varies from language to language, but statically typed languages almost always provide clear syntax for doing so. Dynamically typed or prototype-based languages may not always make the relationship explicit.

In C++:

```
  class Superclass {
2 public:
      Superclass( );
4 };

6 class Subclass : public Superclass {
  public:
8     Subclass( );
  };
```

In Python:

```
1 class Superclass(object):
      def __init__(self):
3         pass

5 class Subclass(Superclass):
      def __init__(self):
7         Superclass.__init__(self)
```

Related Patterns

Inheritance is ubiquitously used. It is a core component of any EDP that uses object type similarities of Subtype or Sibling. In particular, see *Trusted*

Delegation, *Deputized Delegation*, *Trusted Redirection*, *Deputized Redirection*, *Revert Method*, and *Extend Method*. In addition, *Inheritance* is used in the *Fulfill Method* pattern. Because each of these patterns is fundamental to many other composed patterns, *Inheritance* is an EDP you should make sure you understand thoroughly.

Also see *Delegation* and *Redirection* for further information on how to use those patterns to work around some limitations of *Inheritance*.

Abstract Interface   **Type Relation**

Intent

To provide a common interface for applying a behavior in a family of object types but without providing an implementation of the actual operation. In this scenario, subclasses are forced to provide a proper implementation of their own because no default method exists.

Also Known As

Virtual Method, Polymorphism, Defer Implementation

Motivation

Often, when we have a hierarchy of classes using the *Inheritance* pattern that conforms to our conceptual design, we run into a situation where we simply cannot provide a meaningful method implementation at the root of the class hierarchy. We know what we want to do *conceptually*, but we are not entirely sure how to go about doing it.

Assume that we are modeling animals. Animals all, roughly speaking, have certain behaviors and needs. They eat, they age, and they (usually) move. What they eat depends on the species, but eating is almost always an act of ingestion of some sort. Some animals may not actually ingest food, but they are rare and special cases. Animals pass through a number of phases as they mature, such as gestation, juvenile, and adult. The details and timing of each stage vary across species, but at least a broad default process of aging can be modeled.

Movement, however, is a bit trickier. We can give a destination location for the animal to move to, but implementing this behavior is a more complex task: fish, birds, and terrestrial animals all have very different modes of locomotion and kinds of locations that they can get to. There's no overly broad behavior that we can really model here, at least not without requiring a *lot* of special cases immediately from the beginning. However we choose to implement a `moveTo` method, we're going to end up overriding and replacing the implementation more or less completely in most of the subclasses. We're likely going to end up with something such as in Listing 5.13.

This tells us that perhaps we shouldn't offer an implementation at all, because no matter what we choose, it's almost certainly going to be wrong.

Listing 5.13 Animals almost all move but in very different ways.

```
 1  public class Animal {
        public void eatFood( FoodItem f ) {
 3          this.ingest(f);
            this.digest(f);
 5      };
        public void matureTo ( TimeDuration age ) {
 7          if (age > gestation) {
                this.beAJuvenile(age);
 9          } else if (age > maturation) {
                this.beAnAdult(age);
11          } else if (age > longevity) {
                this.die();
13          }
        };
15      public void moveTo( Location dest ) {
            // Um... what to put here?
17      };
    };
```

We want to ensure that every `Animal`, no matter which subclass describes it, can be *asked* to move, but we can't come up with a reasonable default for *how* to move that would apply to all or even most animals. We want to provide an *interface*—a defined way of invoking the behavior—but no implementation to define the behavior itself.

Recall from the discussion in *Inheritance* that behaviors in types are provided by the methods that are defined on a type. Therefore, to provide the behavior evenly across all the subclasses, we should provide a method definition, but we're then stuck because we have no implementation to define the method with.

If we provide an empty implementation body as in Listing 5.13, then we've provided a default implementation that simply does nothing. If a subclass fails to override this method, then the poor animal being modeled by that class won't be able to move at all. Although there are some truly stationary animals, they are the exceptions. Therefore, in cases such as this, we would also like to ensure that the implementors of subclasses are reminded to define a proper implementation, even though we can't. The solution is to create an *Abstract Interface* for that method.

Applicability

Use *Abstract Interface* when:

- Implementation of a method either is not known at class definition time or no reasonable default implementation can be determined.

- The interface for that method *can* be determined.

- You expect subclasses to handle the functionality of the method according to their special needs.

Structure

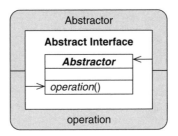

Participants

> **Abstractor**
> The class type that declares an interface for `operation`.
>
> **operation**
> The method being abstracted out: no method definition can be given.

Collaborations

> Abstractor defines an interface for a method that all subclasses will implement. (An implicit collaboration occurs between `Abstractor` and an as-yet unknown subclass here.)

Consequences

> The *Create Object* pattern lets us instantiate objects, and the *Retrieve* pattern shows how to fill in the fields of that newly created object. *Abstract Interface* is unusual in that it indicates the *absence* of a method implementation; instead of showing us how to fill in the method, it shows us how to defer the method definition until another point in the design. See the related *Fulfill Method* pattern for the rest of the solution.
>
> In this case, the method is declared in order to define the proper interface for our conceptual needs, yet the method body is left undefined. This does *not* mean that we simply define an empty method, one that does nothing; the method has *no definition at all*. This is a critical point, and one that is often missed by programmers new to object-oriented languages. How it is done varies from language to language, as you can see from the examples in the Implementation section.

Different languages have different uses of this pattern as well. C++, for instance, asserts that any class type with even a single method that is an *Abstract Interface* is an *abstract class* and therefore incapable of being instantiated directly. Only subclasses that provide a definition for the abstract method via the *Fulfill Method* pattern may be instantiated into objects using *Create Object*.

Java takes it even further. As with C++, a class may contain one or more abstract methods, making the class abstract. If it contains nothing but abstract methods, however, Java offers the *interface* construct instead. The term interface here refers to a classlike entity collecting many abstract methods, not the interface of a single method. Like an abstract class, a Java interface cannot be instantiated. Unlike abstract classes, which can have both defined and abstract methods, a Java interface is not allowed to have any defined methods at all. Classes should have at least one defined method, and interfaces are composed of only abstract methods. Although Java has only single inheritance of classes, it offers multiple inheritance of interfaces to allow the composition of new class interfaces at a very fine granularity. See *Inheritance* for more information on inheritance models.

Python added support for abstract methods only in version 2.6 of the library as a standard library addition in the abc module, which stands for abstract base class. Python 3.0 introduced a slightly more straightforward notation, which you will see in the Implementation section. Unlike Java or C++, Python's approach allows for a default implementation, which can be called by subclasses, most often using the *Extend Method* EDP. Subclasses, however, still must override the method and provide their own implementation.

Implementation

In C++ the method is set equal to zero and called a *pure virtual method*:

```
  class AbstractOperations {
2 public:
      virtual void operation() = 0;
4 };

6 class DefinedOperations :
      public AbstractOperations {
8 public:
      void operation();
10 };

12 void
   DefinedOperations::operation() {
```

```
14    // Perform the appropriate work
   };
```

In Java the method is included in an *interface* or is in an *abstract class*:

```
1 public interface AbstractOperations {
      public void operation();
3 };

5 public abstract class SemiDefinedOperations {
      public abstract void operation2();
7     public void operation3() {};
  };
9
  public class DefinedOperations
11    extends SemiDefinedOperations
      implements AbstractOperations {
13    public void operation() {
          // Perform the appropriate work
15    }
      public void operation2() {
17        // Perform the appropriate work
      }
19 };
```

In Python 3.x:

```
1 class AbstractOperations(metaclass=ABCMeta):
     @abstractmethod
3    def operation(self, ...):
         // Default implementation allowed
5        return

7 class DefinedOperations(AbstractOperations):
     def operation(self, ...):
9        // Perform the appropriate work
         pass
```

Related Patterns

Inheritance will obviously be used in conjunction with this EDP to set up the subclass that will provide an implementation for the method used in *Abstract Interface*. See the *Fulfill Method* pattern in Chapter 6 for the complete story on how to go about doing so.

Delegation   Object Behavioral

Intent

To parcel out, or delegate, a portion of the current work to another method in another object.

Also Known As

Messaging, Method Invocation, Calls, The Executive

Motivation

In the course of working with objects, the situation often arises that "some other object" can provide a piece of functionality we want to have. *Delegation* embodies the most general form of a method call from one object to another, allowing one object to send a message to another, to perform some bit of work. The receiving object may or may not send back data as a result.

As a real-world example, consider how a corporation works. The CEO's goal is to successfully run a company. She assigns subordinates to handle different parts of it, and rarely are any two subordinates in charge of the same part of the operation. The vice president of finance, for instance, ensures that the financial reporting meets government standards, the CTO makes sure the technology needs of the company are addressed, and so on. Each job is discrete and differs greatly from the others as well as from the responsibilities of the CEO, but the success of the company as a whole relies on the synergy of all of its parts. Listing 5.14 shows a bit of code that models this approach.

Listing 5.14 CEO delegates out responsibilities.

```
   public class CEO {
2      FinanceExec      vpFinance;
       ResearchExec     vpResearch;
4      TechnologyExec   cto;
       public void runCompany () {
6          vpFinance.ensureFinancialCompliance();
           vpResearch runResearchDivision();
8          cto.manageTechnology();
       };
10 };
```

One interesting point to make here is that the routine in Listing 5.14 is an example of *synchronous* method calling. In this Java code, when runCompany is invoked, the vice president of finance is asked to manage the finances, and *only when he is finished reporting* is the vice president of research asked to *start* his task. The tasks are synchronized by the calling task. First one, then the other, and execution is done in a specific order.

In real life, of course, this isn't how the CEO performs her job. She asks all the executives to go do their jobs and to do them at the same time. Then, when each is done, he or she reports back on his or her own schedule. This is an example of *asynchronous* execution. The delegates are told to go off and do their own thing, in parallel.

Such asynchronous, or parallel, processing is not a simple feature to perform in most object-oriented languages, although some do offer threading libraries, such as Java's FutureTask API, to fulfill this need. Other languages, particularly functional languages such as Go and Erlang, have native support for concurrency and parallel features via asynchronous calls, but their syntax is, as you might expect, radically different. Whether it is referred to as asynchronous calling, concurrent programming, or parallel programming, it is an entire discipline beyond the scope of this book. Note, however, that every EDP described in this text is applicable as an asynchronous call.

Delegation is a common enough component of design and functionality that C# offers the delegate keyword. This language feature encapsulates a function in an object such that it can be passed around as if it were a regular object. This delegate object then becomes callable as a regular method would be. The enclosing object is essentially invisible.[6] The point here is that this feature makes no assertions and imposes no restrictions on the method being wrapped other than that it match a predefined set of types for the arguments and return value. The delegate object being called upon is obviously dissimilar from the calling object, the object types have nothing to do with one another, and the method being wrapped may or may not be named anything like the method doing the calling. This truly is the most general possible case and an example of *Delegation*.

---

6. C++ offers something similar in the *functor* concept using operator() as the calling mechanism, but C# takes the next step to allow for ad hoc wrapping of preexisting methods for passing around in this manner.

Applicability

Use *Delegation* when:

- Another object can perform some work that your current method body wishes to have done.

- The other object does not need access to the private data in the current object to complete the task.

- There is no known relevant type relationship between the two objects.

Structure

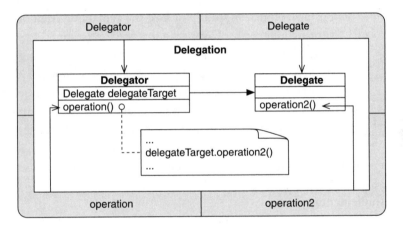

Participants

Delegator
The object type sending the message to the `Delegate`.

operation
The method within the `Delegator` that is currently being executed when the message is sent—the point of invocation of the *opera-tion2* method call.

Delegate
The object type receiving the message, with an appropriate method to be invoked.

operation2
The method being invoked from the call site.

Collaborations

This is a simple binary relationship: one method calls another, just as in procedural systems, and with the same sorts of caveats and requirements. Because we are working in an object-oriented realm, however, we have a couple of additional needs. We require the object being called to be visible at the point of invocation, whether by being a locally scoped object variable, or by access through *Retrieve*. Also, obviously, the method being called must be visible to other objects.

Consequences

All operations between any two objects can be described as an instance of the *Delegation* pattern, but being able to describe further attributes of the relationship is much more useful. See the remaining Method Invocation EDPs for refinements of *Delegation* that are better suited to specific tasks and needs. This generalized form of a method call, however, is a crucial concept in some of the higher abstractions such as *Bridge*, or *Adapter* in its object-variant form, where the point is to create a well-formed and effective translation between two interfaces that are otherwise unrelated. If the interfaces are related in a methodical manner, then these patterns are not necessarily the right ones to use. The lack of relation between the interfaces and types is a required trait, therefore, and *Delegation* fulfills that need.

Implementation

The most generalized and basic style of method invocation in object-oriented programming, *Delegation* describes how two objects communicate with each other, as the sender and receiver of messages, performing work and returning values.

In C++:

```
   class Delegator {
 2 public:
       Delegatee   target;
 4     void operation() {
           // Work may be done before...
 6         target.operation2();
           // Work may be done after...
 8     };
   };
10
   class Delegatee {
12 public:
       void operation2();
14 };
```

Related Patterns

Delegation is ubiquitous in object-oriented programming. If no other Method Invocation EDP applies, this is the most general form that will be the default. Immediately related EDPs include those reached through minor changes to *Delegation*. By altering the method similarity to similar, you arrive at *Redirection*. Changing the object type similarity to similar gives you *Delegated Conglomeration*. Modifying only the object similarity doesn't give us anything particularly meaningful, because it would result in a single object having two dissimilar types imposed on it simultaneously. *Delegation* is often found in conjunction with *Retrieve*, which provides the object to be called upon.

Method Call Classification

Object: Dissimilar   **Object Type:** Dissimilar   **Method:** Dissimilar

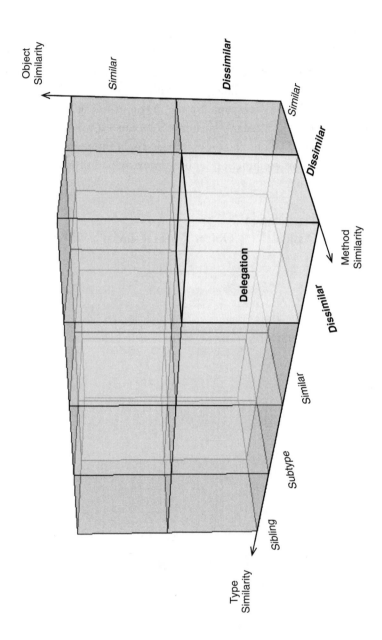

Redirection   **Object Behavioral**

Intent

To request that another object perform a tightly related subtask to the task at hand, perhaps performing the basic work.

Also Known As

Tom Sawyer, Shop Foreman

Motivation

A small refinement to *Delegation*, *Redirection* takes into consideration that methods performing similar tasks are often named similarly. We can take advantage of this to clarify the intent of this pattern over the more general form and show cases where it is applicable.

An example for this pattern is *Tom Sawyer*, a literary figure who was famous for convincing other people to do his tasks for him [39]. Unlike the *Executive* alias of *Delegation*, Tom generally sought to have others do exactly the task he was asked to do. The common anecdote involves Tom being asked to paint his aunt's fence. He didn't want to do the work himself, so he convinced a group of friends to do it for him. He could have had one friend handle paint buckets, another prep the fence, and so on, and the workflow would have looked a lot like that of an executive. Instead, he decided the best way of dividing the work was to have each friend perform the *same* task: paint the fence. Tom made sure that each person had the right tools and enough paint and that the task was completed, but he did not perform the task himself. Those he asked to paint the fence each did the same task Tom was asked to do—they just did smaller portions of it.

So it is with *Redirection*. Use *Redirection* when a job can be broken down into smaller subtasks that have the same basic motivation and intent as the main task. Note that the behavior may be radically different across the methods but that intent is the same. Tom didn't paint—he handed out paint and brushes—but his intent was to get the fence painted. Likewise, the people working for him intended to paint the fence—they were just concerned with smaller sections of it. Listing 5.15 shows an example in Java: Tom directs each of his friends to paint the fence when he's asked to do it.

Listing 5.15 Tom paints the fence with help.

```java
public class Friend {
    public void paintTheFence(int beg, int end) {
        // Do the painting
    };
};

public class TomSawyer {
    // Friends are collected elsewhere
    java.util.ArrayList<Friend> friends;

    // Paint the fence from beg to end
    public void paintTheFence(int beg, int end) {
        int fenceLength = end - beg;
        int subfence = fenceLength / friends.size();
        int friendBeg = beg;
        for (Friend f : friends) {
            int friendEnd = friendBeg + subfence - 1;
            f.paintTheFence(friendBeg, friendEnd);
            // ^--- Redirect
            friendBeg = friendEnd + 1;
        }
    };
};
```

This setup is similar to what we saw back in Chapter 2, Section 2.2.4, with the shop foreman painting cars. Notice that in neither case is the calling method actually doing the work requested, although it certainly is possible. Whether the calling method is acting purely as a router, a foreman, or a manager, or whether it is involved in actually performing the task is immaterial.

At other times, the caller may have a slightly different idea of what the task to be completed is and ask someone else to do the bulk of the work, and the caller will then either perform prep work or do cleanup afterwards. If you're painting a room, there are two ways you can go about doing it. You can either dive in and start painting with a brush—and hope you don't slop too much paint on lightswitches, molding, outlets, and the like—or you can take time to carefully prepare the room by laying down tarps properly taped to the baseboards, removing the lightswitch and outlet plates, taping all the molding edges, and carefully replacing everything and removing the tape and tarps afterwards.

Someone who is lightning fast and good at applying a coat of paint isn't necessarily going to be the person who is careful and methodical about prep work and cleanup. They're both painting the room, but one person's

Listing 5.16 Prep work and cleanup are important.

```
 1  class SloppyFastPainter {
    public:
 3      void paintRoom( Room r ) {
            // Paint the walls
 5      };
    };

 7
    class CarefulPainter {
 9      SloppyFastPainter sloppy;
    public:
11      void paintRoom( Room r ) {
            // Laydown tarps in room
13          // Remove hardware from room
            sloppy.paintRoom( r ); // Redirect
15          // Replace hardware in room
            // Clean up room
17      };
    };
```

concept of how to go about doing it is to maximize speed, while the other person's focus is on quality. It would be great to do both where you can. In cases such as this, you can have the careful person perform the prep work and cleanup, and then that person can ask someone else to do the actual painting for speed. Now the prep and cleanup person is free to go prep another room while the first one is being painted. This process can be modeled synchronously as something like Listing 5.16.

Unfortunately, there is an opportunity for confusion here. Used in the general sense, the word *delegate* simply means to hand off part of a workload to someone else. That most general sense is what the *Delegation* EDP defines. Every method-call EDP is a specialization of delegation, but *Redirection* is the most likely one to be mistakenly described as *Delegation*. This confusion is quite understandable, as the term *delegation is* used in a number of ways in software engineering. Just remember that even C# has adopted the term *delegate* for the most general case, using it as a keyword wrapping a method to be passed around while leaving open all three of the similarity axes we defined in this text. *Delegation* is used for handing off to *any* other method, while using *Redirection* is a bit more specific.

Applicability

Use *Redirection* when:

- Another object can perform some work that your current method body wishes to have done.

- The other object does not need access to the private data in the current object to complete the task.

- There is no known relevant type relationship between the two objects.

- That target object has a method that has a similar intent, expressed through its signature name after Kent Beck's **Intention Revealing Selector** pattern.

Structure

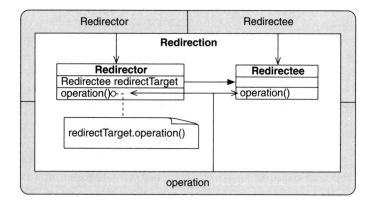

Participants

Redirector

The originating site of the method call contains a method named *operation*, which has a subtask to be parceled out to another object. This object, redirectTarget, is a field element of type Redirectee.

Redirectee

The type of the receiver of the message, which performs the subtask asked of it.

operation

Redirector's *operation* calls redirectTarget.*operation* to perform a portion of its work, and thereby invokes Redirectee's version of *operation*.

Collaborations

As with *Delegation* (and indeed all the Method Invocation EDPs), *Retrieve* describes a binary relationship between two objects and their enclosed methods. In this case, it defines a relationship between two dissimilar objects of dissimilar types, using a call between similar methods. The similarity of the naming, and therefore assumed intent, provides a clue to the nature of their relationship.

Consequences

Even though *Retrieve* is almost identical to the *Delegation* pattern, the seemingly small additional requirement that the methods be similar has some far-reaching effects. We will see in later patterns that when this pattern is combined with other EDPs and typing information, complex interactions can quickly be formed and described simply.

By leveraging the facts that both methods have the same name and that this is a common way of declaring the intent of a method, we can deduce that the two methods have a common functional intent. Furthermore, it becomes obvious that this is an appropriate way to indicate that our originating call-site method is requesting the invoked method to do some portion of work, and that work is tightly related to the core functionality of the original method.

The object being called upon may reside in or be owned by the calling method, the object enclosing the calling method, or it may come from elsewhere via a use of *Retrieve*. The Implementation section shows multiple forms.

If done carefully, this behavior can be used to form an ad hoc variant of *Inheritance* by stitching one object to another with the same (or very similar) interface using multiple *Redirection* instances with a single target object. The calling methods may just pass through to the `Redirectee`, mimicking an inherited implementation, or they may provide their own method body, mimicking the overriding of an inherited implementation, but breaking the *Redirection*. If they both provide their own method body, and in that body call the appropriate target method in the `Redirectee`, then not only is this a *Redirection*, but it is also an ad hoc form of the related *Extend Method*.

Implementation

In Java:

```java
public class Foo {
    public void operation();
};

public class Bar {
    Foo f;
    public void operation() {
        Foo f2;
        f.operation(); // Redirect
        f2.operation(); // Redirect
    };
};
```

In Objective-C, illustrating the use of *Retrieve* to get the reference to the Redirectee:

```objc
@interface Foo
{
}
- (void) operation;
@end

@implementation Foo
- (void) operation {
    // Do work
};
@end

@interface Goo
{
    Foo* f;
}
- (Foo*) getFoo;
@end

@implementation Goo
- (Foo*) getFoo {
    return f;
};
@end

@interface Bar
{
    Goo* g;
}
- (void) operation;
@end

@implementation Bar
- (void) operation {
    [[g getFoo] operation]; // Redirect on Retrieve
}
@end
```

Related Patterns

Redirection is another very general EDP. It differs from *Delegation* only in that the methods now have a similarity of intent and naming. Alter that similarity, and you're back to *Delegation*. Also see *Retrieve* for advice on how to let the target object vary at runtime by tightening the object type similarity. As with *Delegation*, changing just the object similarity to similar while leaving the object type similarity as dissimilar results in an unknown state.

Method Call Classification

Object: Dissimilar   **Object Type:** Dissimilar   **Method:** Similar

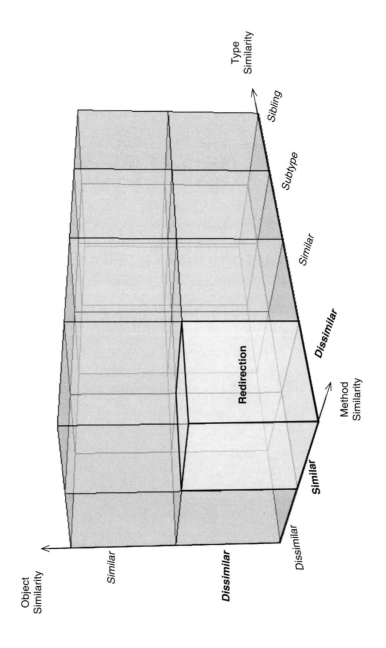

Conglomeration   **Object Behavioral**

Intent

To bring together, or conglomerate, diverse operations and behaviors in order to complete a more complex task within a single object.

Also Known As

Decomposing Message, Helper Methods

Motivation

An object is often asked to perform a task that is too large or unwieldy to be performed within a single method. Usually, it makes conceptual sense to break the task into smaller parts to be handled individually as discrete methods, and then build them back into a whole result by the method responsible for the larger task. Kent Beck refers to this as the **Decomposing Message** pattern [5]. It may also happen that related subtasks can be unified into single methods, resulting in the reuse of code inside a *single* object.

The recomposition of smaller actions by *Conglomeration* has several benefits. It refines the granularity of actions that can be triggered by having each method perform less work. This can improve maintainability by allowing these methods to be reused in multiple places without copying and pasting the code in several places. Additionally, other objects may be able to use portions of the behavior in new ways if these fine-grained methods are made publicly visible.

Consider the example in Listing 5.17, which builds on one of the code examples from *Redirection*. We recognized that the method for painting a room is simply too long; there are too many steps to be taken, and the code is easier to read if it is broken up into smaller tasks. We make the subtask methods publicly available because it becomes obvious that the actions of setting up and cleaning up a room are valuable and can be requested independently of the act of painting a room. Now, the `CarefulPainter` can do the preparation before a ceiling refinisher or a drywall sander comes in and can also perform the cleanup afterwards. What was once inextricably part of the `paintRoom` behavior is now broken out into useful smaller actions.

Listing 5.17 Prep work and cleanup are decomposable.

```
 1  class SloppyFastPainter {
    public:
 3      void paintRoom( Room r ) {
            // Paint the walls
 5      };
    };
 7
    class CarefulPainter {
 9      SloppyFastPainter sloppy;
        Room currentTarpRoom;
11      Room currentHardwareRoom;
    public:
13      void paintRoom( Room r ) {
            this->laydownTarps( r ); // Conglomeration
15          this->removeHardware( r ); // Conglomeration
            sloppy.paintRoom( r );
17          this->replaceHardware();// Conglomeration
            this->cleanUp(); // Conglomeration
19      };
        void laydownTarps( Room r ) {
21          this->currentTarpRoom = r;
            // Laydown tarps
23      };
        void cleanUp() {
25          // Clean currentTarpRoom
            // Relinquish currentTarpRoom
27      };
        void removeHardware( Room r ) {
29          this->currentHardwareRoom = r;
            // Remove hardware
31      };
        void replaceHardware() {
33          // Replace hardware in currentHardwareRoom
            // Relinquish currentHardwareRoom
35      };
    };
```

In doing so, we had a decision to make. We could have allowed the room to be sent along as a parameter to each and every of the subtasks. This allows for the greatest flexibility, but let's assume for a moment that there are employer and union regulations at work here, and one is that, for accountability reasons, the same person must perform the preparation and finalization tasks. This prevents, say, hardware lost during removal from being blamed on the person replacing it, and so on. Each person finishes the job he or she initiated. Not properly tracking this data can, however, lead to confusion.

If an unorganized site manager had several `CarefulPainters` running around and was responsible for telling them which room to go do each step in, they could accidentally send one to clean up a room that another had prepped. Instead, we choose to make the room information private to each `CarefulPainter`. Think of this as if the site manager tells a worker to go `laydownTarps` and hands him or her a chit with the room number. The chit is kept in the worker's pocket, and when told to `cleanUp`, he or she simply refers to the chit to make sure the right room gets cleaned up. Once completed, the worker relinquishes the chit and is ready for another room. The data the chit represents is private to the worker and ties together separate tasks that worker can be asked to do.

Conglomeration is powerful, but it can cause issues if taken too far. The illogical conclusion would be to place every statement within its own method, but it should be obvious why that's a bad idea. Any time *Conglomeration* is applied, a balance must be struck between the necessity for fine granularity and the simplification and efficiency of directly expressed code. Finding the proper "atomic behavior" requires knowing how large your atoms must be.

Applicability

Use *Conglomeration* when:

- A large task can be broken into smaller subtasks.

- The subtasks must be performed on a single object instance, usually due to shared private data or state.

- Several subtasks may be unified into a single method body.

Structure

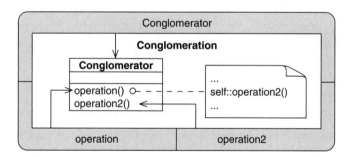

Participants

Conglomerator
Enclosing object type.

operation
Master controlling method that parcels out subtasks.

operation2
Subservient method performing a particular subtask.

Collaborations

In a specialization of *Delegation*, the object calls a method of itself. The calling site is `operation`, and the method being called is `operation2`.

Consequences

As with *Delegation*, this pattern ties two methods into a reliance relationship in which `operation` relies on the behavior and implementation of `operation2`. In this case, unlike *Delegation*, there may be immediate side effects on shared data within the confines of the object that they share.

Implementation

In Java:

```
  public class Conglomerate {
2     public void operation() {
          // Optional prep work
4         operation2();
          // Optional finish work
6     };
      public void operation2() {};
8 }
```

In Python:

```
  class Conglomerate:
2     def operation(self):
          # Optional prep work
4         self.operation2();
          # Optional finish work
6     def operation2(self):
          # Requested behavior
8         pass
```

Related Patterns

Conglomeration ties methods within a single object together and therefore is the first EDP we've seen that doesn't have a form that relies on *Retrieve*. Modifying the object similarity so that the call is to another object, while retaining the same object type similarity, results in a use of *Delegated Conglomeration*. Reversing this to retain the object similarity, and changing the object type similarity to a subtyping relationship leads to *Revert Method*. This may sound a bit bizarre—having the same object but not the same type—but read the *Revert Method* specification for why this is not only possible but also highly useful. On the other hand, keeping the object similarity but changing the object type similarity to completely dissimilar is, at this juncture, ill formed. Finally, changing the method similarity such that the call is to a similar method results in *Recursion*.

Conglomeration will appear anywhere that an object is breaking down a task internally, but for a rather unique use of this EDP, see *Template Method* in Chapter 7.

Method Call Classification

Object: Similar   **Object Type:** Similar   **Method:** Dissimilar

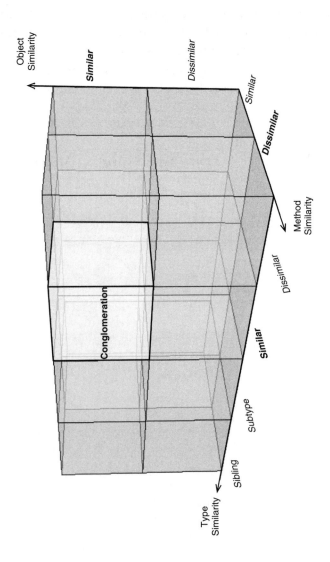

Recursion   **Object Behavioral**

Intent

To accomplish a larger task by performing many smaller and similar tasks while using the same object state.

Motivation

Sometimes, after consideration, we find that a problem can be broken down into subtasks that are identical to the original task, except on a smaller scale. Sorting an array of items using the merge sort algorithm is one such example. Merge sort takes an array and divides it into halves, sorting each individually, and then merges the two sorted arrays into a unified whole. The two half-problems are also sorted using merge sort, so they are subject to the same halving of the problem, and so on. Eventually, arrays of a single item are reached, at which point the merging begins.

The process by which a method calls itself is known as *recursion*, and it is ubiquitous in general programming. The same principle applies in object-oriented programming, but we have the additional requirement that the object must be calling on itself through implicit or explicit use of *self*. You're almost certainly familiar with this concept, but it has a specific placement and context within the EDP catalog.

Generally speaking, recursion is a way of folding a large amount of computation into a small conceptual space. Assume we want to sort an array, and we decide that a simple way to sort a large array is to split it into two arrays of similar size and then merge the two subarrays after they are individually sorted. The merging will be easy: if the head of array A is less than the head of array B, then the head of A is copied to the new, larger array; otherwise, the head of B is copied. The copied item is removed from the appropriate array, and the process is repeated until both arrays are merged.

Because the merge sort scheme relies on the proper sorting of the subarrays, we correctly surmise that we can perform the sort algorithm on the two subarrays by splitting, sorting, and then merging each in turn. We are again faced with the same sorting problem, so we continue in the same manner until we reach the smallest indivisible array: a single item. At that point, the process of merging the sorted subarrays at each step can begin.

Assume we have an `Array` class that contains the usual methods of `add` and `remove`. If the length of the beginning array was 4 items, then we could hardcode the entire sorting as in the following pseudocode, remembering that in an object-oriented system we should have an enclosing class or object by default.

```
class ArrayOfLength4Library {
    Array  sort_merge(Array a) {
        Element a11 = a[0];
        Element a12 = a[1];
        Element a21 = a[2];
        Element a22 = a[3];
        Array a1, a2, res;
        // Sort first half
        if (a11 < a12) {
            a1.add(a11);
            a1.add(a12);
        } else {
            a1.add(a12);
            a1.add(a11);
        }
        // Sort second half
        if (a21 < a22) {
            a2.add(a21);
            a2.add(a22);
        } else {
            a2.add(a22);
            a2.add(a21);
        }
        // Merge
        if (a1[0] < a2[0]) {
            res.add(a1[0]);
            a1.remove(0);
        } else {
            res.add(a2[0]);
            a2.remove(0);
        }
        if (a1[0] < a2[0]) {
            res.add(a1[0]);
            a1.remove(0);
        } else {
            res.add(a2[0]);
            a2.remove(0);
        }
        if (a1.length == 0) {
            res.add(a2[0]);
            res.add(a2[1]);
        }
        if (a2.length == 0) {
            res.add(a1[0]);
            res.add(a1[1]);
        }
        if (a1.length == 1 && a2.length == 1) {
            res.add(a1[0]);
            res.add(a2[0]);
        }
        return a;
    };
};
```

While highly efficient, this solution has an obvious drawback: it is limited to only working for arrays of length 4. A much more flexible version is one using looping. Here we illustrate a `for` loop implementation, assuming for simplicity that the length of the array is a power of 2:

```
1  class ArrayOfPower2LengthLibrary {
       Array sort_array(Array a) {
3          // Slice a into subarrays
           subarray[0][0] = a;
5          for (i = 1 to log_2(a.length())) {
               for (j = 0 to 2^i) {
7                  prevarray = subarray[i-1][floor(j/2)]
                   subarray[i][j] = prevarray.slice(
9                      ((j mod 2) *
                          (prevarray.length() / 2)),
11                     ((j mod 2) + 1) *
                          (prevarray.length() / 2))
13             }
           }
15         // Sort subarrays and merge
           for (i = log_2(a.length()) to 1) {
17             for (j = 2^i to 0) {
                   subarray[i-1][j] =
19                     max(subarray[i][j],
                           subarray[j][i]);
21             }
           }
23         return subarray[0][0];
       };
```

This solution succeeds in making our algorithm much more flexible, but at a cost of making it almost unreadable because of the overhead mechanisms. Note that we are looping inward to the base case (length of array is a single unit), storing state at every step, then looping outward using the state previously stored. This process of enter, store, use store, and unroll is precisely what a function call accomplishes. We can use this fact to vastly simplify our implementation using *Recursion*:

```
   class ArrayLibrary {
2     Array sort (Array a) {
          return sort_array(a,
4                         a.begIndex(), a.endIndex());
      }
6     Array sort_merge(Array a, int beg, int end) {
          if (a.length() > 1) {
8             Array firstHalf =
                  sort_array(a, beg, end-beg/2);
10            // ^--- Recursion (implicit self)
              Array secondHalf =
12                this->sort_array(a,
                                   (end-beg/2) + 1, end);
14            // ^--- Recursion (explicit self)
              return merge(firstHalf, secondHalf);
16        } else {
```

```
              return a;
18        }
     };
20
     Array merge(Array a, Array b) {
22       Array res;
         while (b.length() > 1 || a.length() > 1) {
24           // If a or b is empty, then a[0] or b[0]
             // returns a min value
26           if (a[0] < b[0]) {
                 res.add(a[0]);
28               a.delete(0);
             } else {
30               res.add(b[0]);
                 b.delete(0);
32           }
         }
34       return res;
     };
36 };
```

This version is conceptually cleaner and performs the same task as our looping variation. We allow the runtime of the language to handle the overhead for us. As a bonus, we're no longer limited to certain lengths. Not only is the code cleaner, it is highly generalized.

There are times, such as in a high-performance embedded system, when that manner of overhead handling may be excessive for our needs. In such cases, optimizing away the recursion into loops, or further into linear code, is a possibility. These instances are extreme, however, and tend to be highly specialized. In most cases, the benefits of *Recursion*—conceptual cleanliness and simple code—greatly outweigh the small loss of speed.

Applicability

Use *Recursion* when:

- A task can be divided into highly similar subtasks.

- The subtasks must be, or are preferred to be, performed by the same object, usually because of a need for access to common stored state by both the calling and called methods.

- A small loss of efficiency is overshadowed by the resulting gain in simplicity.

Participants

Recursor

Recursor has a method that calls back on itself within the same instantiation.

operation

`operation` is the method that calls itself, through `self.operation()`, whether implicitly or explicitly.

Structure

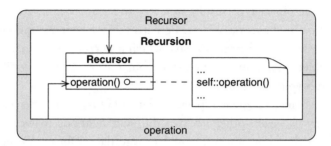

Collaborations

`Recursor`'s method `operation` collaborates with itself, requesting that smaller and smaller tasks be performed at each step, until a base case is reached, at which point results are gathered into a final result.

Consequences

The reliance of *Recursion* on a properly formed base case for termination of the recursion stack is the weakest point of this pattern. It is nearly impossible in most modern systems to wantonly consume all available resources, but recursion can do it easily by having a malformed base case that is never satisfied.

Implementation

In Java:

```
1 public class Recursor {
      public void operation() {
3         // Optional prior work
          self.operation();
5         // Optional finish work
      };
7 }
```

Related Patterns

Recursion is perhaps the least general method-call EDP, in that it specifies that object, object type, and method similarity are all set to similar. Each can be relaxed to reach new EDPs. *Conglomeration* is achieved by using other methods within the same object and object type while using methods that are dissimilar to the caller. (The final sort_merge example from earlier contains instances of *Conglomeration*, including the call from sort to sort_merge and the call from sort_merge to merge.) Retaining the method similarity but allowing the call to occur to other instances of the same object type results in a *Redirected Recursion*, a concept commonly seen in chains of objects. Perhaps the most interesting neighbor EDP of *Recursion* is *Extend Method*, which is encountered when the method and object similarity are preserved but the object type similarity is set to a subtyping relationship.

Finally, there is a specialized use of *Delegation*: when two objects mutually call each other via two different methods to work through a task together, but with separated private data. Object A's method f() calls method g() on object B, and in turn g() calls method f() on object A. This is known as *mutual recursion* because each method calls itself indirectly. While not a true example of *Recursion*, it is conceptually similar enough to warrant mentioning.

Method Call Classification

        Object: Similar   **Object Type:** Similar   **Method:** Similar

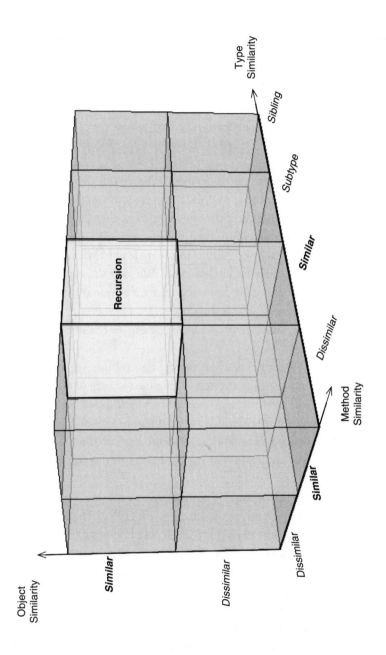

Revert Method   **Object Behavioral**

Intent

Bypass the current class's implementation of a method, and use the super-class's implementation instead, reverting to less specialized method body.

Motivation

Polymorphism sometimes works against us. In the pattern specification for *Inheritance*, you learned how reducing maintenance issues during reuse of an implementation is a driving factor for that pattern. Fixes applied to the base implementation for a method are auto applied to subclasses, but subclasses are allowed either to override existing methods or add new functionality through *Extend Method*. We don't always want fixes to be propagated automatically, however, and we're not always calling a similar method. Sometimes we need to use prior implementations of a method from higher up our inheritance tree instead of the one local to our class definition.

One such instance is when providing multiple versions of classes for simultaneous use within a system. Imagine a library of classes for an Internet data transfer protocol. A base library is shipped as 1.0. With the 1.1 library, changes to the underlying protocol are made, and an application using the 1.1 protocol must be able to fall back to the 1.0 protocol when it detects that the application at the other end of the connection is only 1.0 enabled.

One approach would be to use polymorphism directly and define a base class that abstractly provides the protocol's methods, as in Figure 5.1, and create the proper class item on protocol detection. Unfortunately, this approach does not offer a lot of dynamic flexibility and would not allow a protocol to adapt on the fly to changing demands.

Although it makes setting up a connection with client using the older protocol simple, it makes graceful degradation of the connection in case of an error more problematic. Let's say you're transmitting a video stream, and if network conditions are good and latency is low, then a new processor-intensive compression algorithm for the data can be brought to bear. If

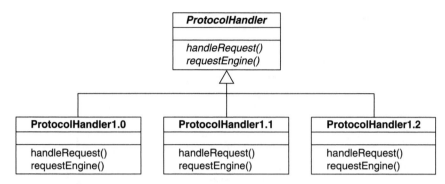

Figure 5.1 Polymorphic approach

latency is high, however, then the CPU time needed for decompression at the other end would cause skipping. If you notice that the network is congested, you drop down to the older compression system.

You could instantiate objects of each protocol type and swap to earlier versions as needed, but protocol state issues might arise and be troublesome. Converting from one protocol handler class to another would require instantiating a new object of the new class and then copying over any private data each and every time a possible protocol shift was needed. Hopefully this data can be held exclusively in the `ProtocolBase` class, but even then there has to be a breaking of strict encapsulation of the private data to accomplish the copy. Further, this splits the protocol knowledge between the `Protocol` classes and the `Controller` class, as shown in Listing 5.18. The former classes implement that actual behavior, but the latter has to know when each behavior is appropriate.

Listing 5.18 Instance swapping for protocol fallback in C++.

```
1 class CommonData{};
  class RawData{};
3 class Video{};

5 class Connection{
  public:
7     bool lowLatency(); // is network in good shape?
      void transmit(RawData);
9 };

11 class RemoteEnd {
  public:
13     int protocolVersion();
   };
15
   // Protocol handler classes:
```

```
17  class ProtocolBase {
    protected:
19      CommonData  data;
        int         d_version;
21      Connection  connection;
    public:
23      virtual
        Connection initConnection(RemoteEnd otherSide);
25      Connection getConnection() {
            return connection;
27      };
        virtual void sendData(Video vid) {
29          connection.transmit(compress(vid));
        };
31      int version() { return d_version; };
        CommonData getData() { return data; };
33      virtual RawData compress(Video vid) = 0;
    };
35
    class Protocol1dot0 : public ProtocolBase {
37  public:
        Protocol1dot0() {
39          d_version = 1.0;
        };
41      Protocol1dot0(ProtocolBase* base) {
            d_version = 1.0;
43          this->data = base->getData();
        };
45      RawData compress(Video vid);
    };
47
    class Protocol1dot1 : public ProtocolBase {
49  public:
        Protocol1dot1() {
51          d_version = 1.1;
        };
53      Protocol1dot1(ProtocolBase* base) {
            d_version = 1.1;
55          this->data = base->getData();
        }
57      RawData compress(Video vid);
    };
59
    class Controller {
61      ProtocolBase*   handler;
    public:
63      void setupConnection(RemoteEnd otherSide) {
            if (otherSide.protocolVersion() == 1.0) {
65              handler = new Protocol1dot0();
            } else {
67              handler = new Protocol1dot1();
            }
69          handler->initConnection(otherSide);
        };
71      void sendData(Video vid) {
            bool networkGood =
73              handler->getConnection().lowLatency();
            if (networkGood &&
75              handler->version() == 1.0) {
                // fall forward
77              handler = new Protocol1dot1(handler);
            } else if (!networkGood &&
79              handler->version() == 1.1) {
                // fall back
81              handler = new Protocol1dot0(handler);
            }
```

```
83          handler->sendData(vid);
      };
85  };
```

This is a tremendous amount of overhead being placed in each of the methods in `Controller`. We could have tried to put all of this controller logic in to the `ProtocolBase` class, and at first glance that looks like it could work. However, it requires that the `ProtocolBase` class know about all of the subclasses, which is fairly poor design in general. It also means that `ProtocolBase` must be updated anytime a new protocol is defined. If this class is shipped in a precompiled library for clients to use, then the clients cannot extend the library for new protocol versions.

In addition, this approach doesn't easily allow for code reuse for the actual implementation. If Protocol 1.1 is just a small tweak off of Protocol 1.0, then it would be nice if we could reuse 1.0's behavior, which would probably be done by hoisting the common code into the base class and allowing it to be called from each subclass. This approach is likely to work well for two subclasses. Once we start getting into more subclasses, protocol versions, and special cases, however, it is likely to become cumbersome. The likelihood of a common core of code being definable goes down quickly.

It fast becomes apparent that graceful dynamic fallback and fallfoward is not well supported by this approach.

Instead, we can have each new protocol version subclass from the prior protocol version so that only the necessary changes to the protocol need to be implemented. This lets us have only a single class to deal with when we first figure out the best possible protocol that each end might be able to support, but we still need to be able to revert to the previous version. Figure 5.2 shows an extended variant of this approach, including several versions.

An example of this approach is shown in Listing 5.19 with just two classes. The supporting classes are as in Listing 5.18. In this case, we can

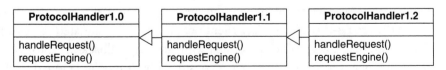

Figure 5.2 Subclassing approach

instantiate an object of just the last class in the chain, and conditional statements in the code will pass the protocol handling back up the chain to the appropriate version if needed. This vastly simplifies further maintenance of the code that supports this protocol because only the instance(s) of the protocol-handling object need to be changed to the latest version anytime a new update to the library comes out, and all the graceful degradation is therefore handled automatically.

Listing 5.19 Auto fallback/forward using *Revert Method.*

```
1  class Protocol1dot0 {
   public:
3      virtual
       void initConnection(RemoteEnd otherSide) {
5          connection = otherSide.connect(1.0);
       };
7      virtual
       void sendData(Video vid) {
9          RawData rawData = compress(vid);
           connection.transmit(rawData);
11     };
   protected:
13     virtual
       RawData compress(Video);
15     Connection connection;
       CommonData data;
17 };

19 class Protocol1dot1 : public Protocol1dot0 {
   public:
21     virtual
       void initConnection(RemoteEnd otherSide) {
23         connection = otherSide.connect(1.1);
       };
25     virtual
       void sendData(Video vid) {
27         RawData rawData;
           if (connection.lowLatency()) {
29             rawData = compress(vid);
           } else {
31             rawData = Protocol1dot0::compress(vid);
           //                ^--- Revert Method
33         }
           connection.transmit(rawData);
35     };
   protected:
37     virtual
       RawData compress(Video);
39 };
```

Now we have eliminated the need for the `Controller` and `ProtocolBase` classes. Any client only needs to instantiate the newest version that it is capable of working with, and any fallback or fallforward happens automatically. The code is considerably cleaner and more directly expresses the intent of the developer.

Applicability

Use *Revert Method* when:

- A class wishes to *reenable* a superclass's implementation of a method that it has overridden in order to use the original behavior.

Structure

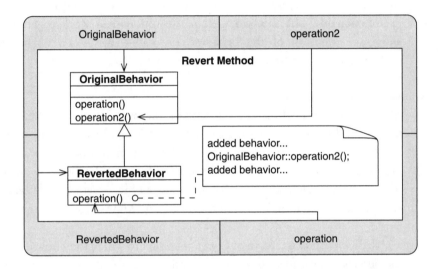

Participants

OriginalBehavior
A base class defining at least the method `operation2`.

operation
`operation` is the method in which the call takes place and is defined in at least the `RevertedBehavior` class.

operation2
`operation2` is the method being called and is defined in at least the `OriginalBehavior` class. If must also be defined in a subclass of `OriginalBehavior`, either in `RevertedBehavior` or in a class defined between them in the class hierarchy. This second definition masks the implementation in `OriginalBehavior` from being the default within `RevertedBehavior` and forcing the selection of the reverted implementation.

RevertedBehavior

A subclass of `OriginalBehavior`, with *operation* defined and *operation2* overridden. *operation* calls the `Original-Behavior` implementation of *operation2* when we would normally expect it to call its own implementation of that method.

Collaborations

In most cases, a subclass overrides a parent class's method to replace its functionality, but the two method definitions can work together to allow an extension of the behavior. `RevertedBehavior` relies on `OriginalBehavior` for a core implementation.

Consequences

There is a conceptual disconnect between the overriding of a base class's method and the utilization of that same method that can be confusing to some students and practitioners. Overriding a method does not erase the old method; it merely hides the old method from public view for objects of the subclass. The object still has knowledge of its parent's methods and can invoke them internally without exposing this knowledge to the external world.

Revert Method is a form of *Conglomeration* to which the knowledge of a superclass's implementation and the ability to access it directly have been added.

Implementation

In C#:

```
 1  public class OriginalBehavior {
        // Optional definition of operation()
 3      public virtual void operation() {};
        public virtual void operation2() {};
 5  };

 7  public class RevertedBehavior : OriginalBehavior {
        public override void operation() {
 9          // Optional work priot
            if (oldBehaviorNeeded) {
11              OriginalBehavior::operation2();
            } else {
13              operation2();
            }
15          // Optional work after
        };
17      // If this were not overridden, there would be
```

```
        // no need to revert to superclass's version
19      public override void operation2();
    };
```

Related Patterns

As noted earlier, *Revert Method* is closely related to *Conglomeration* except that it uses a supertype's implementation of the method to be conglomerated. If the similar method is to be called, then you have an example of *Extend Method*. If the behavior is being provided by the other objects of the supertype defined by `OriginalBehavior`, then that is an instance of *Trusted Delegation*.

Method Call Classification

Object: Similar   **Object Type:** Subtype   **Method:** Dissimilar

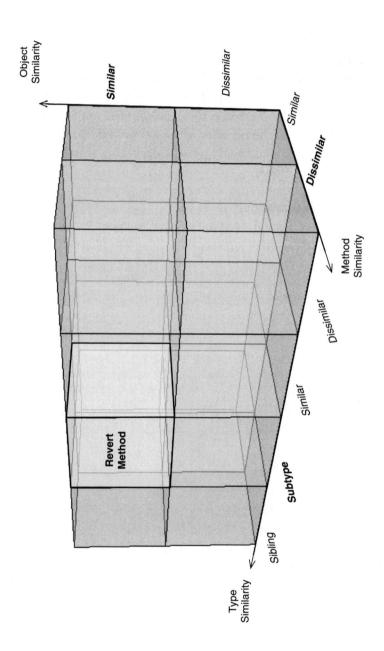

Extend Method   Object Behavioral

Intent

Supplement, not replace, behavior in a method of a superclass while reusing existing code.

Also Known As

Extending Super

Motivation

Two of the most common tasks in software production and maintenance are to fix bugs or add new features. The most straightforward way of doing so is to alter the code directly. Where the bug exists, fix it. Where the new feature is needed, add it.

This isn't always possible, however. Often the code that needs fixing or enhancing is not available in source form because it has been provided as a library. Other times, the original code and behavior must be preserved for use by legacy code. In either case, there will be times when the original method cannot be changed.

If the original source is available, of course, we can just copy and paste the old code into the new method. As shown in the specification for *Inheritance*, however, this presents a host of problems, including inconsistency of methods, and results in a potential maintenance morass. A much less error-prone approach is to have any implementation defined at only a single point and then reuse the existing code, tweaking the input or results as needed. Data can be massaged before being passed to the original implementation, or the results of the original implementation can be used to perform additional steps. Adhering to this principle is a simple way to reduce maintenance complexity and produce clear code.

If the original source is not available, then we're prevented from copying and pasting code in any case and have to find another way to reuse the existing code. It is possible, of course, to create a reference to a delegate object with the original behavior and call into it when needed. This is the approach taken in *Redirection*, but this approach breaks down quickly in certain cases, as shown in Listing 5.20. If the added behavior needs to have access to data that was encapsulated as private by the original code, and the code does not expose it for use or manipulation by outside clients, then this tactic simply isn't possible. Even when it is possible, it may not be clear what the new code is doing and that its relationship to the original code is quite close.

Listing 5.20 Using *Redirection* in Python to add behavior.

```
   class OriginalBehavior:
2      __privateData = True
       # Prepend __ for a private attribute
4      def desiredBehavior(self, data):
           # Do something interesting
6          return data

8  class NewBehavior:
       def addMoreBehavior(self, data):
10         # Perform any necessary pre-call setup
           # Cannot access __privateData of ob
12         ob = OriginalBehavior()
           val = ob.desiredBehavior(data)
14         # Post-call cleanup or more functionality
```

The solution to these problems is to use *Extend Method*, as in Listing 5.21. We implement a new class that subclasses off of the class containing the original desired behavior using *Inheritance* because it provides the mechanisms for reuse of the original code. We then override the original method, adding what implementation of the method we need, but make a call back to the superclass's implementation of the method when we need its behavior to be executed. This provides us with simple maintenance, reuse, and encapsulation of the altered behavior.

Listing 5.21 Using *Extend Method* to add behavior.

```
   class OriginalBehavior:
2      __privateData = True
       # Prepend __ for a private attribute
4      def desiredBehavior(self, data):
           # Do something interesting
6          return data

8  class NewBehavior(OriginalBehavior):
       def desiredBehavior(self, data):
10         # Perform any necessary pre-call setup
           # Can access __privateData!
12         superDelegate = super(NewBehavior, self)
           superDelegate.desiredBehavior(data)
14         # ^--- Extend Method
           # Post-call cleanup or more functionality
```

Applicability
Use *Extend Method* when:

- Existing behavior of a method needs to be extended but not replaced.

- Reuse of code is preferred or necessitated by lack of source code.

- Using *Redirection* is not possible or optimal because the new behavior needs access to data that is private to the original implementation.

Structure

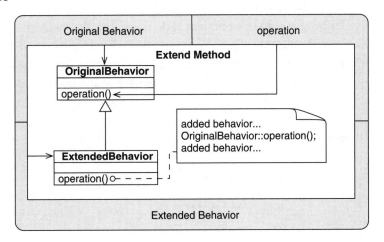

Participants

Original Behavior
Defines interface and contains an implementation of the method `operation` with the desired core functionality.

operation
Defined by `OriginalBehavior` to provide basic behavior. Overridden in `ExtendedBehavior` to provide a new implementation that makes use of the original implementation.

Extended Behavior
Uses interface of `OriginalBehavior`, then reimplements the `operation` method to include a call to the base class code surrounded by added code and/or behavior.

Collaborations

In most cases when a subclass overrides a parent class's method, the purpose is to replace the functionality of that original method. The two method definitions, however, can work together to allow an extension of the behavior of the parent class instead of a replacement. ExtendedBehavior relies on OriginalBehavior for both interface and core implementation.

Consequences

As with *Revert Method*, the concept of calling an overridden version of a method can be confusing. In *Extend Method*, it can be even more confusing because the calling method seems to be invoking a ghost method. Using this pattern optimizes code reuse, but the method operation in OriginalBehavior becomes somewhat fragile—its behavior is now relied on by ExtendedBehavior::Operation to be invariant over time. Behavior is extended polymorphically and transparently to clients of OriginalBehavior.

Implementation

In Java:

```java
1  public class OriginalBehavior {
       public void operation() {
3          // Do core behavior
       };
5  };
   public class ExtendedBehavior
7      extends OriginalBehavior {
       public void operation() {
9          // Optional work before
           super.operation();
11         // Optional work after
       };
13 };
```

In C++:

```cpp
1  class OriginalBehavior {
   public:
3      virtual void operation() {
           // Do core behavior
5      };
   };
7  class ExtendedBehavior : public OriginalBehavior {
   public:
9      void operation() {
           // Optional work before
```

```
11              OriginalBehavior::operation();
                // Optional work after
13          };
        };
```

Related Patterns

Extend Method, like *Recursion*, is defined using a single object. Converting this object similarity to distinct dissimilar objects results in an instance of *Trusted Redirection*, which uses polymorphism to traverse a cluster of trusted related classes for functionality. Relaxing the method similarity to call a different method of the superclass results in *Revert Method*. Because *Revert Method* is a superclass-aware variation of *Conglomeration*, *Extend Method* is a superclass-aware version of *Recursion*, even though the resulting behavior is quite different. *Recursion* can be reached by simply removing that superclass access and invoking the current type's implementation.

Method Call Classification

Object: Similar   **Object Type:** Super   **Method:** Similar

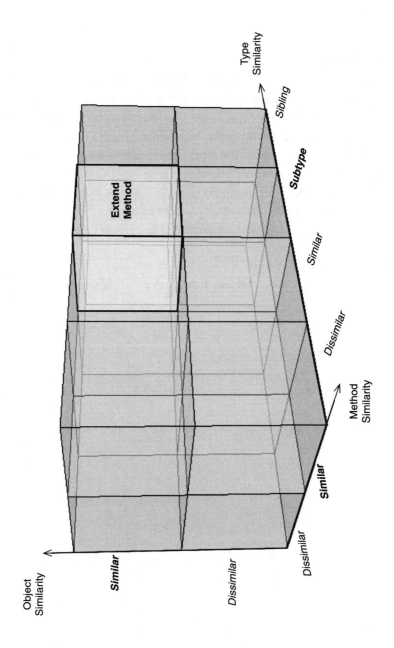

Delegated Conglomeration   **Object Behavioral**

Intent

When multiple objects of the same type must work in concert to complete a task, with each performing different behaviors.

Motivation

Objects of the same type often work in concert to perform tasks. Homogeneous data environments with heterogeneous behavior are frequently coded as a collection of like objects collaborating to produce a larger functionality.

Listing 5.22 presents an example using a social networking site. Each user's account has a list of friends, and one action users are likely to want to do is invite other friends to an event. Users can set their own notification preferences, including the email address they want to be contacted at when they get an invitation.

Listing 5.22 Inviting friends naively in Java.

```
   import java.util.Vector;
 2 import java.lang.String;

 4 public class UserAccount {
       Vector<UserAccount> allMyFriends;
 6     public String        notificationEmail;

 8     public void inviteToEvent (
            Vector<UserAccount> friends, String msg) {
10         for (UserAccount friend : friends) {
               String email = friend.notificationEmail;
12             // send email
           }
14     }
   };
```

This solution works, but it requires each account to expose its email information publicly. Most users do not want to expose their email address on a networking site. To keep this information slightly more private, event planners can request emails from friends, and friends can provide those emails if they wish to, as shown in Listing 5.23.

Listing 5.23 A slightly better approach for inviting friends.

```java
import java.util.Vector;
import java.lang.String;

public class UserAccount {
    Vector<UserAccount> allMyFriends;
    public String        notificationEmail;

    public void inviteToEvent (
            Vector<UserAccount> friends, String msg) {
        for (UserAccount friend : friends) {
            String email = friend.getEmail(this);
            // send email
        }
    }

    public String getEmail (UserAccount requester) {
        String returnVal = "";
        if (allMyFriends.contains(requester)) {
            returnVal = notificationEmail;
        }
        return returnVal;
    };
};
```

This approach still requires users to provide their email address to anyone on their friends list who requests it. Again, most users would probably just like to receive an invitation without having to share their email address. Visibility of an email address can be separated from the capability to receive invitations by use of *Delegated Conglomeration*, as in Listing 5.24. Now when users invite friends, they don't see or access their friends' email information directly. Instead, they send a notification request to their friends' accounts, which ensures the invitation is delivered without exposing the email addresses.

Listing 5.24 *Delegated Conglomeration* in Java.

```java
import java.util.Vector;
import java.lang.String;

public class UserAccount {
    Vector<UserAccount> allMyFriends;
    public String        notificationEmail;

    public void inviteToEvent (
            Vector<UserAccount> friends, String msg) {
        for (UserAccount friend : friends) {
            friend.notify(this, msg);
            // ^--- Delegated Conglomeration
        }
    }

    public boolean notify (UserAccount inviter,
                            String msg) {
```

```
19        // Send email to notificationEmail
          return true;
        };
21  };
```

Listings 5.23 and 5.24 are technically instances of *Delegated Conglomeration*, but the latter shows a much better justification and clearer use case. Listing 5.23 selectively exposes private data based on who requests it; Listing 5.24 shows that *Delegated Conglomeration* can be used to completely hide private data such that it is never shared. The second object is given the sole responsibility to perform a task with private data.

Applicability

Use *Delegated Conglomeration* when:

- A task can be broken into subtasks that are properly handled by the same object type.

- Many objects of the same type work in concert to complete a task.

- A single object cannot complete the task alone.

- The task requires data that is kept private by the other objects.

Structure

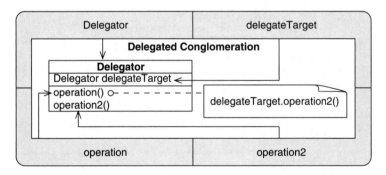

Participants

Delegator
The object type that contains references to other instances of its own type.

delegateTarget
The enclosed instance that is called upon to perform a task.

operation
The calling point within the first object.

operation2
The subtask to be completed by the second object.

Collaborations

Only one object type, `Delegator`, is involved in this pattern, but there are two distinct instances of that type. One object relies on the other to perform some part of the task, as with *Delegation*, and that subtask is not directly associated with the current request, as with *Conglomeration*.

Consequences

As with *Redirected Recursion*, this pattern offers the ability to distribute tasks among a number of objects. Unlike its cousin, however, *Delegated Conglomeration* offers a clear decision-making point, separating the behavior-determining logic from the behavior implementation.

Implementation

In C++:

```
 1  class Delegator {
        Delegator*  delegateTarget;
 3  public:
        void operation() {
 5          // Optional work prior
            delegateTarget->operation2();
 7          // Optional work after
        };
 9      void operation2() {
            // Do something useful
11      };
    }
```

In Objective-C:

```
    @interface Delegator
 2  {
        Delegator* delegateTarget;
 4  }
    - (void) operation;
 6  - (void) operation2;
    @end
 8
    @implementation Delegator
10  - (void) operation
    {
12      // Optional work prior
        [delegateTarget operation2];
```

```
14      // Optional work after
    }
16  - (void) operation2
    {
18      // Do something useful
    }
20  @end
```

Related Patterns

Obviously, *Delegated Conglomeration* can be converted either to *Delegation*, by relaxing the typing relationship between the objects, or to *Conglomeration*, by having the object call back into itself. If the type similarity is changed to subtyping, it means the object is calling into a family of trusted classes, resulting in *Trusted Delegation*. Keeping the type similarity the same and retaining the distinct objects, but instead having the method call into its similar counterpart in the other object to invoke the *same* behavior, brings us to *Redirected Recursion*.

Method Call Classification

Object: Dissimilar   **Object Type:** Similar   **Method:** Dissimilar

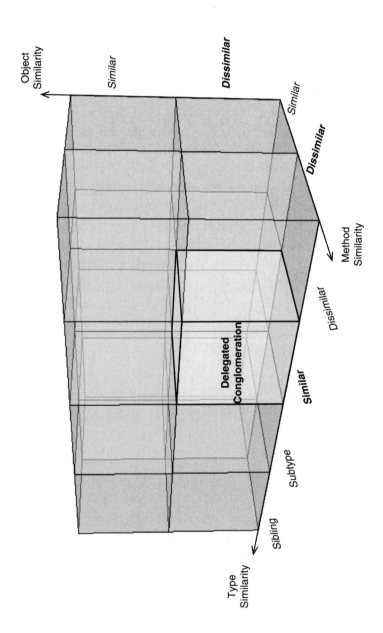

Redirected Recursion   Object Behavioral

Intent

To perform a singular action on multiple objects and have the objects be responsible for distribution and invocation of that action.

Motivation

Often we wish to perform the same action on a lot of data in a system. Sometimes that data is best organized by an external container, and the data can be considered "dumb," with no responsibility for its own organization; it is acted on only by an external entity traversing the container. Iterating over a container and performing an action on each item contained in it is an example of this process. It requires that the structure of the data be imposed from outside and that the flow of invocation of the behavior also be controlled externally. A simple example is provided in Listing 5.25.

Listing 5.25 Traditional iteration and invocation in C.

```
  #include <stdio.h>
2 #define LENGTH 4
  int data[LENGTH] = {1, 2, 3, 4};
4 void printAll() {
     int i;
6   for(i = 0; i < LENGTH; i++) {
        printf("%d\n", data[i]);
8   }
  };
```

This solution is a common way of solving the original problem, but it can be improved on. First, data in an object-oriented system doesn't have to be dumb. It can perform its own actions when requested. We can instead do something more like what is shown in Listing 5.26.

Listing 5.26 Object-oriented iteration and invocation in C++.

```
1 #include <cstdio>

3 class DataItem {
     int data;
5 public:
     DataItem(int val) : data(val) {};
```

```
7      void print() {
           printf("%d\n", data);
9      };
   };
11
   #define LENGTH 4
13 DataItem data[LENGTH] =
       {DataItem(1), DataItem(2),
15      DataItem(3), DataItem(4)};

17 void printAll() {
       int i;
19     for(i = 0; i < LENGTH; i++) {
           data[i].print();
21     }
   };
```

Now the data is responsible for doing the printing. The `printAll()` function doesn't have to know anything about the data, how it is encoded, or even how it is printed. It just has to know how to traverse the organizing container and invoke `print()` on each object.

This solution is better, but we can take it a step further. Instead of an array, the data may be best represented by a graph or a balanced tree. As it currently stands, any piece of code that wishes to perform an operation on each element in the above array would have to be modified to now traverse the new organizational structure. In a large system, this can be a huge undertaking. Because objects can contain references to other objects through the use of *Retrieve*, however, we can have the objects also take care of their own organization, leading us to something like Listing 5.27.

Listing 5.27 Basic *Redirected Recursion* in C++.

```
   #include <cstdio>
2
   class DataItem {
4      int data;
       DataItem* next;
6 public:
       DataItem(int val) : data(val), next(NULL) {};
8      DataItem(int val, DataItem* next) :
           data(val), next(next) {};
10     void print() {
           printf("%d\n", data);
12         if (next) {
               next->print();
14             // ^--- Redirected Recursion
           }
16     };
   };
18
   DataItem data =
20     {DataItem(1,
           new DataItem(2,
22             new DataItem(3,
                   new DataItem(4))))};
```

```
24
   void printAll() {
26      data.print();
   };
```

Now responsibility not only for the printing behavior but also for how to find the next piece of data has been handed over to the data object. Because the data is now responsible for its own organization, it can also be responsible for its own invocation ordering. If the `DataItem` class decides to change its implementation and store its partner objects as a red-black tree, a hashmap, or any other manner of data structure, it is free to do so, and the code in `printAll()` doesn't need to change. This isn't always the right approach to take, but it can be powerful in the right circumstances when objects that a system is dealing with can be trusted to be self-organizing and only need a trigger to initiate a complex sequence of events in tandem.

Imagine, for example, a line of paratroopers getting ready for a jump. Space is tight, so the commander cannot walk down the line to indicate to each trooper to jump individually. Instead, he stands at the back of the line, and when the drop time comes, he taps the last trooper on the shoulder. That trooper knows to tap the shoulder of the trooper in front of him and to jump after that soldier has jumped. This can continue down a line of arbitrary length, from 2 to 200 troopers. The paratroopers' only tasks are to, when they feel a tap on their shoulder, tap the next person in line; wait; shuffle forward as space is available; and when they see the soldier in front of them go, jump next. The commander issues one order instead of one to each soldier. A sample coding of this might look like Listing 5.28.

Listing 5.28 Paratroopers implementing *Redirected Recursion*.

```
 1 class Paratrooper {
      bool          _hasJumped;
 3    Paratrooper*  nextTrooper;
   public:
 5    Paratrooper() : _hasJumped(false) {};
      void jump() {
 7        if (nextTrooper) {
              nextTrooper->jump();
 9            // ^--- Redirected Recursion
              while (! nextTrooper->hasJumped() ) {
11                shuffleForward();
              }
13        }
          leap();
15    };
```

```
        void leap() {
17          _hasJumped = true;
            // Enter gravity's sweet embrace
19      };
        void shuffleForward() {
21          // Take a step
        };
23      bool hasJumped() {
            return _hasJumped;
25      };
    };
27
    class Commander {
29      Paratrooper*     backOfLine;
    public:
31      void greenLight() {
            backOfLine->jump();
33      };
    };
```

The current paratrooper cannot jump until the trooper in front has completed the task, and so on, and so on. Eventually each paratrooper has completed his or her task, in the proper order, and with very little instruction. The order issues down the chain, but the behavior propagates back. The first trooper tapped is the last to jump.

Applicability

Use *Redirected Recursion* when:

- Recursion is a clean way to break up the task into subparts.

- Multiple objects of the same type must interact to complete the task.

- The objects can be responsible for their own organization among themselves.

Structure

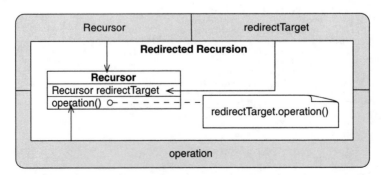

Participants

Recursor

An object type that holds a reference to another instance of its own type.

redirectTarget

The enclosed instance.

operation

A method within `Recursor` that is recursive on itself but through `redirectTarget`.

Collaborations

Multiple instances of the same object type interact to complete a task. Each instance knows how to message the next object for its turn.

Consequences

This is a powerful method for shared recursive behavior when using a number of objects, and it is found in many systems. It allows functionality to be split among disparate data sets that can be self-organized, but it constrains the functionality to a particular behavior. It is analogous to single instruction, multiple data (SIMD) computing in hardware such as a graphics processor, except that in this case the data is responsible for passing along the instruction. This can be a highly flexible approach to solving problems that require a divide-and-conquer algorithm, as changing the method's implementation propagates across all objects equally.

Implementation

In Java:

```java
public class Recursor {
    Recursor    redirectTarget;
    public void operation() {
        // Optional work before...
        redirectTarget.operation();
        // Optional work after...
    };
};
```

In Python:

```python
class Recursor:
    def __init__(self):
```

```
               __redirectTarget = Recursor()
  4
        def operation(self):
  6          # Optional work before...
             redirectTarget.operation();
  8          # Optional work after...
```

Related Patterns

As you might expect from the name, *Redirected Recursion* can be converted into *Redirection* by eliminating the method similarity requirement. Similarly, collapsing the distinct object dissimilarity into one object results in simple *Recursion*. Retaining the object dissimilarity to enforce cooperation between multiple objects while relaxing the method similarity to a method dissimilarity yields *Delegated Conglomeration*. Finally, *Trusted Redirection* is achieved by changing the type relationship to one of subtyping, which lets the method call be handled polymorphically through a trusted collection of classes related to the one initiating the call.

Method Call Classification

Object: Dissimilar   **Object Type:** Similar   **Method:** Similar

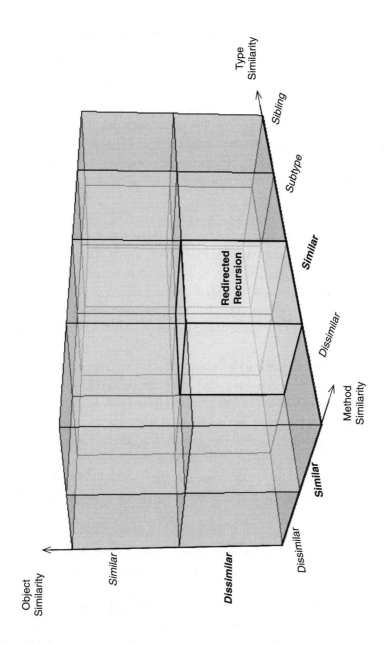

Trusted Delegation   Object Behavioral

Intent

Related classes are often defined as such to perform tasks collectively. In these cases, multiple objects of related types can interact in generalized ways to delegate tasks to one another. If the objects are of related types, the objects can make certain well-formed assumptions about the level of trust they can place in the other object.

Motivation

When objects must act in concert to perform a task, such as in *Delegation*, they are placing a certain amount of trust in the other object to complete its task. One way to ensure trust, or at least to reduce the risk involved, is to delegate the portion of the task that the calling object knows something about to another object. A common way to share information about objects is for their types to be related, and the simplest form of that is the subtyping relationship.

By passing a task to an object of a supertype of the current object, certain aspects of the receiving object can be known ahead of time. The method signatures are necessarily established before the call can be implemented, and the intent can be assumed from the relationship between the method signatures, as with *Delegation*. In addition, however, the intent can be *known* precisely, because the calling object *also has that same method*. The implementation may differ, but the calling object has inherited the basic conceptual intent as well as the signature. It may even have the same default implementation.

Intent and concept, however, are most important here. The calling object knows that the delegate object is going to have *at least* the semantics of the superclass. Through polymorphism (where applicable), the delegate object may restrict these semantics to provide specialization, but in general, it is not allowed to relax them. The calling object knows that the delegate object will conform to a certain set of predeterminable guidelines. Although this is technically true in any strongly typed language—because the calling object must have an idea of the type of the delegate object at the calling site—the fact that the type is the calling object's own supertype offers an entirely different level of knowledge. This additional knowledge enables the calling object to place a higher level of trust in the delegate object.

User interfaces are a familiar type of system in which to find *Trusted Delegation* and related patterns such as *Deputized Delegation*, *Trusted Redirection*, and *Deputized Redirection*. This pattern allows tasks to be parceled out within a family of classes, often called a class cluster, when the interface and method name are known, but the precise object type and, therefore, method body may not be. It is a form of polymorphic delegation in which the calling object is one of the polymorphic types.

Consider a windowing system that includes slider bars and rotary dials as input controls and text fields and bar graphs as display widgets. An input control is tied to a particular display widget and sends that widget updates of values when the control is adjusted by the user. The input controls don't need to know precisely what kind of display widget is at the other end; they just need to know that they must call the `updateValue` method with the appropriate value as a parameter. Because input controls also necessarily display a value, it is possible to programmatically change their adjustment accordingly, so they too need an `updateValue` method. By our *Inheritance* pattern, it seems the input controls and display widgets are of the same family and, in fact, we want to make sure that they can all interact, so we create a class hierarchy accordingly, as in Listing 5.29.

Listing 5.29 UI widgets demonstrating *Trusted Delegation* in C++.

```
    class UIWidget {
 2  public:
        virtual void updateValue( int newValue );
 4  };

 6  class InputControl : UIWidget{
        UIWidget*    target;
 8  public:
        void userHasSetNewValue(int myNewValue)   {
10          target->updateValue(myNewValue);
            // ^--- Trusted Delegation
12      }
    };
14
    class SliderBar : public InputControl {
16  public:
        // Moves the slider bar accordingly
18      void updateValue( int newValue );
        void acceptUserClick() {
20          // Determine new value, set it
            int newVal;
```

```
22          // Update the slider bar graphic
            this->userHasSetNewValue(newVal);
24      };
    };
26
    class RotaryKnob : InputControl {
28  public:
        // Rotates the knob image accordingly
30      void updateValue( int newValue );
        void acceptUserClick() {
32          // Determine new value, set it
            int newVal;
34          // Update the knob image
            this->userHasSetNewValue(newVal);
36      };
    };
38
    class GraphicsContext {
40  public:
        virtual void render(int);
42  };

44  class DisplayWidget : public UIWidget {
    protected:
46      // Each subclass should set the
        // GraphicsContext to something
48      // meaningful for its needs
        GraphicsContext*    gc;
50  public:
        void updateValue( int newValue ) {
52          gc->render( newValue );
        };
54  };

56  class TextWidget : public DisplayWidget {};

58  class BarGraph : public DisplayWidget {};
```

In this example, the `InputControl` and `UIWidget` classes fulfill
the necessary roles in the *Trusted Delegation* pattern, as shown in Figure 5.3. `InputControl` has a greater sense of certainty about what the
call to `updateValue` will do, because it knows about and is intimately
tied with the `UIWidget` class through subclassing. If the `target` object
were of some other type, then `InputControl` would have much less
information about what that call to `updateValue()` would accomplish.
Knowing that it is an instance of `UIWidget` or of one of its subclasses
tells `InputControl` that the delegate object will be involved with the
user, just as it is. It can trust that its delegated task will be handled as
expected.

The `SliderBar` and `RotaryKnob` objects do not have to know anything about where their value is going and, in fact, they could be tied to
each other, with each adjusting the other in sync. You could even have two

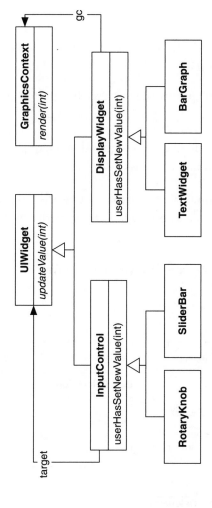

Figure 5.3 UI class cluster showing an instance of *Trusted Delegation*.

objects of the same `InputControl` subclass tied together, such as two `SliderBar` instances. We have separated the concerns of who is sending what data and who is receiving it. Our only concerns are that the data is being sent to a properly receiving client polymorphically and that the current calling object is *of that polymorphic family*. This allows for a single, unified interface for many classes that can work in tandem to perform many tasks.

Applicability

Use *Trusted Delegation* when:

- Delegation is appropriate, with related and/or unrelated subtasks to be performed.

- A level of assumed trust is required in the requirements and/or implementation for the task.

- The actual implementation may not be selectable ahead of time, and polymorphism may be required to properly handle the message request.

- The calling object is of a type in the polymorphic class hierarchy.

Structure

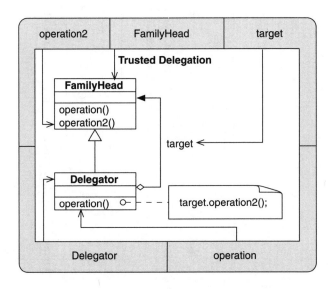

Participants

FamilyHead
The base class for a polymorphic class cluster.

Delegator
A subclass of `FamilyHead`.

target
A polymorphic instance of `FamilyHead` that is contained by `Delegator`.

operation
The calling method that is requesting a trusted delegated task.

operation2
The called method trusted to perform the delegated task.

Collaborations
`FamilyHead` provides a base interface for `Delegator`, and an instance of `FamilyHead` also resides within the `Delegator` to handle requests. This instance is understood to be polymorphic and may handle a request in a number of different ways. *Trusted Delegation* differs from *Trusted Redirection* in that it is a more generalized form and parcels out subtasks that are related to, not refinements of, the initiating method.

Consequences
As with any subtyping relationship, `Delegator` is tied to the interface of `FamilyHead`. The implementation of the `target` method is subject to the particular subclass that it ends up being contained in, via polymorphism. For this reason, *Trusted Delegation* may set up unintended consequences if another class within the class hierarchy implements its methods in an unexpected way. On the other hand, this is a powerful mechanism for extending functionality by adding classes to the class family. If the possible extensions need to be limited in some way, consider using the *Deputized Delegation* pattern instead.

Implementation
The `target` can be defined in either the base class or the subclass; it just needs to be accessible from with the subclass.

In Java, superclass-defined target:

```java
  public abstract class FamilyHead {
2     FamilyHead  target;
      public abstract void operation();
4     public abstract void operation2();
  };

6
  public class Delegator extends FamilyHead {
8     public void operation() {
          // Optional work before...
10        target.operation2();
          // ^--- Trusted Delegation
12        // Optional work after...
      };
14    public void operation2() {};
  };
```

In Python, subclass-defined target:

```python
1 class FamilyHead:
      def operation(self):
3         pass
      def operation2(self):
5         pass
  };

7
  class Delegator(FamilyHead):
9     target = FamilyHead();
      def operation(self) {
11        # Optional work before...
          target.operation2();
13        # ^--- Trusted Delegation
          # Optional work after...
```

Related Patterns

As you might guess from the name, *Trusted Delegation* is a specialized version of *Delegation*, but the delegation is going to an object of a trusted type, by virtue of that type of the delegate object being a supertype of the calling object. Removing this typing relation results in turning this pattern back into a plain *Delegation*. On the other hand, putting even tighter restrictions on this typing relationship and turning it into a sibling type relationship yields *Deputized Delegation*. Putting yet tighter restrictions on the type, making it exactly the same as the calling object, creates an instance of *Delegated Conglomeration*. Keeping the type smiliarity the same but modifying the method similarity such that we're calling the similar method in the delegate object gets us to *Trusted Redirection*. Finally, collapsing the objects into the same one, such that we're calling the supertype implementation of a method on the same object, we arrive at *Revert Method*.

Method Call Classification

Object: Similar   **Object Type:** Subtype   **Method:** Dissimilar

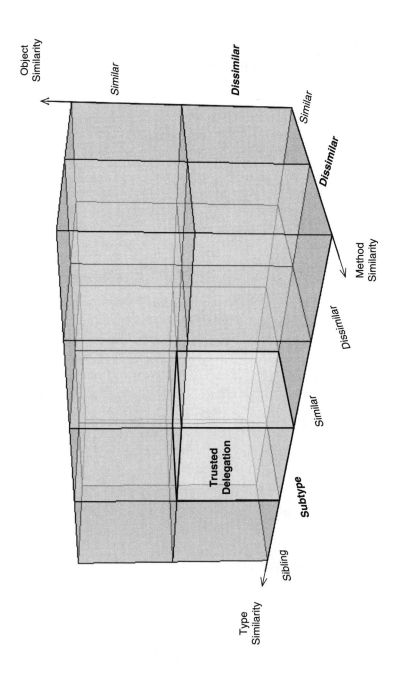

Trusted Redirection   **Object Behavioral**

Intent

Redirect some portion of a method's implementation to a possible cluster of classes of which the current class is a member. The classes are considered trustworthy through the typing relationships.

Motivation

Frequently, a hierarchical object structure of related objects is built at runtime, and behavior needs to be distributed among multiple objects operating with differing implementations. This is an effective way to move responsibility for the handling of a request through a number of objects, and it is a core structure in the *Chain of Responsibility* and *Composite* patterns [21]. *Trusted Redirection* can be considered a single link of such chains.

Although we could simply use *Redirection* in these cases, chains of related behavior assume more stringent requirements than simple method similarity. The intents must be *identical,* not just similar. Frequently, even the implementations are assumed to have some commonality.

Just as in *Trusted Delegation*, a level of trust is built between the calling object and the called object, based on the knowledge that the called object is of a very closely related type. With *Trusted Redirection*, however, that trust is just a little bit stronger.

The use of a *Redirection* implies that the intent behind the calling method and the target method are similar and that a strong correlation exists between the two methods. By ensuring that the type of the recipient object is a supertype of the current object, a much stronger correlation can be established. Declaring that the target object must be of a type that is, or is derived from, a superclass of the current object's type, sets up a pool of trusted types. These types are expected to have behavior that is closer in form and intent to the method triggering the call.

For example, in event-handling systems, such as found in GUIs, it is common to have a hierarchy of event-aware elements. Data views and controls are contained within panes, which are composed into windows, which sit in a global UI environment, perhaps with other elements. Any of these elements may be asked to handle a user-generated event such as a mouse-click, but it may be a context-driven handling. A window that is in the background and currently inactive may react differently to mouse events than one in the foreground, for example. If the window is inactive, it will come to the foreground; but if the window is active, it will redirect the click event to its contents, so they can handle it. Those contents could be a tabbed subpane, a control widget, a text box, anything at all. A tabbed subpane may be similarly active or inactive and decide how to react to the click. A text box may, in turn, elect to pass along the click to the text contents if appropriate, based on its state. The text contents can react to the click, drag, or other event internally while letting the text box handle the visual aspects. Not all event handlers have a visual component. All the visual elements are expected be *able* to handle an event appropriately, but they may not all be asked to handle them the same way *at any specific point in time*. This temporal dynamicism is a common but not necessary constraint leading to the use of *Trusted Redirection*.

Example code for an implementation of an event handler could be defined in C++ as in Listing 5.30 and in Figure 5.4.

Listing 5.30 Event handler in C++ showing *Trusted Redirection*.

```
    #include <vector>
 2  using std::vector;

 4  class Event {};
    class Position {};
 6
    class MouseEvent : public Event {
 8      vector<bool>    modifierKeys;
        Position        position;
10      bool            mouseDown;
    };
12
    class EventHandler {
14  public:
        virtual void handle(Event* e) {
16          // do what is needed
        };
18  };

20  class TextData : public EventHandler {
        // Text storage class
22  };

24  class UIWidget : public EventHandler {
    protected:
26      EventHandler*   nextHandler;
    public:
28      virtual bool isActive();
        virtual void handle(Event* e) {
30          // Possible setup...
```

```
              if ( !(this->isActive()) ) {
32                nextHandler->handle(e);
                  // ^--- Trusted Redirection
34            } else {
                  // Handle it myself
36            }
        };
38 };

40 class Button : public UIWidget {
        // Base class for any clickable button
42 };

44 class TabPane : public UIWidget {
        UIWidget*    contents;
46 public:
        TabPane() {
48          // Setup contents
            nextHandler = contents;
50      };
   };
52
   class TextField : public UIWidget {
54    TextData*    text;
   public:
56    TextField() {
            // Setup text
58          nextHandler = text;
        };
60 };
```

Each visual UI subclass inherits the default behavior from `UIWidget`, although it can be overridden at any time. In this structure, each subclass uses an instance of `EventHandler` as the next item to be asked to handle an event in the case that the current object is not suitable. A common alteration to this behavior includes checking to see what type of event has been passed in before making a decision regarding whether to handle it.

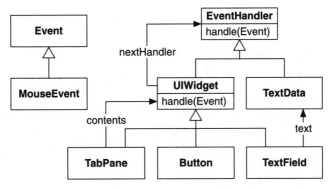

Figure 5.4 UI class cluster showing an instance of *Trusted Redirection*.

Applicability

Use *Trusted Redirection* when:

- An aggregate structure of related objects is expected to be composed at compile or runtime.

- Behavior should be decomposed to the various member objects.

- The structure of the aggregate objects is not known ahead of time.

- Polymorphic behavior is expected but not enforced.

Structure

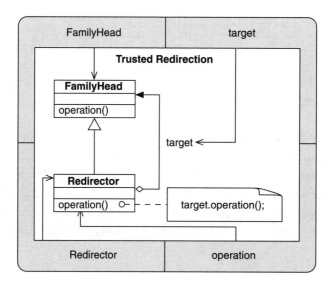

Participants

FamilyHead

Defines interface and contains a method to be possibly overridden.

Redirector

Uses interface of `FamilyHead` and redirects internal behavior back to an instance of `FamilyHead` to gain polymorphic behavior over an amorphous object structure.

target

The object that is being requested to perform the redirected work.

operation

Indicates the intended task to be completed in both the calling and called objects.

Collaborations

`Redirector` relies on the class `FamilyHead` for an interface and an instance of the same for an object-recursive implementation. The *Redirection* relationship is a critical part of this pattern because it drives the concept of "do the same as I was asked to do." The trusted aspect comes in from redirecting the work to a supertype of the current object for polymorphic handling.

Consequences

`Redirector` is reliant on `FamilyHead` for its interface, but it falls to the entirety of the class hierarchy to provide the various implementations. For this reason, other classes in the hierarchy may exhibit unexpected behavior. If unexpected behavior is occurring, consider instead using the *Deputized Redirection* pattern to restrict the possibilities to a manageable set.

Implementation

In C++:

```cpp
   class FamilyHead {
2  public:
       virtual void operation();
4  };

6  class Redirector : public FamilyHead {
   public:
8      void operation();
       FamilyHead* target;
10 };

12 void
   Redirector::operation() {
14     // Optional work before...
       target->operation();
16     // Optional work after...
   }
```

Related Patterns

Trusted Redirection is a specialization of *Redirection* such that the possible targets of the redirected task are from a trusted cluster of classes defined as mutual subclasses of a the target type. As such, relaxing that trust lets you go back to that simpler, more general EDP. Further restricting that trust to a subset of the sibling subclasses of the superclass results in *Deputized Redirection*. If the exact same type of target object is required with no variability, then look to *Redirected Recursion* for how to work with object type similarity set to the same type. Retaining the subtyping relationship but coalescing the calling and target objects into one object gives rise to *Extend Method*. Simply breaking the method similarity moves us to *Trusted Delegation*.

Method Call Classification

Object: Similar   **Object Type:** Subtype   **Method:** Similar

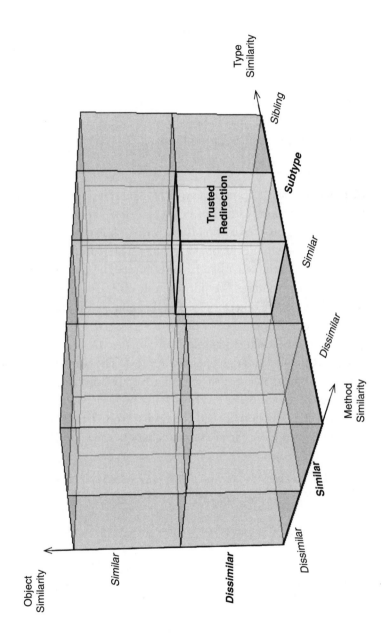

Deputized Delegation   **Object Behavioral**

Intent

When we need the trusted delegation behavior of *Trusted Delegation* but find it too generalized, it is necessary to preselect a subtree of the class hierarchy for a restricted polymorphism.

Motivation

Static typing is a way to preselect types from a well-defined pool and form more concrete notions of an object's type *before* the invocation of a system at runtime. This preselection is a way of adding type safety—we know precisely what capabilities an object will have when used during execution. Polymorphism, on the other hand, is a technique for abstracting out typing information *until* runtime. We purposefully obfuscate many details of the underlying type of the object, providing flexibility at the cost of type safety. Sometimes we need a balance of the two.

Consider the driving example from *Trusted Delegation*. A common data-input control is missing, one to enter text. The way things are set up, a `TextInput` class that subclassed from `InputControl` would be able to alter the value of a `BarGraph` showing numeric values, and this may not be what the designer wants.[7] The design from *Trusted Delegation* can be fine-tuned by adding the classes and changes shown in Listing 5.31.

Listing 5.31 UI widgets demonstrating *Deputized Delegation* in C++.

```
 1  class UIWidget {
    public:
 3      virtual void updateValue( int newValue );
    };
 5
    class InputControl : UIWidget{
 7      UIWidget*   target;
    public:
 9      void userHasSetNewValue(int myNewValue)   {
            target->updateValue(myNewValue);
11      }
```

---

7. A good argument can be made that having a text input widget control a numeric display *does* make rational design sense, assuming a numeric input control that was restricted to numerics only, but there are UI toolkits that went the other way.

```
     };
13
     class SliderBar : InputControl {
15   public:
         // Moves the slider bar accordingly
17       void updateValue( int newValue );
         void acceptUserClick() {
19           // Determine new value, set it
             int newVal;
21           // Update the slider bar graphic
             this->userHasSetNewValue(newVal);
23       };
     };
25
     class RotaryKnob : InputControl {
27   public:
         // Rotates the knob image accordingly
29       void updateValue( int newValue );
         void acceptUserClick() {
31           // Determine new value, set it
             int newVal;
33           // Update the knob image
             this->userHasSetNewValue(newVal);
35       };
     };
37
     class GraphicsContext {
39   public:
         virtual void render(int);
41   };

43   class DisplayWidget : public UIWidget {
     protected:
45       // Each subclass should set the
         // GraphicsContext to something
47       // meaningful for its needs
         GraphicsContext*     gc;
49   public:
         void updateValue( int newValue ) {
51           gc->render( newValue );
         };
53   };

55   class TextWidget : public DisplayWidget {};

57   class BarGraph : public DisplayWidget {};

59   // New class to support Deputized Delegation
     class TextInputControl : public InputControl {
61       TextWidget* textTarget;
     public:
63       void userHasSetNewValue(int myNewValue) {
             textTarget->updateValue(myNewValue);
65           // ^---- Deputized Delegation
         };
67   };
```

Now the `TextInputControl` is available for altering instances of
the `TextField` class, but it will not be able to alter instances of `Bar-Graph` or other nontext display items. `SliderBar` and `RotaryKnob`
could similarly be limited to a class hierarchy based on a `NumericWid-get`, for example. This may be easier to see in Figure 5.5.

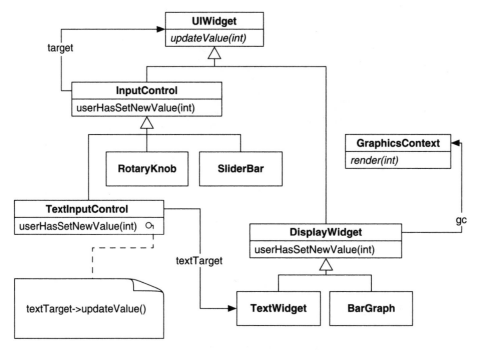

Figure 5.5 UI class cluster showing an instance of *Deputized Delegation*.

Applicability

Use *Deputized Delegation* when:

- *Trusted Delegation* is the appropriate general pattern.

- Greater control over the possible types of objects is required.

- The types to be delegated to do not include the calling object's type.

Participants

FamilyHead

The base class for a polymorphic class cluster, which establishes the basic generalized interface and semantics.

Delegator

A subclass of `FamilyHead` that requires a subtask to be delegated to a trusted delegate.

DelegateSibling

Another subclass of `FamilyHead` that has the appropriate semantics for the subtask.

target
An instance of `DelegateSibling` that is contained by `Delega-tor` and will be asked to perform the subtask.

operation
The calling method sending the request for the subtask to be performed.

operation2
The called method being asked to perform the subtask.

Structure

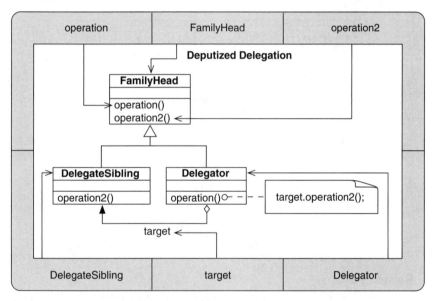

Collaborations

In addition to the collaborations involved in *Trusted Delegation*, this pattern adds the `DelegateSibling` class as the target for the `operation` implementation. By doing so, it limits the possible behavior to a subclass of the common ancestor class and therefore to select refined semantics.

Consequences

This pattern differs from its cousin, *Trusted Delegation*, in that a design decision is made to limit the polymorphism statically to a subtree of the original class family. It can provide large benefits in containing complexity, but it can also lead to issues later if, for example, the chosen sibling class is determined to be *too* limiting. Although the syntactic change to the code is minimal, the addition of a broader set of possible classes and behaviors can have far-reaching effects that should be carefully considered. Also note that unlike *Trusted Delegation*, the `target` cannot be a member of the shared superclass, because the superclass would have to have prior knowledge of one of its subclasses. Although some languages can pull off this particular bit of trickery, it's not a robust design decision and should be avoided whenever possible.

Implementation

In C++:

```
1 class FamilyHead {
  protected:
3     void operation();
      void operation2();
5 };

7 class DelegateSibling : public FamilyHead {
      void operation2();
9 };

11 class Delegator : public FamilyHead {
      DelegateSibling*    target;
13    void operation() {
          // Optional work prior
15        target->operation2();
          // ^--- Deputized Delegation
17        // Optional work after
      };
19 };
```

Related Patterns

Deputized Delegation is rather specialized and can only lead to a couple of more general EDPs. If the criteria of using a trusted class cluster is relaxed slightly such that the object type similarity is set to subtyping, we get back to *Trusted Delegation*. If the method being invoked is changed to one that is similar to the caller, then we slide over to *Deputized Redirection*. This is one case where collapsing the calling and delegate objects into one doesn't make much sense, and we end up with ill-formed EDP design space positions.

Method Call Classification

    Object: Dissimilar   **Object Type:** Sibling   **Method:** Dissimilar

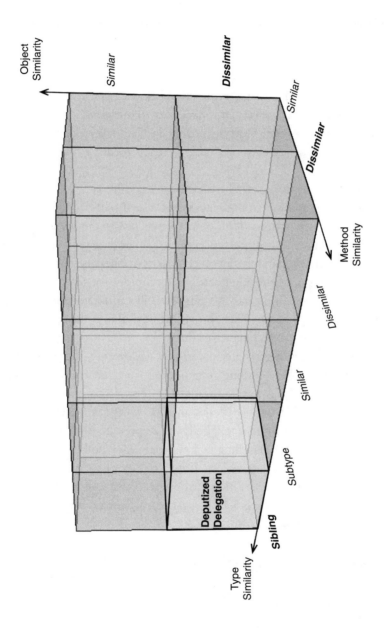

Deputized Redirection   **Object Behavioral**

Intent

When we need the trusted redirection behavior of *Trusted Redirection* but find it still too generalized, it is necessary to preselect a subtree of the class hierarchy for a restricted polymorphism. This selected subtree of classes will not include the class originating the redirection.

Motivation

Static typing is a way to preselect types from a well-defined pool and form more concrete notions of an object's type *before* the invocation of a system at runtime. This preselection is a way of adding type safety—we know precisely what capabilities an object will have when used during execution. Polymorphism, on the other hand, is a technique for abstracting out typing information *until* runtime. We purposefully obfuscate many details of the underlying type of the object, providing flexibility at the cost of type safety. Sometimes we need a balance of the two.

In the driving example for *Trusted Redirection*, the code provided a very general event-handling system. Such an open-ended type hierarchy, however, is not appropriate for all cases. For instance, a slider bar is only going to respond to mouse events, and not, except in special circumstances, to keystrokes. Likewise, a text field will respond to both mouse events and keystrokes, but the handling of keystrokes may be best taken care of by an underlying text data object. Entire classes of events can therefore be eliminated from consideration at runtime by a simple refinement. Starting with the code in Listing 5.30 from *Trusted Redirection*, we can alter it to look like the code in Listing 5.32.

Listing 5.32 UI widgets demonstrating *Deputized Redirection* in C++.

```
1  #include <vector>
   using std::vector;
3
   class Position {};
5  class Key {};
   class Event {
7  public:
```

```
            virtual int getID();
 9  };

11  class MouseEvent : public Event {
        vector<bool>     modifierKeys;
13      Position         position;
        bool             mouseDown;
15  };

17  class KeyEvent : public Event {
        vector<bool>     modifierKeys;
19      Key          key;
        bool             keyDown;
21  };

23  class EventHandler {
    public:
25      virtual void handle(Event* e) {
            // do what is needed
27      };
    };
29
    class TextData : public EventHandler {
31  public:
        // Text storage class
33      virtual void handle(KeyEvent* e) {
            // do what is needed
35      };
    };
37
    class UIWidget : public EventHandler {
39  protected:
        EventHandler*    nextHandler;
41  public:
        bool isActive();
43      virtual void handle(Event* e) {
            // Possible setup...
45          if ( !(this->isActive()) ) {
                nextHandler->handle(e);
47          } else {
                // Handle it myself
49          }
        };
51  };

53  class Button : public UIWidget {
        // Base class for any clickable button
55  };

57  class TabPane : public UIWidget {
        UIWidget*    contents;
59  public:
        TabPane() {
61          // Setup contents
            nextHandler = contents;
63      };
    };
65
    class TextField : public UIWidget {
67      TextData*    text;
    public:
69      TextField() {
            // Setup text
71          nextHandler = text;
        };
73      virtual void handle(Event* e) {
```

```
         // Is e a KeyEvent or subclass?
75       if (dynamic_cast<KeyEvent*>(e)) {
             // Optional work before
77           text->handle(dynamic_cast<KeyEvent*>(e));
             // ^--- Deputized Redirection
79           // Optional work after
         } else { .
81           // Handle MouseEvents
         }
83   };
   };
```

The new structure is shown in Figure 5.6. We added the `KeyEvent`
class, and `TextField` now overrides `handle()`. It handles instances
of `MouseEvent` on its own, but previously it simply set the `next-`
`Handler` to the `TextData` instance `text`. There was the chance that
a `MouseEvent` could slip through via a bug and trip up `TextData`'s
implementation of `handle()`, but this way the only events handed to
`TextData` are those of `KeyEvent`. `TextField` and `TextData` have a
higher level of trust than do `TextField` and other subclasses of `Event-`
`Handler`.

Now, `TextField` ensures that it handles the `MouseEvents` while
the underlying `TextData` only handles raw text interactions. `TextData`
is trusted to handle the `KeyEvent` events, because `TextField` knows
more precisely what to expect `TextData` will do with them. In addition,
`TextField` is specifically *not* including itself as the type of the possible
recipient, as is the case in *Trusted Redirection*. `TextField` is insisting that
someone else it is related to take care of that portion of the job.

Applicability

Use *Deputized Redirection* when:

- *Trusted Redirection* is the appropriate general pattern.

- Greater control over the possible types of objects is required.

- The types to be redirected to do not include the calling object's type.

Participants

FamilyHead
Defines interface, contains a method possibly to be overridden, and
is the base class for both `Redirector` and `RedirectSibling`.

Redirector
Uses interface of `FamilyHead`; redirects internal behavior back to

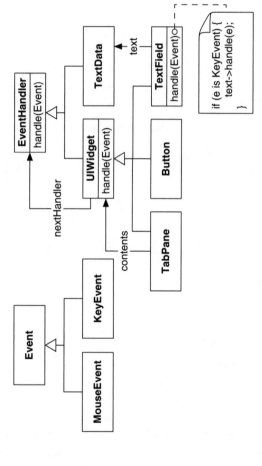

Figure 5.6 UI class cluster showing an instance of *Deputized Redirection.*

an instance of `RedirectSibling` to gain polymorphic behavior over an amorphous *but limited-in-scope* object structure.

RedirectSibling

The head of a new class tree for polymorphic behavior.

target

A polymorphic instance of `RedirectSibling` that is contained by `Redirector`.

operation

The calling site.

Structure

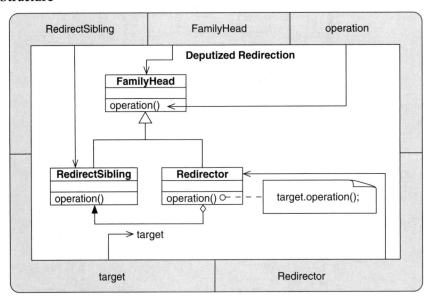

Collaborations

As with *Trusted Redirection*, `Redirector` and `FamilyHead` are tied by interface and intent. The `RedirectSibling` provides a conceptual starting point for a particular type of implementation. In this case, `Redirector` specifically reduces the set of possible classes that can be polymorphic targets of the request to either classes or subclasses of `Redirect-Sibling`. The fact that `Redirector` and `RedirectSibling` have a common base class in `FamilyHead` means that each may make stronger assumptions about the other.

Consequences

This pattern differs from its cousin *Trusted Redirection* in that a design decision has been made to limit the polymorphism statically to a subtree of the original class family. It can provide large benefits in containing complexity, but it can also lead to issues later if, for example, the chosen sibling class is determined to be *too* limiting. Although the syntactic change to the code is minimal, the addition of a broader set of possible classes and behaviors can have far-reaching effects that should be carefully considered.

Implementation

In C++:

```
    class FamilyHead {
 2  protected:
        virtual void operation();
 4  };

 6  class RedirectSibling : public FamilyHead {
        void operation();
 8  }

10  class Redirector : public FamilyHead {
    public:
12      RedirectSibling*    target;
        void operation() {
14          // Optional work prior
            target->operation();
16          // ^--- Deputized Redirection
            // Optional work after
18      };
    };
```

Related Patterns

Because *Deputized Redirection* is a specialization of *Trusted Redirection*, we can return to that EDP if we relax the trust a bit by changing the type similarity from a sibling relationship back to the more general subtyping relationship. Or, we can change the method similarity to call a dissimilar method and arrive at *Deputized Delegation*. Finally, it should be noted that attempting to change the object similarity to be similar makes no sense in this case, and we arrive at one of our undefined coordinates in the EDP design space.

Method Call Classification

Object: Dissimilar   **Object Type:** Sibling   **Method:** Similar

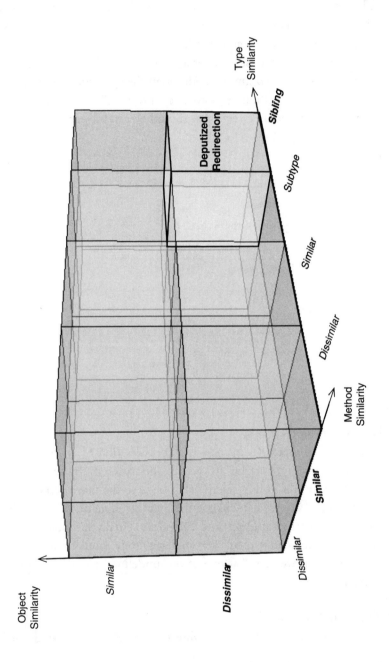

Intermediate Pattern Compositions

T his chapter establishes the first level of patterns composed directly from EDPs. We saw this process in Chapter 4, and here we flesh out several common, simple, but not-yet-elemental design patterns. As before, the Pattern Instance Notation (PIN) from Chapter 3 is used to illustrate the component portions that form these patterns. With the EDPs, the PIN notation was used to show the internal relationships using UML. From here on out, both UML and PINboxes appear in the PIN diagrams. A PINbox-only version is also included to illustrate the purely conceptual connections.

These patterns are extremely common, and developers keep coming back to them because they are both effective and because they also combine a small number of simple concepts in novel ways. The intermediate patterns are not EDPs because they are decomposable and can be discussed as the composition of more fundamental concepts. Frequently, however, the intersection of the underlying concepts is not made explicit in discussions of these patterns. It is left up to the student or developer to have that eureka moment of comprehension into the deeper semantics of the pattern. This assumes that the reader of the pattern has sufficient practice with the underlying concepts to recognize them when they occur.

Using the EDPs as a basis, we can make the composition and connection points of the concepts that form each pattern much more explicit. This chapter shows you how small concepts can quickly build into more complex abstractions and demonstrates how to analyze already published patterns for new insights. Studying the inner workings of these intermediate patterns will give you a strong foundation for understanding how EDPs and other patterns can be used in conjunction to form larger and richer design patterns.

The pattern specifications in this chapter do not contain the method-call Classification section, as that was specific to the method-call EDPS.

Fulfill Method   **Object Structural**

Intent

To provide an implementation for a previously abstracted method, thereby fulfilling the contract made by *Abstract Interface* that a later subclass would provide such an implementation.

Motivation

Abstract Interface promises that some subclass will provide a proper method implementation to a method interface declared in a class intended to be a superclass. *Inheritance* lets us define that subclass, and *Fulfill Method* describes how to go about fulfilling that prior promise by combining the two pattern instances.

This approach lets us cleanly separate the abstraction of the method in the superclass from any number of possible subclasses that may (or may not) provide an implementation for it.

Applicability

Use *Fulfill Method* when:

- Implementation of a method has been deferred using *Abstract Interface*.

- A subclass of the class specified in *Abstract Interface* is able to handle the functionality of the method as promised.

Participants

Abstractor
The class type that declares an interface for `operation`.

Fulfiller
The class type that defines a method body for `operation`; inherits from `Abstractor`.

operation
The method that was declared in `Abstractor` and defined in `Fulfiller`.

Structure

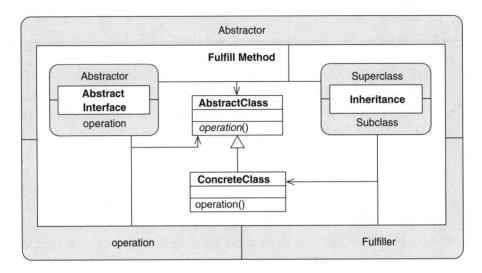

PINbox-only version (also used in Figure 4.4):

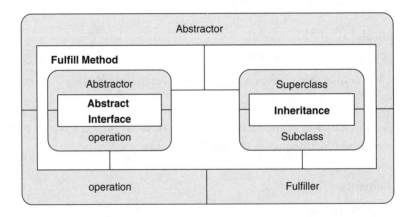

Collaborations

Abstractor defines an interface for a method, and Fulfiller provides the implementation. Fulfiller subclasses from Abstractor to gain the appropriate typing and interface.

Abstractor is the primary class in the instance of *Abstract Interface*, and Abstractor and Fulfiller are related through an instance of *Inheritance*.

Consequences

Fulfiller relies on Abstractor for the interface to the implemented method. These two must be kept in sync, and there are times when a shuffling interface at the top of a class hierarchy can have far-reaching effects on its subclasses. In cases where this is expected, a solution utilizing *Delegation* may be preferred. A solution using *Delegation* allows the external interface to be independent of the implementation object. Alternatively, if only one class/object is mandated, *Conglomeration* can be used to hand off the task to private methods internal to the type, thereby preserving the interface/implementation encapsulation.

Implementation

Every language that supports inheritance and abstract methods, regardless of expression, supports *Fulfill Method*. Following are some examples based on the examples from *Abstract Interface*.

In C++:

```cpp
1  class Abstractor {
   public:
3      virtual void operation() = 0;
   };
5
   class Fulfiller :
7      public Abstractor {
   public:
9      void operation() {
           // Perform the appropriate work
11     };
   };
```

In Java, the method is included in an *interface* or is in an *abstract class*:

```java
   public interface Abstractor {
2      public void operation();
   };
4
   public abstract class AnotherAbstractor {
6      public abstract void operation2();
       public void operation3();
8  };

10 public class Fulfiller
       extends AnotherAbstractor
12     implements Abstractor {
       public void operation() {
14         // Perform the appropriate work
       }
16     public void operation2() {
```

```
                // Perform the appropriate work
18      }
    };
```

In Python 3.x:

```
1  class Abstractor(metaclass=ABCMeta):
       @abstractmethod
3      def operation(self, ...):
           // Default implementation allowed
5          return

7  class Fulfiller(Abstractor):
       def operation(self, ...):
9          // Perform the appropriate work
           pass
```

Related Patterns

Fulfill Method is composed of two of the core EDPs: *Abstract Interface* and *Inheritance*. Because *Fulfill Method* fulfills the promise made by *Abstract Interface*, it is found in almost every case where *Abstract Interface* is. In those cases where *Fulfill Method* doesn't accompany *Abstract Interface*, the resulting abstract class isn't usable in code until a subclass completes the promise. Multiple *Fulfill Method* instances can be found later in this chapter under *Objectifier*. *Fulfill Method* can also be found as a necessary component of most of the Gang of Four patterns, including *Proxy, Command, Iterator, Observer, State, Decorator, Prototype, Template Method*, and many others [21].

Retrieve New   **Object Management**

Intent

Used when a new instance is needed and the creation of that instance is a complex or expensive procedure that needs to be encapsulated in another object. The returned object is guaranteed not to have any other references to it.

Motivation

Often, a newly created object needs to be a pristine object with well-defined ownership. Creating such an object locally is always an option, but it can be a suboptimal decision if, for instance, the object to be created is determined by a rather complex behavior. An example would be deciding which object to create on the basis of which reply is given in response to a database query. Any object creation process that is wrapped in complex logic or transactions that may take significant time isn't code that lends itself to copy and paste reuse. We want to both centralize such logic and encapsulate it into its own method.

This encapsulation of logic leads to other issues, of course. If the created object can be referenced by a number of sources and the memory model is an unmanaged one such as in C++, then any piece of code with such a reference to the object can request its destruction, leaving the remainder of the references pointing to an invalid object. Alternatively, none of the referring objects may request its destruction, leading to a memory leak because the object becomes unreachable while still resident. Garbage collection can help with this issue, but well-defined memory management starts with small decisions.

One such decision is to make sure that only the recipient of a *Retrieve* has access to the object being retrieved, thereby establishing a clear and precise ownership. This can be done almost transparently by returning a copy of an object, because the copy will create a fresh instance. Other schemes involving passing back a method-local reference that is destroyed on method exit can be used, but they are more error prone during later maintenance unless there is a strong sense for, and enforcement of, the ownership issues involved. In all cases, this requires an instance of *Create Object* to be applied as well.

Applicability

Use *Retrieve New* when:

- A remote object provides an object that is required for local computation and is provided by an exposed field object or return value from an exposed method.

- The object returned needs to be a fresh copy without other references to it.

Structure

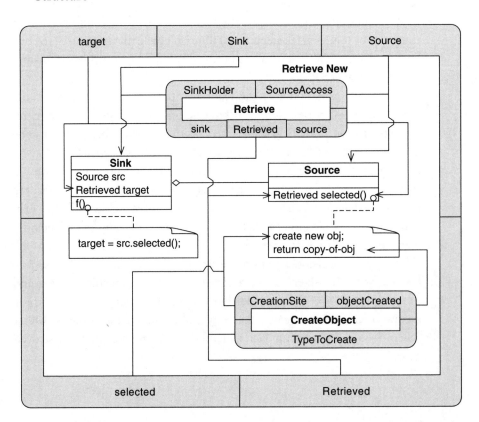

PINbox-only version (identical to *Retrieve Shared*):

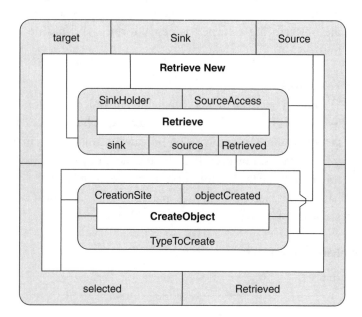

Participants

Source

The type of the object tasked with handing off the retrieved object. It serves as the initial source, creating the object.

Sink

The object (or class) type that requests the retrieved object and includes the item, `target`, to be given a new value.

Retrieved

The type of the value to be updated and the value that is returned.

target

The field that is updated to the retrieved object for local use.

selected

The method or field that produces and returns the new value. In this scenario, the returned object is guaranteed to not have any other references to it.

Collaborations

There are only three objects in this collaboration, and they simply play the parts of the request originator, the request fulfiller, and the passed object.

The critical portions of *Retrieve New* occur within the implementation of the retrieval method `selected`. This method is tasked with ensuring that the object being returned is newly formed and has no other references to it.

Consequences

Separation between object ownership and object creation has some advantages. For example, the type of the created object can be determined in a flexible manner, possibly using polymorphism, such as in an *Abstract Factory*. It means, however, that the recipient object is solely responsible for the lifetime of the created object. If references to the created object are handed out, a good reference management policy must be in place unless garbage collection is allowed.

Implementation

In C++:

```
   class Retrieved {};
 2
   class Source {
 4 public:
       Retrieved giveMeAValue() {
 6         Retrieved ret;
           return ret;
 8     };
   };
10
   class Sink {
12     Retrieved target;
       Source srcobj;
14 public:
       void operation() {
16         target = srcobj.giveMeAValue();
       ;}
18 };
```

In Python:

```
 1 class Source:
       def giveMeAValue(self):
 3         ret = Retrieved()
           return ret
 5
   class Sink:
 7     def __init__(self):
           srcobj = Source()
 9         return self
```

```
11    def operation(self):
          target = srcobj.giveMeAValue()
```

Related Patterns

Retrieved New is closely related to *Retrieve Shared*, and if you look at the the PINbox-only diagrams, they are equivalent. The distinctive portion is a behavior-level aspect because of how the requested object is returned to the caller, either with clean ownership characteristics, as here, or with possible references being retained, as in *Retrieve Shared*.

Many of the creational patterns from the original *Design Patterns* [21] use *Retrieve New* in some manner. *Prototype* uses *Retrieve New* explicitly to ensure that fresh copies of an object are always returned, and *Builder* provides an excellent example of *Retrieve New*'s ability to encapsulate complex creation logic. *Abstract Factory* and *Factory Method* also end up using *Retrieve New* in many cases.

Retrieve Shared   **Object Management**

Intent

To obtain a reference to a shared object without holding explicit ownership of that object. Ubiquitous in object-oriented programming.

Motivation

Objects are conceptual entities, and any particular instance may encapsulate state or provide functionality that may be of interest to many other objects simultaneously. Consider a printer queue, for example. Many applications want to have access to the queue, but there is no reason for each application to have its own queue. In fact, this would certainly lead to eventual resource collisions as differing queues competed. Instead, a queue can be shared among many applications simultaneously. Requests from disparate objects can be handled in the order best suited by the queue. The queue is a shared resource, and must be available for whoever needs it.

Retrieve Shared uses both *Create Object* and *Retrieve*, as does *Retrieve New*, but differs in that it is free to cache or otherwise hand off references to the newly created object for other purposes. Not only is there no guarantee that the newly created object has no other references, it is explicitly assumed that it does have other references to it. Ownership is ill-defined among those entities holding references.

Retrieve Shared is so common that many languages support it directly on some level. C++, for example, has the `shared_ptr` construct, which is included in Section 20.7.2.2 of the recently adopted 2011 C++ standard [18].

Other languages and environments have idioms and assumed library support for quasi-manual management of referenced objects, such as Objective-C's `autorelease` feature. Many others use garbage collection to automatically detect and remove "dead" objects from the system during runtime. Java, C#, Python, and most scripting languages are examples of this last case. Automated memory management is becoming more popular and common among programming languages, but it is still far from universal. All developers should have the basics of manual memory management under their belt.

Applicability

Use *Retrieve Shared* when:

- A remote object provides a value object that is required for local computation and is either:

  – provided by a method call's return value or

  – provided by an exposed field object.

- The object should be shared with other objects and not considered a private resource.

Structure

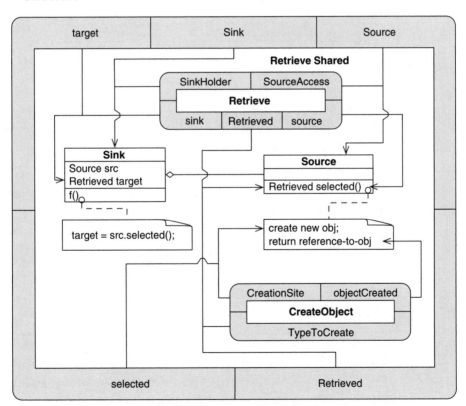

PINbox only version (identical to *Retrieve New*):

```
┌─────────────────────────────────────────────────────┐
│  target          │      Sink        │      Source    │
│  ┌──────────────────────────────────────────────┐    │
│  │              Retrieve Shared                  │    │
│  │  ┌────────────────────────────────────────┐   │    │
│  │  │ SinkHolder      │   SourceAccess        │   │    │
│  │  │  ┌──────────────────────────────────┐  │   │    │
│  │  │  │          Retrieve                │  │   │    │
│  │  │  └──────────────────────────────────┘  │   │    │
│  │  │   sink    │    source    │  Retrieved  │   │    │
│  │  └────────────────────────────────────────┘   │    │
│  │  ┌────────────────────────────────────────┐   │    │
│  │  │ CreationSite     │   objectCreated      │   │    │
│  │  │  ┌──────────────────────────────────┐  │   │    │
│  │  │  │       CreateObject               │  │   │    │
│  │  │  └──────────────────────────────────┘  │   │    │
│  │  │          TypeToCreate                  │   │    │
│  │  └────────────────────────────────────────┘   │    │
│  └──────────────────────────────────────────────┘    │
│      selected              │      Retrieved           │
└─────────────────────────────────────────────────────┘
```

Participants

Source
The object tasked with handing off the retrieved object. It serves as the initial source, creating the object.

Sink
The object (or class) type that requests the retrieved object and includes the item, `target`, to be given a new value.

Retrieved
The type of the value to be updated and the value that is returned.

target
The field that is updated to the retrieved object for local use.

selected
The method or field that produces and returns the new value. In this scenario, the returned object is a reference to an object, and the reference is not guaranteed to be associated with ownership in any way.

Collaborations

This collaboration has only three objects and they merely play the parts of the request originator, the request fulfiller, and the passed object. Compare and contrast this pattern with *Retrieve New*. The differences between the elements of the patterns are extremely minor, but the effects can ripple outwards quickly.

Consequences

In a garbage-collected language or environment, the retrieved object gains a reference count by using this pattern but does not restrict the generation of new references. Generating new references can lead to memory leaks fairly readily, so be certain a well-defined ownership policy exists elsewhere. Consider *Retrieve New* instead if an object needs to be retrieved with assured uniqueness or wishes to be the primary owner of a newly allocated shared resource.

Implementation

In Java:

```
   class Retrieved {
 2 };

 4 class Source {
       public Retrieved giveMeAValue() {
 6         Retrieved ret = new Retrieved();
           // Do something with ret, such as
 8         // cache elsewhere
           return ret;
10     };
   };
12
   class Sink {
14     Retrieved target;
       Source srcobj;
16     public void operation() {
           target = srcobj.giveMeAValue();
18     };
   };
```

Related Patterns

Retrieve Shared and *Retrieve New* obviously share much of the same conceptual plumbing when looking at the structure diagrams. The distinguishing feature is the uniqueness of the ownership of the returned object.

    Singleton is perhaps the most common design pattern that utilizes *Retrieve Shared*.

Objectifier

This specification briefly recaps Walter Zimmer's *Objectifier* pattern and shows how it is a multiplicity of a single smaller pattern. The full definition and original discussion of this pattern can be found in [43]. Please refer to that text for the base document if necessary.

Intent

Objectifier is, according to the original specification, intended to "objectify similar behaviour in additional classes, so that clients can vary such behaviour independently from other behaviour" [43, p. 363]. Note the phrase "similar behaviour in additional classes." From this we might expect to see some form of *Redirection*, but the "in additional classes" qualification is a clue that we are probably dealing with a subclassing situation here. We know from *Fulfill Method* that we can implement an abstract method in a subclass as long as we have similar intent between the abstract and concrete methods. Multiple concrete subclasses may implement the behavior slightly differently, but the overall intent among the subclasses will remain similar.

Motivation

We find in Zimmer's original Motivation section that our analysis was correct. "A frequent problem in design is the separation of an abstraction from its implementation, and the interchange of implementations" [43, p. 363]. Zimmer is describing a single superclass with an *Abstract Interface*, and multiple subclasses that provide implementations. This tells us that we have multiple *Fulfill Method* instances but that they all share a common superclass in the Abstractor role. This can be shown graphically using a stacked PINbox, as we saw back in Chapter 3, Section 3.2.4.

Zimmer adds one critical piece to the above collection of subclass implementations. He specifies that "to objectify the varying behaviour, [...] have independent implementation objects that can be interchanged at runtime" [p. 363]. By this he means that the developer should create a reference to an object typed to be of the `Abstractor` class and then swap out actual instances of the subclass as needed. All calls made to that instance will now invisibly and automatically get sent to the correct implementation via polymorphism. How the call is made is not particularly relevant; the important thing is that some client object can do so.

Applicability

There is little to add to Zimmer's description of the applicability of *Objectifier*, so I quote it here in full:

Use the *Objectifier* pattern when

- Behaviour should be decoupled from classes to have independent behaviour objects which can be interchanged, saved, changed, shared or invoked.

- Run-time configuration of behaviour is required.

- There are several almost identical classes that differ only in one or a few methods. Objectifying the different behaviour in additional classes allows to unify the former classes in one common class, which can then be configured with a reference to the new, additional classes

- There is a large amount of conditional code to select behaviour [43, p. 363].

Two items stand out here in deciding when to use *Objectifier*. First, that run time configuration is required, and second, that there is a large amount of conditional code to select behavior.

Any time you run across a situation that looks something like Listing 6.1, it should make you pause to consider using *Objectifier*. If you find multiple such conditional structures using the same triggers, then it is a strong sign that you may be able to refactor the conditional blocks into classes with a common superclass to provide an interface. The conditional blocks are then replaced with a simple invocation of the requested method, as in Listing 6.2. This should look a bit familiar: it is related to the example provided back in the specification for *Abstract Interface* in Chapter 5.

Note that the external interface to `feedCritterInEnvirons()` did not change, but the code underneath is now much cleaner. Adding a new animal type just requires defining it as a subclass of `Animal` and making a change at *one* point in the code, where the animal kind is being selected in `feedCritterInEnvirons()`. Previously, adding a new animal type would have required adding conditional blocks to each place that it might be applicable, scattered throughout the code.

Listing 6.1 Conditionals to select behavior.

```
1
   typedef enum{FISH, HORSE, CHEETAH} CritterKind;
3  CritterKind critter;

5  void eatFood(CritterKind critter, FoodItem f) {
       if (critter == FISH) {
7          swimToFood(critter, locationOfFood(f));
           ingest(critter, f);
9          digest(critter, f);
       } else if (critter == HORSE) {
11         checkHerdSafety(critter);
           ingest(critter, f);
13         digest(critter, f);
       } else if (critter == CHEETAH) {
15         turboMode(critter, locationOfFood(f));
           if (caughtPrey(f)) {
17             ingest(critter, f);
               digest(critter, f);
19         }
       } else {
21         ingest(critter, f);
           digest(critter, f);
23     }
   };
25
   void ingest(CritterKind critter, FoodItem f) {
27     if (critter == FISH) {
           ...
29     } else if (critter == HORSE) {
           ...
31     } else if (critter == CHEETAH) {
           ...
33     } else {
           ...
35     }
   };
37
   typedef enum {OCEAN, PLAINS, SAVANNAH} Environment;
39
   void feedCritterInEnvirons(Environment env) {
41     if (Environment == OCEAN) {
           if (isHungry(FISH)) {
43             FoodItem f = findFood(FISH);
               if (f) {
45                 eatFood(FISH, f);
               }
47         }
       } else if (Environment == PLAINS) {
49         if (isHungry(HORSE)) {
               FoodItem f = findFood(HORSE);
51             if (f) {
                   eatFood(HORSE, f);
53             }
           }
55     } else if (Environment == SAVANNAH) {
           if (isHungry(CHEETAH)) {
57             FoodItem f = findFood(CHEETAH);
               if (f) {
59                 eatFood(CHEETAH, f);
               }
61         }
       }
63 };
```

Listing 6.2 Using *Objectifier* to select behavior.

```
 1  class Animal {
    public:
 3      void eatFood(FoodItem f) {
            this->ingest(f);
 5          this->digest(f);
        };
 7      void ingest(FoodItem f);
    };
 9
    class Fish : public Animal {
11  public:
        void eatFood(FoodItem f) {
13          this->swimToFood(locationOfFood(f));
            this->ingest(f);
15          this->digest(f);
        };
17      void ingest(FoodItem f);
    };
19
    class Horse : public Animal {
21  public:
        void eatFood(FoodItem f) {
23          checkHerdSafety(critter);
            ingest(critter, f);
25          digest(critter, f);
        };
27      void ingest(FoodItem f);
    };
29
    class Cheetah : public Animal {
31  public:
        void eatFood(FoodItem f) {
33          turboMode(critter, locationOfFood(f));
            if (caughtPrey(f)) {
35              ingest(critter, f);
                digest(critter, f);
37          }
        };
39  };

41  typedef enum {OCEAN, PLAINS, SAVANNAH} Environment;

43  void feedCritterInEnvirons(Environment env) {
        Animal* critter;
45      if (Environment == OCEAN) {
            critter = new Fish();
47      } else if (Environment == PLAINS) {
            critter = new Horse();
49      } else if (Environment == SAVANNAH) {
            critter = new Cheetah();
51      }
        if (isHungry(critter)) {
53          FoodItem f = findFood(critter);
            if (f) {
55              eatFood(critter, f);
            }
57      }
    };
```

Structure

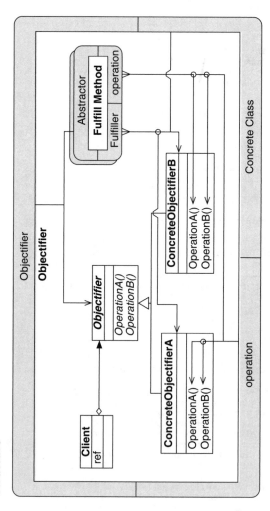

PINbox-only version:

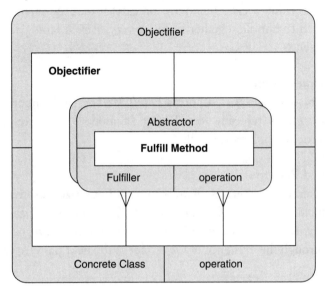

Participants

We can add the following to the participants that Zimmer provides:

operation

The method that is being abstracted out and requested by the client.

Concrete Class

One of the subclasses providing an implementation.

Collaborations

There is little to add to Zimmer's brief discussion, so I quote it here in its entirety.

- A client may use *Objectifier* to delegate parts of its behaviour. The *Objectifier* receives the information needed to fulfill its task during its initialization, or the client passes the information as a parameter when calling the *Objectifier*.

- A client can be configured with a concrete *Objectifier* to adapt the behaviour to fulfil a certain task [43, p. 364].

Consequences

Overall, this pattern is highly useful. It offers a great degree of flexibility and extensibility in most systems, while enhancing the comprehensibility and clarity of a body of code. It can, however, lead to confusion if the intent of behavior is not explicitly stated or is intertwined with unrelated behaviors within a class hierarchy. Be careful that the intents of methods you wish to bundle together in an *Objectifier* class family are compatible and clear.

Implementation

Any language that supports *Fulfill Method* can support *Objectifier*. This pattern is typically found in most modern software that uses a class structure polymorphically.

Related Patterns

Zimmer enumerates many Gang of Four patterns that use *Objectifier*, including *Bridge, Builder, Command, Iterator, Observer, State*, and *Strategy*. To these we can add *Chain of Responsibility, Composite*, and *Decorator*, through the existence of *Objectifier* in the next pattern, *Object Recursion*.

Object Recursion

This specification briefly recaps Bobby Woolf's *Object Recursion* and demonstrates that it is a simple intersection of two smaller patterns. The full definition and original discussion of this pattern can be found in Woolf's "The Object Recursion Pattern" [41]. Please refer to that text for the base document if necessary.

Intent

Booby Woolf states the intent as follows: "Distribute processing of a request over a structure by delegating polymorphically. Object Recursion transparently enables a request to be repeatedly broken into smaller parts that are easier to handle" [41, p. 41]. This says nothing about those smaller parts, however, and from our discussions of *Delegation* and *Redirection*, we know that the relationship between subtasks of a behavior can significantly affect how a system is implemented. After reading the entire specification, we can add that these "smaller parts" are closely related in intent and behavior.

Motivation

In the original specification, Woolf used a driving example for this pattern of comparing two objects by having them tell their respective members to compare themselves, recursively working down an object tree. This is a good use case and illustrates a necessary component of *Object Recursion*: that the task being performed at each level is the same kind of work. This is an example of redirection, so we expect to find some form of *Redirection* in any decomposition of *Object Recursion*.

The use of the word *polymorphism* in the Intent section indicates two things to us. First, it tells us that we're going to see at least one instance of *Fulfill Method* as well as the underlying *Inheritance* and *Abstract Method* EDPs. Second, it tells us that there almost certainly will be more than one such instance, that is, one for each potential subclass target. We therefore expect to see an instance of *Objectifier*.

At this point, we have a duo of well-defined and simple concepts that we can use to help us understand the *Object Recursion* pattern. We just need to see how they might be refined as we continue analyzing this pattern and how they come together to form this more complex behavior and concept.

Applicability

The Applicability section in Woolf's original specification states that *Object Recursion* is appropriate when:

- passing a message through a linked structure where the ultimate destination is unknown.

- broadcasting a message to all nodes in part of a linked structure.

- distributing a behavior's responsibility throughout a linked structure [41, p. 44].

It's interesting to note that if we were to limit the applicability to *only* these constraints, the problem would be solvable without using the solution that Woolf provided. Specifically, nothing in the applicability addresses the relative intents of the behavior that is distributed or the level of trust that the objects can place in each other to perform that behavior. The above constraints, as stated, could just as easily be handled by a chain of unrelated objects through uses of *Redirection*, or, with a bit of creative interpretation of the criteria, *Delegation*.

From the information in the Intent and Motivation sections, we can deduce some other key characteristics of *Object Recursion* and enhance this section. For instance, we know that polymorphism will figure prominently and that the "linked structure" described previously likely has some very specific requirements, primarily that the linked structure is composed of objects whose types are related to one another via a common ancestor, as evidenced by the polymorphism mentioned in the Intent section. This assumption is borne out by the later sections in the original specification.

This common ancestor clue leads us to expect to see the subtyping-relation form of our *Redirection*. In other words, we can specify that instead of a generalized *Redirection*, we will expect to see *Trusted Redirection*.

Using this information, we can refine the applicability as follows:

- A linked structure such as a tree exists, and the elements in the structure have a shared intent and purpose, each with common defined behaviors.

- A message needs to be sent through this linked structure to invoke one of the common behaviors; the intent of the message needs to remain essentially unaltered in intent during passage.

- The ultimate destination of the passed message is unknown within the linked structure.

- The message may need to be broadcast to all nodes in just a portion of the linked structure.

- Responsibility for fulfilling the behavior requested by the message is distributed throughout the linked structure.

Now it is clear that the linked structure does not contain random elements, but each node in the structure is related in nature and intent. It is also clearly stated that common behaviors can be invoked, that behavior can be distributed through objects in the structure, and/or that the behavior may or may not be applicable to the *entire* structure. All of these points are important for shaping what the solution will eventually look like.

Structure

We can use these deductions during an inspection of the original UML diagram provided by Woolf and annotate it with PINboxes, as shown. The *Objectifier* and *Trusted Redirection* instances do exist, as we surmised.

Participants

Woolf's original specification lists four participants: Initiator, Handler, Recursor, and Terminator. To these, we can add two more for the structure PIN diagrams and for clarity in the discussion: handleRequest and successor. The participants then can be listed as:

Initiator
– initiates the request.
– usually not a subtype of `Handler`; `makeRequest()` is a separate message from `handleRequest()`.

Handler
– defines a type that can handle requests that initiators make.

Recursor
– defines the `successor` link.
– handles a request by delegating it to its successors.

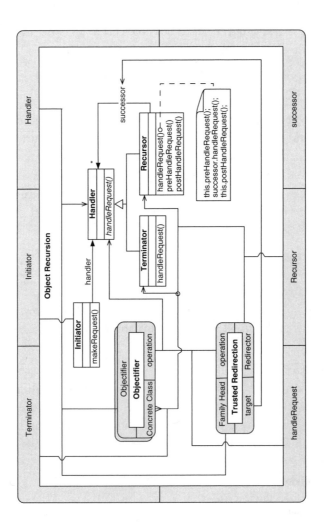

We can reduce this down to a much more readable PINbox-only version:

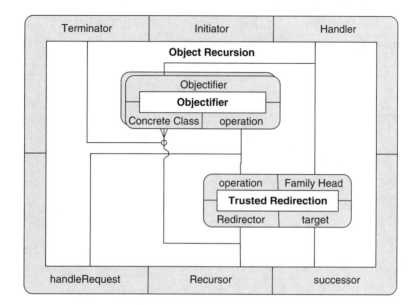

    – successors relevant to a request can vary by request.
    – can perform extra behavior before or after delegating the request.
    – may be a terminator for a different request.

Terminator
– finishes the request by implementing it completely and not delegating any of its
    implementation.
– may be a recursor for a different request [41, p. 44].

handleRequest
The method that handles the requested behavior at each stage and is
responsible for passing it along to a successor as necessary.

successor
The object that receives the `handleRequest` message from an
instance of `Recursor`; it is of type `Handler`.

Collaborations
Adding PINboxes to the original UML sequence diagram lets us see the
exact demarcation between the responsibilities of *Objectifier* and *Trusted
Redirection* in implementing the behavior of *Object Recursion*. Each is taking half of the sequence diagram, and they meet in the `aRecursor` object.

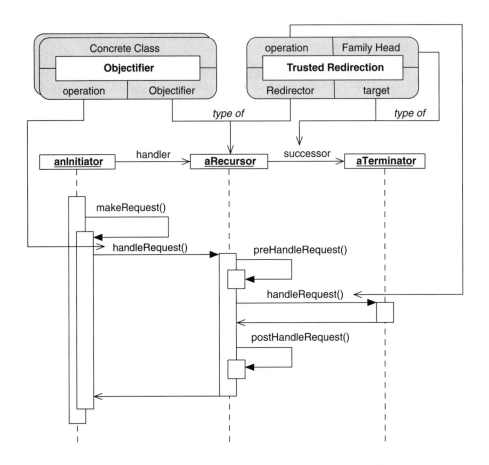

Consequences

The one disadvantage that Woolf lists under Consequences is: "Programming complexity. Recursion, procedural or object-oriented, is a difficult concept to grasp. Overuse can make a system more difficult to understand and maintain" [41, p. 46]. While true, the situation can be clarified by dividing the two essential elements of this style of recursion into the structure of the polymorphism via *Objectifier* and the recursive-style call into that polymorphic system via *Trusted Redirection*. Now the two aspects of this distributed recursion technique are explicitly shown, aiding comprehension.

Implementation

The original *Object Recursion* specification states in its Implementation section that "The Initiator.makeRequest() message must not be polymorphic with the Recursor.handleRequest() message" [41, p. 47]. The earlier discussion, where the *Objectifier* and *Trusted Redirection* instances are made explicit, shows this distinction clearly.

Related Patterns

Object Recursion is commonly used in design patterns with a family class cluster structure, including *Chain of Responsibility*, *Decorator*, *Composite*, and *Interpreter*. *Abstract Factory* can use *Object Recursion* to enable the building of multilayered objects, with each subcomponent requesting an appropriate callback through the factory interface as needed.

Gang of Four Pattern Compositions

At this point, you have seen the full method-call EDP catalog and several examples of patterns that are formed by combining them. In this chapter, we take that process to the next level, showing how the patterns in Chapters 2 and 6 can be combined to form a few of the Gang of Four (GoF) design patterns that developers are most familiar with.

Six GoF patterns are discussed in this chapter, two each from the Creational, Structural and Behavioral families as defined in *Design Patterns*. These additional patterns provide a foundation for working with other design patterns on this level. Why only six? Although every design pattern can be described in terms of EDPs, not all design patterns can be adequately described using only the EDPs presented *in this book*. Remember that this book only covers EDPs based on method calls, and method calls are only one of the four kinds of reliance relationships among entities of object-oriented programming. Refer back to Chapter 2, Table 2.3, in Section 2.2.2 for a refresh on the remainder. These six were selected because they are nicely related to others in the group in ways that are not obvious at first glance but become apparent once the underlying conceptual structure is revealed.

The discussions in this chapter do not follow the pattern specification template that the previous two chapters used. These design patterns are well documented in numerous sources, and there is no need to duplicate the structure here. Instead, the discussions outline each design pattern and the composition in a more casual way. PIN and UML diagrams, of course, are used to illustrate relevant relationships and connections.

7.1 Creational Patterns

The creational patterns are all concerned with object creation and management. As you might expect, *Create Object* features heavily in their definitions, as do the *Retrieve*-related patterns. How these two EDPs are connected to each other and to the other EDPs creates a wide array behaviors that distinguish the Creational patterns from each other. The two we decompose and compare are *Abstract Factory* and *Factory Method*. They provide an interesting reminder of how small differences in composition can lead to large changes in implementation and intent.

7.1.1 Abstract Factory

The first creational pattern, *Abstract Factory*, is a perfect example of how simple concepts can relate in complex ways to produce an interesting concept. Only three basic patterns are needed to capture most of the semantics of *Abstract Factory*: *Fulfill Method*, *Retrieve*, and *Create Object*. The manner in which they connect establishes the rich behavior.

The intent for *Abstract Factory* states that it "provides an interface for creating families of related or dependent objects without specifying their concrete classes" [21, p. 87]. From this statement, we can deduce that we are likely to see uses of *Inheritance* to produce that interface and of *Fulfill Method* to provide the implementation of the relevant methods.

Figure 7.1 shows the structure diagram for *Abstract Factory* wrapped within an expanded PINbox. Each role in the PINbox border is connected to just one interconnection of elements that lead to *Abstract Factory*: the `createProductA()` method as implemented in `ConcreteFactory2` is used to produce an instance of the `ProductA2` concrete class, which is subclassed from the `AbstractProductA` class. Similar connections exist for the other three product classes.

This is a rather complex diagram, and it is difficult to see exactly what the relationships at work are. The single interconnection is shown more clearly in Figure 7.2, in which we have removed the elements of the structure diagram that are

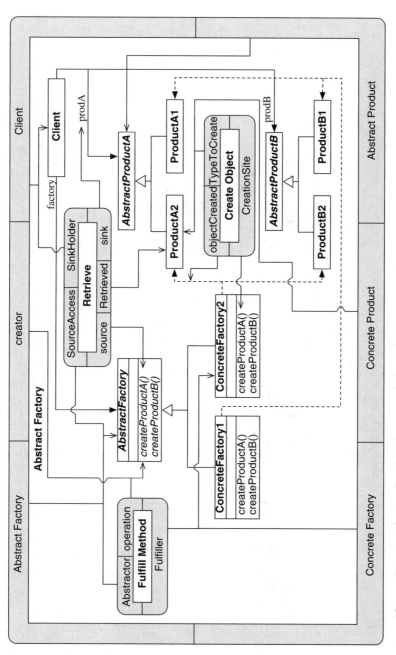

Figure 7.1 *Abstract Factory* subsumed within the expanded PINbox.

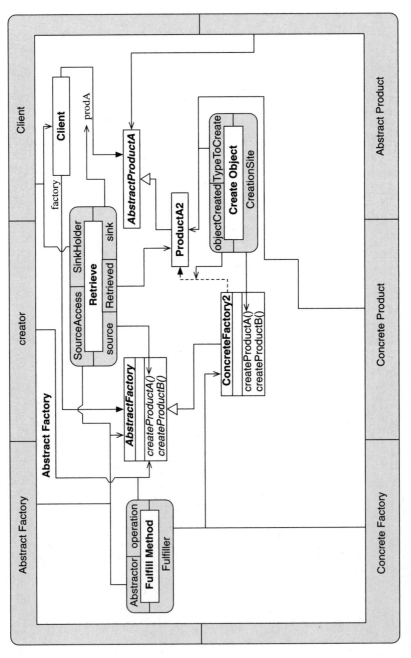

Figure 7.2 Reducing the diagram to just one instance of *Abstract Factory*.

not directly involved in this single *Abstract Factory* instance. Figure 7.3 simplifies it further by cleaning up the internals of the PINbox a bit, leading us finally to Figure 7.4, which illustrates the simple conceptual structure at the core of *Abstract Factory*.

At this point, we can see that a fairly simple connection is at work here. *Retrieve* is returning an instance from *Create Object* and is doing so *through* a call to an abstract method that is being implemented in a subclass via *Fulfill Method*. Although it may look like we could simply collapse the instances of *Retrieve* and *Create Object* into a *Retrieve New*, in some situations, *Abstract Factory* may use a pattern such as *Flyweight* for space-efficient backing of the objects it is returning, resulting in *Retrieve Shared* being implemented instead. Remember also that these two forms of *Retrieve* have identical PIN diagrams, so we can't distinguish between them on this basis alone. Because we can't determine this situation ahead of time but should leave up to the designer or implementor, we keep the two EDPs visible at this point for clarity and flexibility.

7.1.2 Factory Method

This pattern defers creation of an actual object to a subclass while providing a firm interface and a base method for creating the object and using it internally. To begin our analysis, we recognize that because this is a Creational pattern, we expect to see both *Create Object* and *Retrieve* in use. Reading off the items from *Factory Method*'s Participants section gives us the necessary cues to continue the decomposition. For instance, the description for Creator states that it "declares the factory method" [21, p. 108], whereas ConcreteCreator "override[s] the factory method." This is a clear example of a *Fulfill Method*. It is also indicated that Creator "may call the factory method." There's a bit of subtext here, but we can figure out what this means for our analysis with a bit of thought. If Creator is calling the factory method that it declares, it can only do so in one of two ways. Either the factory method is calling itself or the factory method is being called from another method. The former is an example of *Recursion* and is important enough that it almost certainly would be mentioned by name if it were part of the collaborations of *Factory Method*. This leads us to believe that the factory method is being called from another method, as an instance of *Conglomeration*. Inspecting the structure UML diagram for *Factory Method* (Figure 7.5) confirms that the intent is the latter case.

Factory Method weaves the EDPs *Create Object*, *Retrieve*, *Fulfill Method*, and *Conglomeration* together within one type hierarchy, as shown in Figure 7.5. This structure can be made clearer by reducing it to the PIN-only diagram in Figure 7.6.

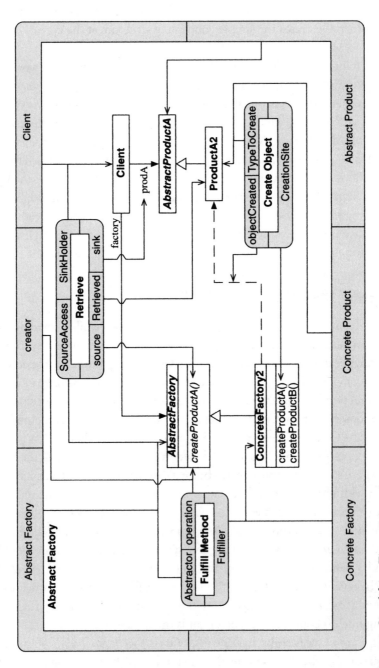

Figure 7.3 Simplifying Figure 7.2.

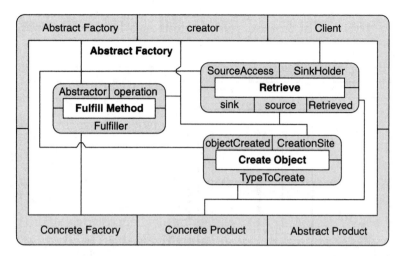

Figure 7.4 *Abstract Factory* as PIN only.

Factory Method is an interesting example in that it is a GoF pattern that explicitly uses another GoF pattern in its definition. In their discussion of *Factory Method*, GoF mentions that "Factory methods are usually called within Template methods" [21, p. 116]. Now we have a clear understanding of how they interact. Figure 7.19 at the end of this chapter and the accompanying discussion of *Template Method* explain how the instances of *Fulfill Method* and *Conglomeration* could be replaced with an equivalent *Template Method*. A *Factory Method* is an extension of a *Template Method* that adds the creation and retrieval of an object.

7.2 Structural Patterns

The two patterns selected from the Structural group are *Decorator* and *Proxy*. Despite their quite different intents and apparent structures, they share some surprising commonalities.

7.2.1 Decorator

Decorator was the driving pattern in Chapter 4, Section 4.2, and there you saw a detailed discussion of how to analyze this pattern. Now we can give it a proper context within its companion design patterns. Figure 7.7 encapsulates Figure 4.17 from Section 4.2 in a PINbox.

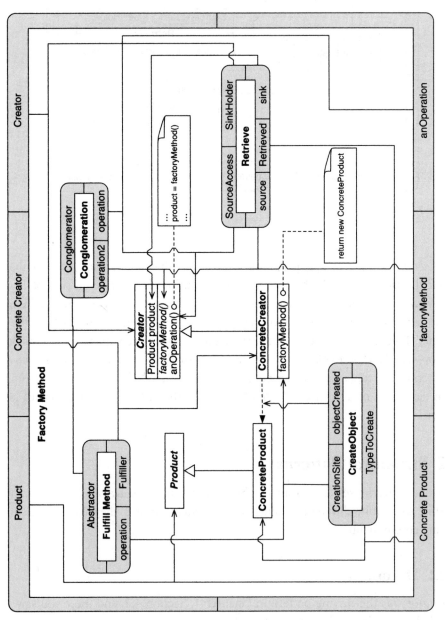

Figure 7.5 *Factory Method* subsumed within the expanded PINbox.

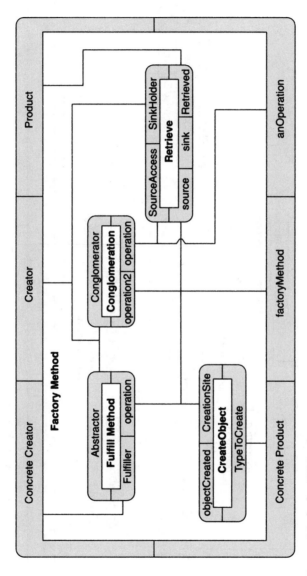

Figure 7.6 *Factory Method* as PIN only.

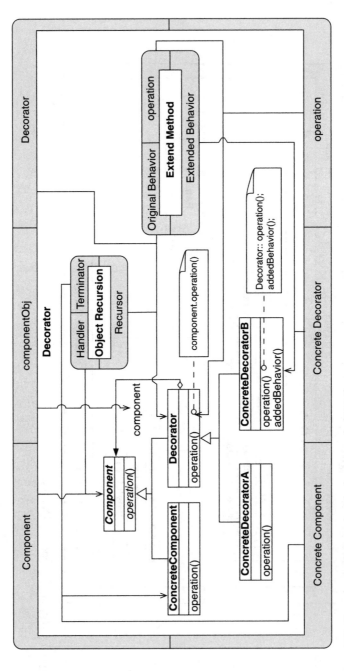

Figure 7.7 *Decorator* subsumed with the expanded PINbox.

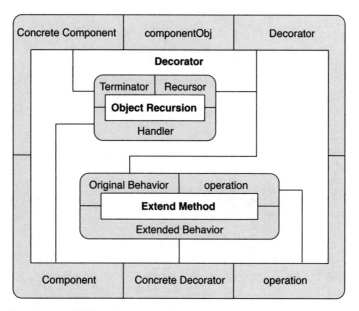

Figure 7.8 *Decorator* as PIN only.

By reducing Figure 7.7 to just the PIN diagram from Figure 4.18, similarly wrapped, we can produce a simple diagram, as in Figure 7.8. Now the underlying concepts are clearly stated, and their connections to each other are explicit.

This simple and straightforward figure shows us the internal composition of *Decorator* from *Object Recursion* and *Extend Method*. For the purposes of this discussion, however, it is useful to continue the deconstruction further. We can present the information from Figure 4.22 in a flattened form, as in Figure 7.9. We've now peeled off the *Object Recursion* and *Objectifier* PINboxes and directly exposed the *Fulfill Method* and *Trusted Redirection* instances.

7.2.2 Proxy

Proxy limits access to an object or object structure, hiding details from the clients. It is a simple enough pattern that we can perform our analysis by simply looking at the structure diagram, as shown in Figure 7.10. We can easily see that there is an instance of *Fulfill Method*, and the call from `Proxy::request()` to the same method in `RealSubject` is an instance of *Deputized Redirection*.

The use of *Deputized Redirection* is the important characteristic of this pattern. It indicates that the objects to which we are redirecting a task are of highly trusted types. We can reduce this diagram to just the PIN for clarity, in Figure 7.11, and then reorganize the diagram a bit, as in Figure 7.12.

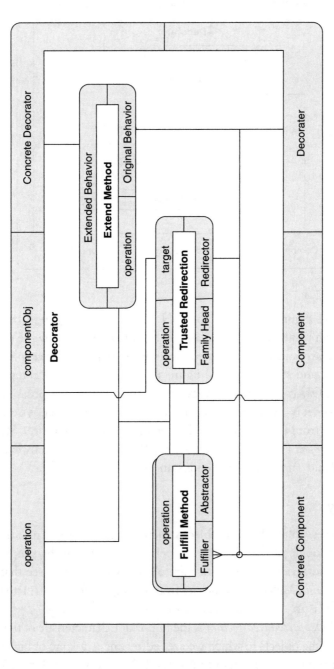

Figure 7.9 *Decorator* expanded three levels deep and flattened.

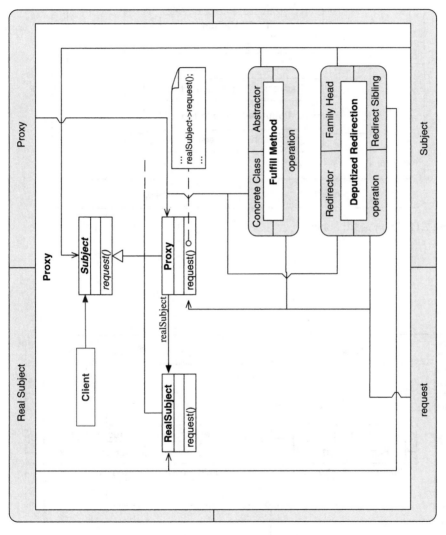

Figure 7.10 *Proxy* subsumed with the expanded PINbox.

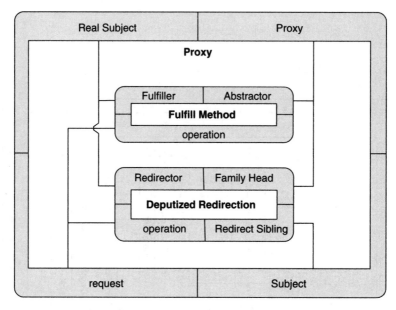

Figure 7.11 *Proxy* as PIN only.

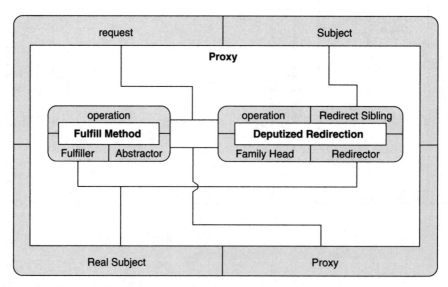

Figure 7.12 *Proxy* PIN reorganized to better match *Decorator*.

The reason for the shuffling is that now the definition for *Proxy* more closely matches the section of *Decorator* that we expanded out of *Object Recursion* in Figure 7.9. If we look at those two closely, we can see that *Proxy* is essentially a highly trusted variant of *Object Recursion*, with one significant difference. When the instance of the recipient object is placed within one of the subclasses, the deeply recursive nature of *Object Recursion* is disrupted. Instead, we have a single linkage, a one-time redirection from the proxy to the final object. Additionally, we can see that *Proxy* lacks the instance of *Extend Method* that *Decorator* has. This indicates that while *Decorator* has the addition of behavior as a prime consideration, *Proxy* does not. These two points are verified by GoF: "Unlike Decorator, the Proxy pattern is not concerned with attaching or detaching properties dynamically, and it's not designed for recursive composition" [21, p. 200]. These differences are now clearly shown in the PIN diagrams and compositions of these two patterns.

7.3 Behavioral Patterns

The Behavioral patterns from GoF provide an interesting challenge given that the only one of the four kinds of basic reliances fleshed out in this text is the method-call reliance, and we're relying solely on the method call EDPs. The design space defined by our three axes, as in Section 2.2.2, however, provides enough contextual information that many of these patterns can be given surprisingly robust definitions. In particular, *Chain of Responsibility* and *Template Method* are worth investigating.

7.3.1 Chain of Responsibility

Chain of Responsibility is a pattern that has much in common with *Proxy* and *Decorator*. We start as usual by showing the structure diagram wrapped in a PINbox, as in Figure 7.13. The overall construct is fairly straightforward, being composed of only two EDPs. There are multiple instances of *Extend Method*, but this diagram is simple enough that we can forego the intermediate step and jump directly to the PIN-only diagram, as in Figure 7.14.

In fact, if you inspect the EDP-derived definition of *Chain of Responsibility* against *Decorator*, it becomes apparent that the salient difference is that the *Redirected Recursion* of *Chain of Responsibility* replaces the *Object Recursion* of *Decorator*. If one of the variants on *Chain of Responsibility* is used such that the ConcreteHandlers define the successor explicitly [21, p. 225], then *Object Recursion* will be found here as well. The only difference, then, is where in the pattern *Object Recursion* occurs. It is an interesting exercise in extremely small

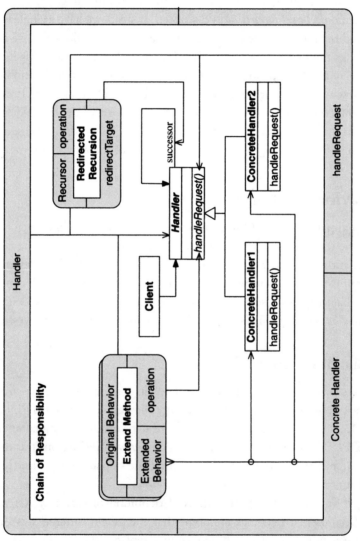

Figure 7.13 *Chain of Responsibility* subsumed within the expanded PINbox.

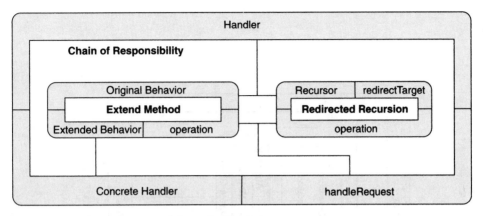

Figure 7.14 *Chain of Responsibility* as PIN only.

conceptual changes resulting in greatly different outcomes. *Chain of Responsibility* and *Decorator* are extremely close in their conceptual makeup, yet so different in the end that they were not even placed the same category by their creators.

7.3.2 Template Method

Finally, *Template Method* is another excellent example of combining two simple concepts in a very specific way to produce a much more powerful construct.

Figure 7.15 shows the original structure diagram encapsulated within an expanded PINbox. You can see multiple instances of both *Conglomeration* and *Fulfill Method*, so let's reduce it down to a simple combination for clarity, as in Figure 7.16. Notice that operation2 of *Conglomeration* and operation of *Fulfill Method* point to the same method: the abstract `primitiveOperation1()` of `AbstractClass`.

Now the resultant PIN diagram can be extracted easily. Figure 7.17 clearly shows that the *Conglomeration* instance is calling into an abstract method that will be handled by a subclass through *Fulfill Method*. The calling method of *Conglomeration* is the `templateMethod`, and the method it is calling is the abstract `primitiveOperation` method in the same class. Necessarily, this means that this class is abstract, and the Abstract Class of both the *Template Method* and the *Fulfill Method*, which ensures that a subclass will provide the proper functionality. This subclass therefore fulfills the Concrete Class role of *Fulfill Method* and the same role of *Template Method*. Requiring the target method of a *Conglomeration* to be the abstract method in an instance of *Fulfill Method*, however, forces a subclass

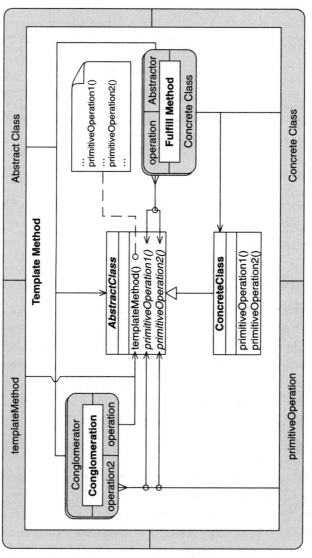

Figure 7.15 *Template Method* subsumed within the expanded PINbox.

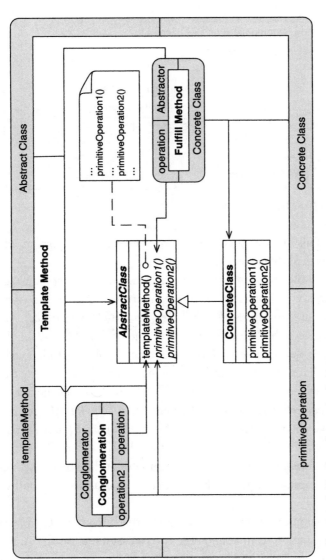

Figure 7.16 *Template Method* reduced to a single instance.

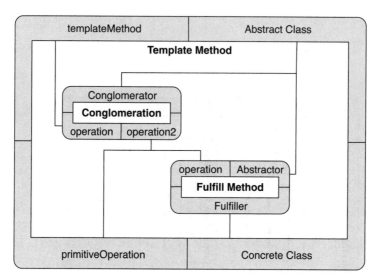

Figure 7.17 *Template Method* as PIN only.

to handle the details in a way such that the implementation of portions of the algorithm can be adjusted dynamically.

Figure 7.18 shows the same PIN diagram information, reorganized to again show congruences with our previous three pattern discussions. Now you can see that where *Proxy* uses instances of *Fulfill Method* and *Deputized Redirection*, *Template Method* replaces the latter instance with one of *Conglomeration*. This eliminates the trusted objects aspect of *Proxy* and instead pulls the functionality within the single object. However, it is worth noting that in the *Proxy* pattern, the primary relationship is that the abstract methods fulfilled in the Proxy element are *initiating* the *Deputized Redirection* relationship. In contrast, in *Template Method* the primary feature is that the abstract methods fulfilled in the Concrete Class element are the *targets* of the *Conglomeration* instances. Neither the shift from *Deputized Redirection* to *Conglomeration* nor swapping of the initiator and target of the method-call relationship is complex or unusual, but together they lead to profoundly different results.

In the discussion of *Factory Method*, you learned that *Template Method* was a possible implementation feature, and now you can see how this fits in. Figure 7.19 shows *Factory Method* redefined with *Template Method* replacing the previously individual instances of *Fulfill Method* and *Conglomeration*. Now the relationship between these two patterns is clearly defined and obvious. *Factory Method* uses a *Template Method* to flexibly handle the infrastructure within which it embeds a combined use of *Retrieve* and *Create Object*, much as is done in *Abstract Factory*.

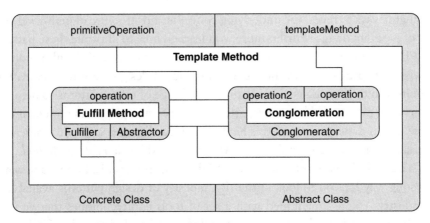

Figure 7.18 *Template Method* PIN reorganized to better match *Decorator*.

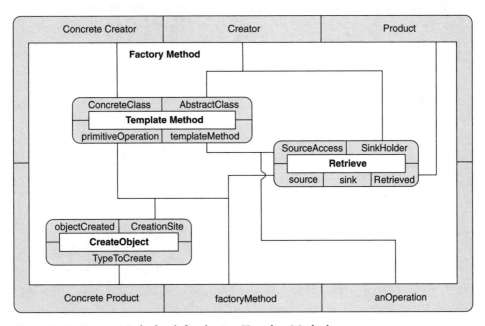

Figure 7.19 *Factory Method* redefined using *Template Method*.

7.4 Conclusion

In this chapter, we drew together the concepts and techniques from the prior chapters, synthesizing analyses of the most common design patterns you will encounter in your practice. The discussions combined the EDPs and intermediate patterns in meaningful ways to reveal the underlying concepts and structure of high-level concepts of program design. Furthermore, you learned how to illustrate these patterns with PIN in a number of variations depending on what level of detail or context you wish to express. You saw how clues and cues in design pattern specifications can point you to leveraging your existing knowledge of other patterns to help you form a better picture of what a new pattern does. You also gained an understanding of how design patterns, even at this higher level, can be used with and inside each other, such as the instance of *Template Method* buried inside *Factory Method*.

This concludes your introduction to EDP, PIN, and what is, I hope, a new and interesting way for you to look at the rich tapestry of design patterns available in our industry. You're now armed with a set of tools and techniques that you can use to further your own knowledge and skill in software design and to further our collective understanding of design patterns by helping document what we have.

Welcome to the community. I look forward to seeing what we do next.

ρ-Calculus

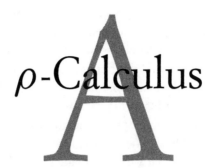

This appendix is designed to be a brief introduction to the formalisms behind the Elemental Design Patterns, the rho-calculus, or ρ-calculus. For those of you with an inclination for theory or research and who are interested in a more complete treatise, the following publications provide formal treatments of the topics. I hope you find them a suitable entry point to a richer world of programming possibilities. You may find it useful to refer back to Chapter 2 occasionally while reading this discussion.

- Martín Abadi and Luca Cardelli. *A Theory of Objects*. Springer-Verlag, New York, 1996.

- Jason McC. Smith. *SPQR: Formal Foundations and Practical Support for the Automated Detection of Design Patterns From Source Code*. PhD thesis, University of North Carolina at Chapel Hill, Dec 2005.

In Section 2.2.2, you were introduced to the idea that all of object-oriented programming can be modeled using just four things: objects, methods, fields, and types. Methods, fields, and types are rather obvious pieces to include because they represent, respectively, the three basic elements of programming: functionality, data storage, and data description. No computation can occur without all three of those elements, regardless of language paradigm. Why we added objects was sort of waved aside at the time.

Although it may still seem self-referential, the formal reason for adding objects is that they form the heart and focal point of object-oriented programming. Without objects, there is no object-oriented programming. Not satisfying? Look to Abadi and Cardelli's ς-calculus (sigma-calculus) instead. [1] ς-calculus is the underlying denotational semantics that forms the core of ρ-calculus. Using ς-calculus, we can reduce any object-oriented programming language's semantics[1] to the four elements: objects, methods, fields, and types.[2] The resulting set of the elements of programming is sufficiently small that we can provide a complete enumeration of the ways in which they can combine and interact. In other words, we can describe any relationship in object-oriented programming, and there can be no others. We have a complete coverage of the possible object-oriented programming relationships.

From another perspective, object-oriented programming has resisted being reliably and sufficiently modeled by using just the methods (as functions), fields, and types of traditional procedural programming. Something fundamental is lost in attempting to do so. Scholars have argued about this particular point for three decades now, but every attempt that I know of to extend the semantics of the lambda-calculus underlying procedural programming to encompass object-oriented techniques has fallen short in some way. In every case, regardless of how closely the procedural extensions model the semantics of object-oriented systems, the mathematical machinations required to come close are extremely cumbersome, obtuse, and fail to show any coherence with the conceptual elegance of using object-oriented programming languages. ς-calculus, on the other hand, by adding objects as first-class entities in their own right, successfully created a mathematical model that mirrors the mental model of object-oriented programming and gives a solid and elegant approach for working with objects in a formal manner.

A.1 Reliance Operators

ς-calculus also swept aside everything but the four required and necessary entities—objects, method, fields, and types—opening the way for simple analyses

---

1. With some exceptions, notably Eiffel; the details are too much for here, but are covered in [35]. If you wish to dive further, investigate covariant versus contravariant return types of methods as a starting point.
2. Yes, this appears to be playing a bit fast and loose with types. I refer you to the text for ς-calculus [1], which should quickly make clear that this is not the case. The foundation is sound.

that are truly comprehensive. For example, given only four items to work with, there
are only sixteen ways they can be combined. This point was illustrated in Table 2.2,
which is reproduced here in Table A.1.

This table is small enough that we can pick it apart piece by piece. We can
address most of this table at one shot by investigating *Defines*. An object defines a
method inside of it, or a field, or perhaps a type. Objects such as namespaces or
package objects can also define other objects within them. Methods can, in some
languages, define inner methods and types within them but can almost always define
objects and fields. Fields, by their nature, do not readily wrap or define other elements, but the *type* of the field, such as a class, can define any of the four elements.

This defining of inner entities is also known as *scoping*. A class that defines
a method is scoping that method inside itself. You must go through the class to
get to the method, either directly or through an object or field instantiated from
that class. Objects scope their children, as do methods. Examples of these in
C++ include scoping a static method in a class or a field in a namespace: `Some-`
`Class::aMethod()` and `ANamespace::aField` respectively. Java eschews
the double colon scoping operator and unifies the scoping notation across the board
to use a simple dot, as in `SomeClass.aMethod()` or `APackage.aField`.
This is the same notation that ς-calculus uses. In all cases, scoping is indicated
by the *dot operator*. It should look very familiar to most programmers because it is
used both to scope through bound instances and select entities out of a definition.
There's really no difference in practice. In fact, *defines* is just a synonym for
scopes.

So why didn't I just use *Scopes* instead? The critical difference between the
traditional denotational calculus of procedural programming, λ-calculus, and ς-
calculus is that selecting an element from a field brings into play the σ operator.
This is what binds an instance to a type, allowing for proper lookup of the selected
item out of the scoping provided by the field, even when polymorphism is present.

Table A.1 All interactions between entities of object-oriented programming

	Object	Method	Field	Type
Object	Defines	Defines	Defines	Defines *or* is of type
Method	N/A	Defines *or* method call	Defines *or* field use	Defines *or* returns of type
Field	N/A	State change	Cohesion	Is of type
Type	Defines	Defines	Defines	Defines *or* subtyping

This binding is unique to ς-calculus and, combined with the treatment of objects as first-class entities, is what makes it extremely effective and elegant. We can, however, ignore this binding for the purposes of this text.

Eliminating *defines* as a known concept leaves us with Table 2.3, again reproduced here, as Table A.2.

Objects and fields are declared to be "of a type." ς-calculus displays this as *anObject : itsType*. This notation is also used to indicate the return type of a method. Types subtype or inherit from one another. This is shown in ς-calculus as *Subtype <: Supertype*.[3] That eliminates the entirety of Table A.2 except for the four *reliance operators*: method call, field use, state change, and cohesion.

There are four reliance operators—relops for short—in ρ-calculus, based on the four relationships described above. The method-method relop (that is, a method call) is the mu-form. This is the single reliance operator discussed in this book. The method-field—a field use—is the phi-form. The field-method is a state change—in other words, the state of the field depends on a method call in some manner—known as the sigma-form. Finally, a field-field reliance is the traditional cohesion, or kappa-form. These are denoted in the mathematics of ρ-calculus as $<_\mu$, $<_\phi$, $<_\sigma$, and $<_\kappa$, respectively. The notation comes from the subtyping operator <:, which you can think of as stating, "The subtype relies on the supertype for its existence and intent." Because : is a typing operator, we can reinterpret < as "relies on." This basic notation is then subscripted with the appropriate indicator to form the four reliance operators. They are binary operators that form a reliance from the left-hand side of their use on their right-hand side. In other words, *someMethod* $<_\mu$ *anotherMethod* should be read as *someMethod* relies on *anotherMethod*.

Table A.2 Nonscoping interactions between entities of object-oriented programming

	Object	Method	Field	Type
Object				Is of type
Method		Method call	Field use	Returns of type
Field		State change	Cohesion	Is of type
Type				Subtyping

---

3. Subtyping, subclassing, and inheritance are *not* all the same from a formal point of view, but for the purposes of this book, we can use the terms interchangeably. See [1] for details.

A.2 Transitivity and Isotopes

In Section 4.1.1, you learned about isotopes and how they are formed from indirect reliances. We can use ρ-calculus to give this process a formal basis through transitivity. The following source example reproduces our code example from Section 4.1.1. We can state, as before, that f.foo relies on b.bar, but now we can write this as $f.foo <_\mu b.bar$. So far, so good. In our example on the right side, we can say that $f.foo <_\mu g.goo$ and that $g.goo <_\mu b.bar$.

```
1 class F {
      B b;
3     void foo() {
          b.bar();
5     };
  };
7 F f;
  f.foo();
```

```
  class F {
2     G g;
      void foo() {
4         g.goo();
      };
6 };
  class G {
8     B b;
      void goo() {
10        b.bar();
      };
12 };
  F f;
14 f.foo();
```

f.foo() relies on b.bar()   f.foo() **still** relies on b.bar()

We can use these two bits of information in a *reduction rule*. This is the primary form of inference in ς-calculus and ρ-calculus. Given a set of clauses that we know to be true, we can infer a new property. We say that we are *reducing* the clauses to the result. For instance, in this case, there is a reduction rule for $<_\mu$ transitivity, as in Equation A.1.

$$
\begin{array}{c}
E \vdash x, y, z \\
x \equiv [m = b_0] \\
y \equiv [n = b_1] \\
z \equiv [o = b_2] \\
x.m <_\mu y.n \\
\underline{y.n <_\mu z.o} \\
x.m <_\mu z.o
\end{array}
\tag{A.1}
$$

This reduction rule begins by stating that we have an environment E such that we have defined in this environment x, y, and z. The next three clauses state that these elements are defined as having subelements m, n, and o, respectively, which are indicated to be methods. The next two clauses specify relops such that $x.m$ relies on $y.n$, and $y.n$ relies on $z.o$. Given this set of clauses, the inferred result is that $x.m$ relies on $z.o$. This is just one of the many transitivities in ρ-calculus, and they are what give ρ-calculus much of its analytic strength. Extremely large systems can be reduced to simple sets of relops, and the existence of high-level abstractions such as design patterns can be searched for by looking in the simplified views of the results. Without this technique, we would have to continually work with or examine all of the intervening pieces. If, for example, we were looking for proof that $x.m$ called $z.o$, a simple examination of this system would fail to find it. By using the transitivities of ρ-calculus and stating that we are looking for a situation where $x.m$ relies on $z.o$ instead, we can prove the existence of the relationship quickly and cleanly.

More precisely, this transitivity allows us to create specific reliance-based definitions for design patterns that can match a tremendous number of structural implementations. These are the isotopes of the canonical, most basic and direct implementation. This is what makes this approach so powerful and flexible.

A.3 Similarity

Our three axes of similarity from Section 2.2.2 can likewise be given a formal basis in ρ-calculus. As a quick reminder, there are three possible ways in which a single relop can have similarities between its two sides. For instance, given the reliance $f.foo <_\mu b.bar$, we can talk about the object similarity between f and b, the similarity between the *types* of f and b, and the similarity between the methods *foo* and *bar*. We use $\sim$ to indicate similarity in ρ-calculus and $\not\sim$ for dissimilarity. For instance, $A \sim B$ for "A is similar to B" or $B \not\sim C$ for "B is dissimilar to C."

The similarity between the types is found in the ρ-calculus definition of f and b. For us to use f and b in a ρ-calculus definition, they must be defined, and they must be given types. Therefore, the typing information of f and b must already be defined. We can talk about this typing relationship, however, as one of the following: unrelated, which we will just call dissimilar, and denote by $\not\sim$; the same exact type, which we call similar and mark as $\sim$; subtyping, denoted by the previously seen $<:$; and sibling typing, in which two types share a common supertype, indicated by $<:>$. All of this information is already present in ρ-calculus.

We can talk about the similarity between objects and methods as either similar or dissimilar as well, using the same $\sim/\not\sim$ notation. For brevity, however, and because this information is unique to specific reliance operator instances, we can add this information to the reliance operator notation directly as a superscript, albeit in a slightly modified form.

Although the $\sim/\not\sim$ notation is easily distinguishable at normal text sizes, at small font sizes it presents readability problems, so $+/-$ is used instead for clarity.[4]

---

4. The $\sim$ and $\not\sim$ notations were, pardon the pun, too similar at the small font sizes found in subscripts to be useful in this manner. User feedback led to the adoption of the $+/-$ as a more visible version.

The selection notation of the dot operator is mimicked in the similarity notation: the object similarity is placed on the left of a dot and the method similarity is placed on the right. For instance, a method call relop with object dissimilarity and method similarity would be noted as $<_\mu^{-.+}$. A relop with object similarity and method dissimilarity would be shown as $<_\mu^{+.-}$, and so on. This lets us collapse a tremendous amount of information into a concise form. Combined with the transitivities, it lets us describe relationships between any two entities in a system quickly, precisely, and cleanly.

It might occur to you that we may not always know the similarity or dissimilarity between two elements of a system. You are correct. In such cases, a circle, ∘, is used to convey a truly unknown relationship.

A.4 EDP Formalisms

We now have the basis for formally defining and working with ρ-calculus to create the foundation for the EDPs. We can revisit the EDP design space diagrams from Section 4.4 and reannotate them with our new notation, as in Figures A.1 and A.2.

Let's establish a simple setup for this discussion. Assume we have an object o of type A and an object p of type B. We can write these as $o : A$ and $p : B$, respectively. Type A defines a method f and type B defines a method g. This setup could be shown in code something like in Listing A.1.

We can now define the EDPs on the basis of their placement within the design space, using our similarity notation and reliance operators.

Looking at Figure A.1, we can see that *Recursion* is at the intersection of the axes of object, type, and method similarity. This means that *Recursion* can be expressed formally as $o.f <_\mu^{+.+} p.g, A \sim B$. Recall that the superscript indicates what the relationship is between the two elements on either side of the matching scoping dot operator. In this case, that o is similar to p and f is similar to g.

You can see that *Delegation* can be written as $o.f <_\mu^{-.-} p.g, A \nsim B$, and, as you might expect, *Redirection* is written $o.f <_\mu^{-.+} p.g$. The claim from Section 2.2.4 that

Listing A.1 Simple code example

```
   class A {
2      void f();
   };

4
   class B {
6      void g();
   };

8
   A o;
10 B p;
```

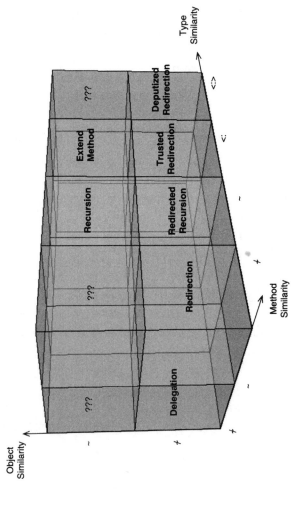

Figure A.1 The full method call EDP design space: similar method.

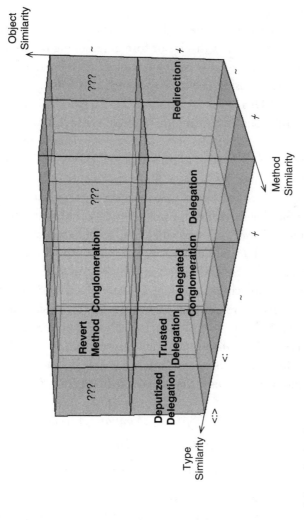

Figure A.2 The full method call EDP design space: dissimilar method.

Redirection and *Delegation* together form the concept of coupling can be stated, therefore, as $o.f <_{\mu}^{-.\circ} p.g$. Our "unknown" notation finally comes into play, albeit in a minor way.

I'm pretty sure you can guess what *Conglomeration* looks like at this point: $o.f <_{\mu}^{+.-} p.g$, and now the cohesion discussed in Section 2.2.4 reduces to $o.f <_{\mu}^{+.\circ} p.g$, as the similarity from *Recursion* and the dissimilarity from *Conglomeration* cancel each other out.

For *Redirected Recursion*, the method reliance is what you'd expect for a *Redirection*: $o.f <_{\mu}^{-.+} p.g$. By the way, this is our formal reasoning for going with *Redirected Recursion* as a name—this is a refinement of *Redirection*, not *Recursion*. As a result, only the type relationship needs to be changed, to $A = B$.

For the final two EDPs along the bottom row of Figure A.1, we add our subtyping and sibling relationships. Again, the method reliance is what you'd expect for a *Redirection*, $o.f <_{\mu}^{-.+} p.g$, and once more we only change the type relation. This time it is set to $A <: B$, which indicates that A is a subtype of B, giving rise to the *Trusted Redirection* EDP.

We can arrive at *Deputized Redirection* by again starting with *Redirection*, this time making a simple change to the type reliance relationship, such that $A <:> B$.

Finally, let's revisit *Recursion*. Start with its call reliance operator and type statements: $o.f <_{\mu}^{+.+} p.g, o : A, p : B$. Change the type relationship to $A <: B$. That's all there is to modifying *Recursion* to evolve it into *Extend Method*.

We can use this approach to define any of the EDPs within this design space, elegantly and concisely expressing their core relationships using the ρ-calculus. Section A.7 provides full definitions for each EDP using our reduction rule notation from Section A.2. Given the proper set of clauses, we can infer that the fact at the bottom of a reduction rule is evident and in turn use it as a new clause in other reduction rule inferences. For instance, take the definition for *Recursion*:

$$Recursor : [l_i : B_i^{\,i \in 1...m}, operation : B_{m+1}],$$
$$r : Recursor,$$
$$r.operation <_{\mu}^{+.+} r.operation$$

Recursion(Recursor : *Recursor*, operation : *operation*)

The clauses above the line are analogous to what we saw when we defined *Recursion*. The first clause states that *Recursor* is a type and that it has at least one method, which is named *operation*, with other optional methods and/or fields. The second clause establishes that the object r is of type *Recursor*. The third clause states that *r.operation* has a method call reliance on itself, with both object and method similarity. The final line states that the elements in the prior clauses form an instance of

Recursion. We use the names in the formal definition as the names of the roles for the pattern. These are used both when discussing the pattern and for defining the structure of its equivalent PIN representation, as you'll see in Section A.6. The slots that are bound to these roles are variables in the mathematical sense. Once an entity is bound to a role, that role is said to be *fulfilled* by that entity. In the preceding case, any class that satisfies the needs of *Recursion* as stated in the definition is said to be bound to the Recursor role of *Recursion*.

A.5 Composition and Reduction Rules

Starting with these definitions, we can compose them into more complex patterns, just like we did in the earlier chapters. Let's reexamine the building of *Decorator* that we undertook in Section 4.2. To recap, we introduced *Fulfill Method* as a combination of *Inheritance* and *Abstract Method*, and then used *Fulfill Method* to define *Objectifier*. We combined *Objectifier* and *Trusted Redirection* to define *Object Recursion*, which was then brought together with *Extend Method* to create *Decorator*.

Let's start by defining *Fulfill Method* as:

$$\frac{\begin{array}{l} \textbf{AbstractInterface}(\text{Abstractor}: \textit{Abstractor},\ \text{operation}: \textit{operation}_n), \\ \textbf{Inheritance}(\text{Superclass}: \textit{Abstractor},\ \text{Subclass}: \textit{ConcreteClass}), \\ \textit{ConcreteClass} \equiv [\textit{operation}_i \Leftarrow b_i^{\,i \in 1..n-1,n+1..m},\ \textit{operation}_n \Leftarrow b_n] \end{array}}{\begin{array}{c} \textbf{FulfillMethod}(\text{Abstractor}: \textit{Abstractor},\ \text{Fulfiller}: \textit{ConcreteClass}, \\ \text{operation}: \textit{operation}_n) \end{array}}$$

The first clause declares an instance of *Abstract Interface*, which takes two arguments, the first a type entity, and the second a method entity. It establishes the relationship between them as defined in the *Abstract Interface* pattern but allows us to replace the full formal definition with this shorter version. The second clause establishes that *ConcreteClass* is a subclass of *Abstractor* through an instance of the *Inheritance* EDP. The third line is the new piece of the puzzle. It states that the method stated in *Abstract Interface* is defined by *ConcreteClass*, fulfilling the promise made by *Abstract Interface*. Note that this piece is crucial, as there is no need for a subclass to actually define the abstract method—it may just be another abstract class in the class hierarchy. The names provided in the clauses are not accidental. If a name appears in more than one position in a reduction rule, then the same entity in the system is being used in each role. This is what ties together the smaller patterns into a larger composition.

We can continue the reduction rules process and define *Objectifier* by adding a Client class to a plurality of operations to abstract:

$$ObjectifierBase : [l_i : B_i^{i \in 1...n}],$$
$$Client : [ref : Objectifier],$$
$$Client.someMethod <_\mu Client.ref .l_i,$$
$$\textbf{FulfillMethod}(Abstractor : ObjectifierBase,$$
$$\text{Fulfiller} : ConcreteObjectifier, \text{operation} : l_i)^{i \in 1...n}$$

$$\textbf{Objectifier}(Objectifier : ObjectifierBase,$$
$$\text{ConcreteClass} : ConcreteObjectifier, \text{operation} : l_i)$$

Trusted Redirection looks rather like our earlier definition for *Recursion*:

$$Redirector <: FamilyHead,$$
$$r : Redirector,$$
$$fh : FamilyHead,$$
$$r.operation <_\mu^{-,+} fh.operation,$$

$$\textbf{TrustedRedirection}(Redirector : Redirector, \text{FamilyHead} : FamilyHead,$$
$$\text{target} : fh, \text{operation} : operation)$$

The formal definition of *Object Recursion* is then:

$$\textbf{Objectifier}(Objectifier : Handler, \text{ConcreteClass} : Recursor_i^{i \in 1...m},$$
$$\text{operation} : handleRequest),$$
$$\textbf{Objectifier}(Objectifier : Handler, \text{ConcreteClass} : Terminator_j^{j \in 1...n},$$
$$\text{operation} : handleRequest),$$
$$init.someMethod <_\mu obj.handleRequest,$$
$$init : Initiator,$$
$$obj : Handler,$$
$$\textbf{TrustedRedirection}(Redirector : Recursor, \text{FamilyHead} : Handler,$$
$$\text{target} : obj, \text{operation} : handleRequest),$$
$$\textbf{!TrustedRedirection}(Redirector : Terminator, \text{FamilyHead} : Handler,$$
$$\text{target} : obj, \text{operation} : handleRequest)$$

$$\textbf{ObjectRecursion}(Handler : Handler, \text{Recursor} : Recursor_i^{i \in 1...m},$$
$$\text{Terminator} : Terminator_j^{j \in 1...n}, \text{Initiator} : Initiator,$$
$$\text{handleRequest} : handleRequest, \text{successor} : obj)$$

We're establishing that some *Objectifier* ConcreteClasses are involved in *Trusted Redirection* and some are not. If all such classes were involved in redirection, a call into this architecture would never terminate.

Next, we can use a shorthand notation for establishing that an element is a method of a class as in *aMethod* ∈ **meth**(*aClass*) and define *Extend Method* as:

$$
\begin{array}{c}
operation \in \mathbf{meth}(OriginalBehavior), \\
ExtendedBehavior <: OriginalBehavior, \\
eb : ExtendedBehavior, \\
eb.operation <_{\mu}^{+,+} eb{\wedge}operation \\
\hline
\mathbf{ExtendMethod}(OriginalBehavior : OriginalBehavior, \\
ExtendedBehavior : ExtendedBehavior, \\
operation : operation)
\end{array}
$$

Finally, we can define *Decorator* as:

$$
\begin{array}{c}
\mathbf{ObjectRecursion}(Handler : Component,\ Recursor : Decorator_i^{i \in 1...m}, \\
Terminator : ConcreteComponent_j^{j \in 1...n},\ Initiator : \mathbf{any} \\
handleRequest : operation_k^{k \in 1...o},\ successor :), \\
\mathbf{ExtendMethod}(OriginalBehavior : Decorator \\
ExtendedBehavior : ConcreteDecoratorB_k^{k \in 1...o}, \\
operation : operation_k^{k \in 1...o}) \\
\mathbf{!ExtendMethod}(OriginalBehavior : Decorator \\
ExtendedBehavior : ConcreteDecoratorA_l^{l \in 1...p}, \\
operation : operation_l^{l \in 1...p}) \\
\hline
\mathbf{Decorator}(Component : Component,\ Decorator : Decorator_i^{i \in 1...m}, \\
ConcreteComponent : ConcreteComponent_j^{j \in 1...n}, \\
ConcreteDecorator : ConcreteDecoratorB_k^{k \in 1...o}, \\
Terminator : ConcreteDecoratorA_l^{l \in 1...p}, \\
operation : operation_k^{k \in 1...o+p})
\end{array}
$$

Note that these equations can be correlated closely with the PIN diagrams used in Section 4.2 to illustrate the compositions. In fact, as we'll see next, PIN and the uses of pattern instances in reduction rules go hand in hand.

A.6 Pattern Instance Notation and Roles

One design goal of PIN is to allow the simple display of composed patterns through expanded PINboxes. The rules for PIN closely mirror those for the reduction rule compositions in this appendix. For instance, Figure A.3 is a repeat of

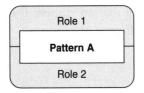

Figure A.3 Standard PINbox.

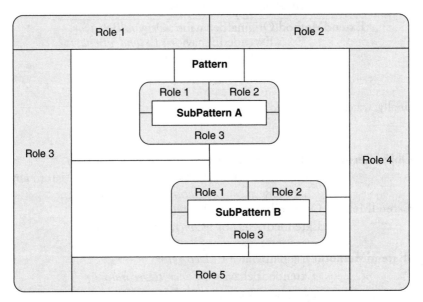

Figure A.4 Expanded PIN instance.

Figure 3.9, and instances of those patterns in the formalism of ρ-calculus would appear as **PatternA**(Role1 : a, Role2 : b) and **PatternB**(Role1 : a, Role2 : b, Role3 : c, Role4 : d, Role5 : e, Role6 : f), where a through f represent unbound roles.

Likewise, Figure A.4 shows our expanded PINbox example from Figure 3.14, which we can now define formally as:

$$\frac{\textbf{SubPatternA}(\text{Role1} : x, \ \text{Role2} : y, \ \text{Role3} : z)}{\textbf{SubPatternB}(\text{Role1} : z, \ \text{Role2} : a, \ \text{Role3} : b)}$$
$$\overline{\textbf{Pattern}(\text{Role1} : x, \text{Role2} : y, \text{Role3} : z, \text{Role4} : a, \text{Role5} : b)}$$

There is a one-to-one correlation between the roles ringing a PINbox and the roles in the formal definition. Also, each connection in the PINbox diagram illustrates a point at which the same bound variable is used in multiple role fulfillments within the definition.

A.7 EDP Definitions

This section provides fully formal definitions of each of the EDPs in this text, using ρ-calculus. Not every aspect of these definitions is explained in full, although you have seen most of the notation used. If you would like a deeper treatment, refer to the base publications for the complete reference, in particular *A Theory of Objects* [1], which provides the comprehensive foundation you need, as well as *SPQR: Formal Foundations and Practical Support for the Automated Detection of Design Patterns from Source Code* [35], which provides the original definitions and a much deeper discussion of each. Some minor details have changed since original publication, such as the addition of the explicit naming of the roles in pattern instances. This was found to be of great utility after the original references were published. Each of the following definitions is accompanied by its equivalent PIN diagram so you can immediately see the correlation with the formalism.

A.7.1 Create Object

This definition is the closest to its foundations in ς-calculus, and studying that foundation is recommended if you wish to truly understand this definition in detail. Or, you can accept that this is a very specific definition for a very simple concept.

$$
\frac{
\begin{aligned}
A &\equiv \textbf{Object}(X)[l_i v_i : B_i^{i \in 1..n+m}] \\
\overline{A} : \textbf{Class}(A) &\triangleq \textbf{subclass of } \overline{A'} : \textbf{Class}(A') \\
&\qquad \textbf{with } (\textbf{ self } : \lfloor A \rfloor) \\
&\qquad\qquad l_i = b_i^{i \in n+1..n+m} \\
&\qquad \textbf{override} \\
&\qquad\qquad l_i = b_i^{i \in Ovr} \\
&\qquad \textbf{end} \\
a &= \textbf{new} \overline{A}
\end{aligned}
}{
\textbf{CreateObject}(\text{CreationSite} : l_i, \ \text{TypeToCreate} : A, \ \text{ObjectCreated} : a)
}
$$

where $A' = \textbf{Object}(X)[l_i v_i : B_i^{i \in 1..n}]$ (and may be *Root*), $\lfloor A \rfloor = A$ for O-1, $X <: A$ for O-2, and $X < \#A$ for O-3-compliant languages, respectively, according to the classifications established in [1].

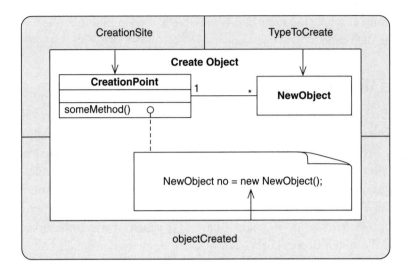

Note that it may very well be easier to consider this as an axiomatic output directly from a language model than to try to derive it from ς-calculus constructs. In particular, if attempting to perform analysis of source code, use the language semantics instead of trying to derive this from ς-calculus primitives.

A.7.2 Retrieve

Most object-oriented languages do not allow the updating of methods with new values (method bodies). Instead, only data fields can be updated in this manner. From a theoretical point of view, there is no appreciable difference between these two scenarios. We allow for both, relying on language semantics to govern which cases are valid and which are not. By deferring our definition until we have a set of well-formed ρ-calculus facts, we avoid much of the complexity of handling the myriad of language quirks. There are two basic forms for the *Retrieve* pattern:

$$o : SinkHolder$$
$$o' : SourceAccess$$
$$o.s \Leftarrow o'.s'$$
$$x : ReturnType$$
$$o'.s' \overset{v}{\leadsto} x$$

$\overline{\qquad\qquad\qquad\qquad\qquad\qquad\qquad\qquad\qquad\qquad\qquad}$

Retrieve(SinkHolder : *SinkHolder*, sink : *s*, SourceAccess : *o'*,
         source : *s'*, Retrieved : *ReturnType*)

$$o : SinkHolder$$
$$o' : SourceAccess$$
$$o.s \Leftarrow o'.s'$$
$$x : ReturnType$$
$$o'.s' \overset{n}{\leadsto} x$$

Retrieve(SinkHolder : *SinkHolder*, sink : *s*, SourceAccess : *o'*, source : *s'*, Retrieved : *ReturnType*)

Both forms are composed of an update in the first clause and a return of a value in the second clause, either by name, indicating a shared reference, or by value, indicating a fresh copy.

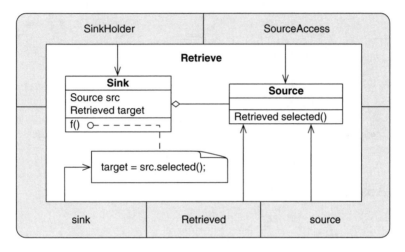

A.7.3 Inheritance

$$\frac{E \vdash Subclass, Superclass, \ Subclass <: Superclass}{\textbf{Inheritance}(Superclass : Superclass, \ Subclass : Subclass)}$$

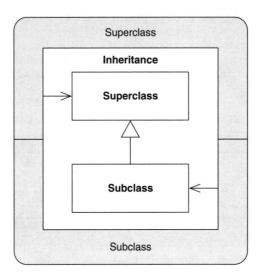

A.7.4 Abstract Interface

$$\frac{E \vdash C, \ C : [l_i : B_i^{i \in 1..n}]}{C \equiv [l_i = b_i^{i \in 1..m-1, m+1..n}, l_m = []]}$$
$$\textbf{AbstractInterface}(Abstractor : C, \ operation : l_m)$$

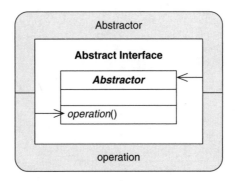

A.7.5 Delegation

$Delegator : [target : Delegator, operation : B_i]$
$Delegator \equiv [operation \Leftarrow ..., target.operation2, ...]$
$Delegatee : [operation2 : B_i]$
$del : Delegator$
$del.operation <_{\mu}^{-.-} target.operation2$

Delegation(Delegator : *Delegator*, Delegatee : *Delegatee*,
             operation : *operation*, operation2 : *operation2*)

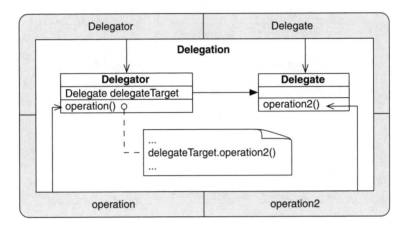

A.7.6 Redirection

$$Redirector : [target : Redirectee, operation : B_i]$$
$$Redirector \equiv [operation \Leftarrow ..., target.operation, ...]$$
$$Redirectee : [operation : B_i]$$
$$red : Redirector$$
$$redirector.operation <_{\mu}^{-.+} target.operation$$

Redirection(Redirector : *Redirector*, target : *target*, operation : *operation*)

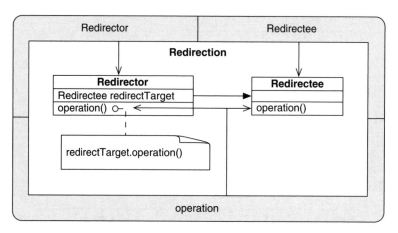

A.7.7 Conglomeration

$$c : Conglomerator$$
$$c.operation <_{\mu}^{+.-} c.operation2$$

Conglomeration(Conglomerator : *Conglomerator*,
operation : *operation*, operation2 : *operation2*)

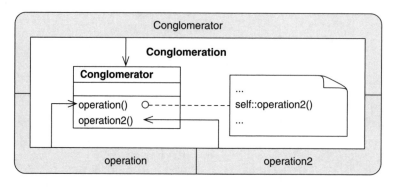

A.7.8 Recursion

$$Recursor : [l_i : B_i^{i\in 1...m}, operation : B_{m+1}],$$
$$r : Recursor,$$
$$r.operation <_\mu^{+.+} r.operation$$

Recursion(Recursor : *Recursor*, operation : *operation*)

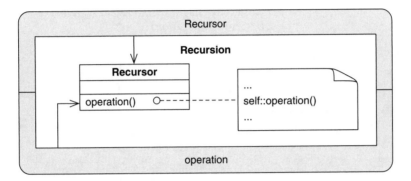

A.7.9 Revert Method

$$OriginalBehavior : [l_i : B_i^{i\in 1...m}, operation : B_{m+1}, operation2 : B_{m+2}],$$
$$RevertedBehavior : [l_i : B_i^{i\in 1...m}, operation : B_{m+1}, operation2 : B_{m+2}],$$
$$RevertedBehavior <: OriginalBehavior,$$
$$rb : RevertedBehavior,$$
$$rb.operation <_\mu^{+.-} rb{\wedge}operation2$$

RevertMethod(OriginalBehavior : *OriginalBehavior*,
                 RevertedBehavior : *RevertedBehavior*,
                 operation : *operation*, operation2 : *operation2*)

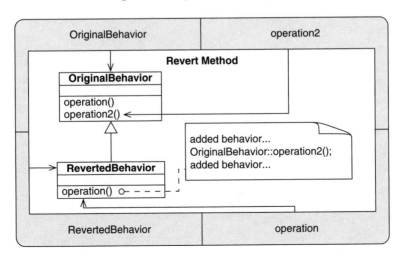

A.7.10 Extend Method

$$operation \in \mathbf{meth}(OriginalBehavior),$$
$$ExtendedBehavior <: OriginalBehavior,$$
$$eb : ExtendedBehavior,$$
$$eb.operation <_{\mu}^{+.+} eb{\wedge}operation$$

ExtendMethod(OriginalBehavior : *OriginalBehavior*,
              ExtendedBehavior : *ExtendedBehavior*,
              operation : *operation*)

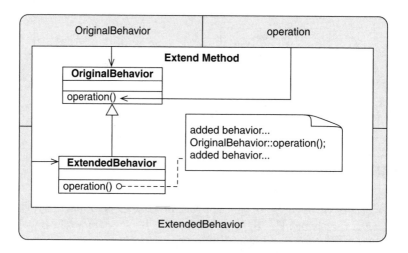

A.7.11 Delegated Conglomeration

del : $DelConglomerator$
$delegateTarget$: $DelConglomerator$
$del.operation <_{\mu}^{-\cdot-} delegateTarget.operation2$

DelegatedConglomeration(Delegator : $DelConglomerator$,
                                        delegateTarget : $delegateTarget$,
                                        operation : $operation$, operation2 : $operation2$)

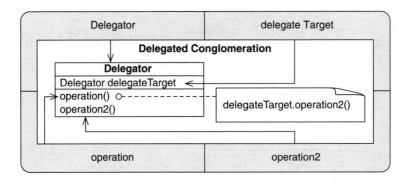

A.7.12 Redirected Recursion

rec : $Recursor$
$redirectTarget$: $Recursor$
$rec.operation <_{\mu}^{-\cdot+} redirectTarget.operation$

RedirectedRecursion(Recursor : $Recursor$,
                                    redirectTarget : $redirectTarget$, operation : $operation$)

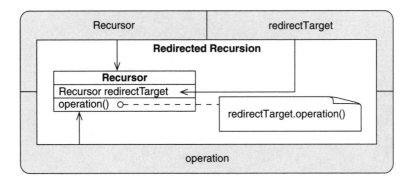

A.7.13 Trusted Delegation

$Delegator <: FamilyHead,$
$d : Delegator,$
$fh : FamilyHead,$
$d.operation <_{\mu}^{-\cdot-} fh.operation2,$

TrustedDelegation(Delegator : $Delegator$, FamilyHead : $FamilyHead$,
target : fh, operation : $operation$ operation2 : $operation2$)

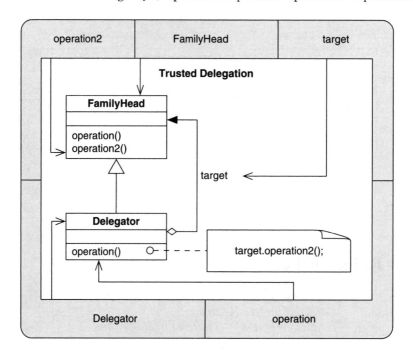

A.7.14 Trusted Redirection

$$Redirector <: FamilyHead,$$
$$r : Redirector,$$
$$fh : FamilyHead,$$
$$r.operation <_{\mu}^{-.+} fh.operation,$$

TrustedRedirection(Redirector : *Redirector*, FamilyHead : *FamilyHead*, target : *fh*, operation : *operation*)

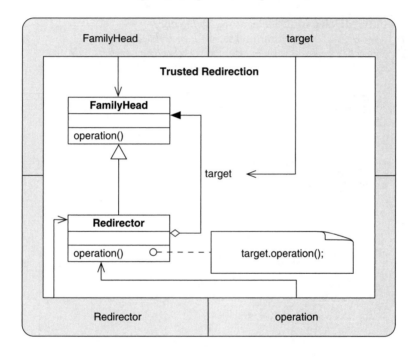

A.7.15 Deputized Delegation

$$
\begin{array}{l}
Delegator <: FamilyHead, \\
Sibling <: FamilyHead, \\
Delegator \neq Sibling, \\
Delegator \not<: Sibling, \\
d : Delegator, \\
sib : Sibling, \\
d.operation <_{\mu}^{-\cdot-} sib.operation2,
\end{array}
$$

DeputizedDelegation(Delegator : *Delegator*,
                            FamilyHead : *FamilyHead*,
                            DelegateSibling : *Sibling*, target : *sib*,
                            operation : *operation*, operation2 : *operation2*)

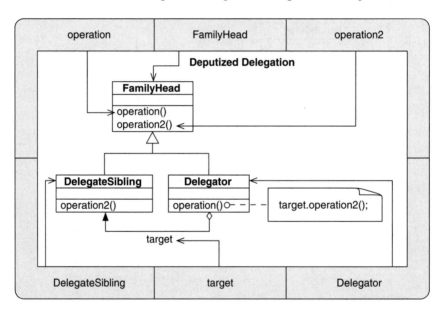

A.7.16 Deputized Redirection

$$Redirector <: FamilyHead,$$
$$Sibling <: FamilyHead,$$
$$Redirector \neq Sibling,$$
$$Redirector \not<: Sibling,$$
$$r : Redirector,$$
$$sib : Sibling,$$
$$r.operation <_\mu^{-.+} sib.operation,$$

DeputizedRedirection(Redirector : *Redirector*,
FamilyHead : *FamilyHead*,
RedirectSibling : *Sibling*, target : *sib*,
operation : *operation*)

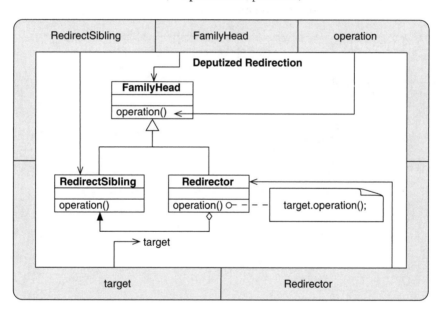

A.8 Intermediate Pattern Definitions

Here you will find the definitions for the patterns presented in Chapter 6. These are the initial patterns demonstrating composition reduction rules from prior pattern instances. Again, each definition is presented along side its equivalent PIN diagram.

A.8.1 Fulfill Method

$$\frac{\begin{array}{c}\textbf{AbstractInterface}(\text{Abstractor}: Abstractor, \; \text{operation}: operation_n),\\ \textbf{Inheritance}(\text{Superclass}: Abstractor, \; \text{Subclass}: ConcreteClass),\\ ConcreteClass \equiv [operation_i \Leftarrow b_i{}^{i \in 1..n-1, n+1..m}, \; operation_n \Leftarrow b_n]\end{array}}{\begin{array}{c}\textbf{FulfillMethod}(\text{Abstractor}: Abstractor, \; \text{Fulfiller}: ConcreteClass,\\ \text{operation}: operation_n)\end{array}}$$

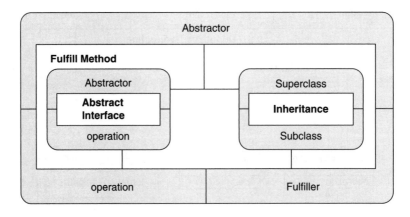

A.8.2 Retrieve New

$o : SinkHolder$
$o' : SourceAccess$
$x : TypeToCreate$
$o'.s' \overset{n}{\rightsquigarrow} x$
CreateObject(CreationSite : $o'.s'$, TypeToCreate : $TypeToCreate$,
          ObjectCreated : $o'.s'.x$)
Retrieve(SinkHolder : $SinkHolder$, sink : s, SourceAccess : $SourceAccess$,
      source : s', Retrieved : $TypeToCreate$)

RetrieveNew(Sink : $SinkHolder$, target : s, Retrieved : $TypeToCreate$,
        Source : o', selected : s')

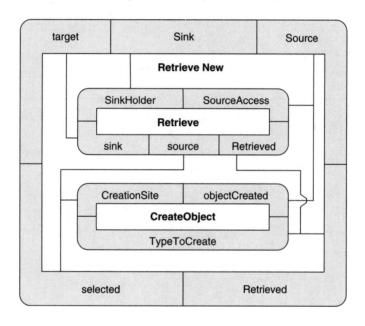

A.8.3 Retrieve Shared

$o : SinkHolder$
$o' : SourceAccess$
$x : TypeToCreate$
$o'.s' \overset{v}{\rightsquigarrow} x$
CreateObject(CreationSite : $o'.s'$, TypeToCreate : $TypeToCreate$,
            ObjectCreated : $o'.s'.x$)
Retrieve(SinkHolder : $SinkHolder$, sink : s, SourceAccess : $SourceAccess$,
    source : s', Retrieved : $TypeToCreate$)

RetrieveShared(Sink : $SinkHolder$, target : s, Retrieved : $TypeToCreate$,
        Source : o', selected : s')

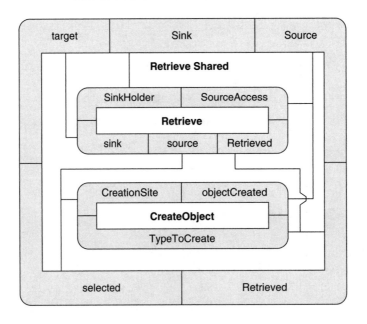

A.8.4 Objectifier

$ObjectifierBase : [l_i : B_i{}^{i \in 1...n}],$
$Client : [ref : Objectifier],$
$Client.someMethod <_\mu Client.ref.l_i,$
FulfillMethod(Abstractor : $ObjectifierBase,$
                    Fulfiller : $ConcreteObjectifier,$ operation : $l_i)^{i \in 1...n}$

Objectifier(Objectifier : $ObjectifierBase,$
                    ConcreteClass : $ConcreteObjectifier,$ operation : l_i)

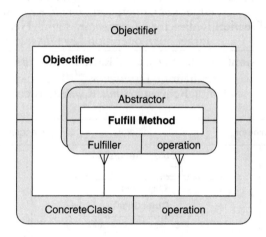

A.8.5 Object Recursion

Objectifier(Objectifier : *Handler*, ConcreteClass : $Recursor_i^{i \in 1...m}$,
                operation : *handleRequest*),
Objectifier(Objectifier : *Handler*, ConcreteClass : $Terminator_j^{j \in 1...n}$,
                operation : *handleRequest*),
init.someMethod $<_\mu$ *obj.handleRequest*,
init : Initiator,
obj : Handler,
TrustedRedirection(Redirector : *Recursor*, FamilyHead : *Handler*,
                target : *obj*, operation : *handleRequest*),
!**TrustedRedirection**(Redirector : *Terminator*, FamilyHead : *Handler*,
                target : *obj*, operation : *handleRequest*)

ObjectRecursion(Handler : *Handler*, Recursor : $Recursor_i^{i \in 1...m}$,
                Terminator : $Terminator_j^{j \in 1...n}$, Initiator : *Initiator*,
                handleRequest : *handleRequest*, successor : *obj*)

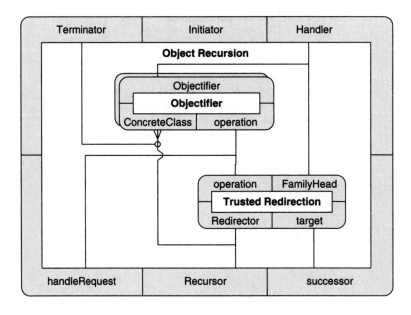

A.9 Gang of Four Pattern Definitions

Finally, this section presents definitions and PIN diagrams for each of the Gang of Four patterns discussed in Chapter 7.

A.9.1 Abstract Factory

Client.prodA : *AbstractProductA*
ProductA2 <: *AbstractProductA*
Retrieve(SinkHolder : *Client*, sink : *someMethod*, SourceAccess : *Client*,
      source : *prodA*, Retrieved : *ProductA2*)
CreateObject(CreationSite : *ConcreteFactory2.createProductA*,
        TypeToCreate : *ProductA2*,
          objectCreated : *ConcreteFactory2.CreateProductA.rtnVal*)
FulfillMethod(Abstractor : *AbstractFactory*, Fulfiller : *ConcreteFactory2*,
      operation : *createProductA*)

    AbstractFactory(AbstractFactory : *AbstractFactory*,
         ConcreteFactory : *ConcreteFactory2*,
         creator : *createProductA*,
         AbstractProduct : *AbstractProductA*,
         ConcreteProduct : *ProductA2*)

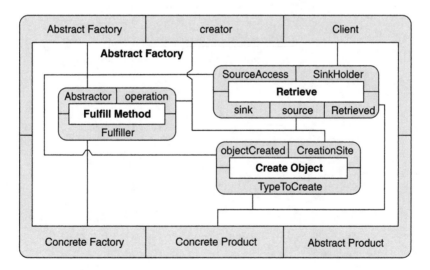

A.9.2 Factory Method

Conglomeration(Conglomerator : *Creator*, operation : *anOperation*,
                    operation2 : *factoryMethod*)
FulfillMethod(Abstractor : *Creator*, Fulfiller : *ConcreteCreator*,
                    operation : *factoryMethod*)
Creator.product : *Product*
ConcreteCreator.factoryMethod ⤳ *retVal*
Retrieve(SinkHolder : *Creator*, sink : *operation.any*,
            SourceAccess : *Creator*, source : *operation2*, Retrieved : *Product*)
ConcreteProduct <: *Product*
CreateObject(CreationSite : *ConcreteCreator.factoryMethod*,
                TypeToCreate : *ConcreteProduct*, objectCreated : *retVal*)

  FactoryMethod(Creator : *Creator*, ConcreteCreator : *ConcreteCreator*,
                    anOperation : *anOperation*,
                    factoryMethod : *factoryMethod*,
                    Product : *Product*, ConcreteProduct : *ConcreteProduct*)

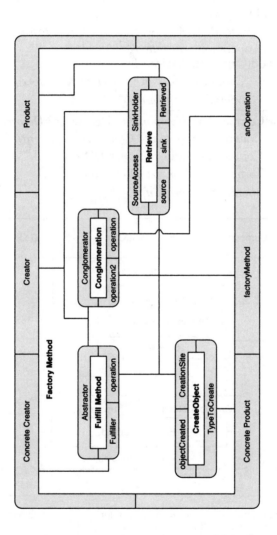

A.9.3 Decorator

ObjectRecursion(Handler : *Component*, Recursor : *Decorator*$_i^{i \in 1...m}$,
           Terminator : *ConcreteComponent*$_j^{j \in 1...n}$, Initiator : **any**
           handleRequest : *operation*$_k^{k \in 1...o}$, successor :),
ExtendMethod(OriginalBehavior : *Decorator*
           ExtendedBehavior : *ConcreteDecoratorB*$_k^{k \in 1...o}$,
           operation : *operation*$_k^{k \in 1...o}$)
!**ExtendMethod**(OriginalBehavior : *Decorator*
           ExtendedBehavior : *ConcreteDecoratorA*$_l^{l \in 1...p}$,
           operation : *operation*$_l^{l \in 1...p}$)

   Decorator(Component : *Component*, Decorator : *Decorator*$_i^{i \in 1...m}$,
           ConcreteComponent : *ConcreteComponent*$_j^{j \in 1...n}$,
           ConcreteDecorator : *ConcreteDecoratorB*$_k^{k \in 1...o}$,
           Terminator : *ConcreteDecoratorA*$_l^{l \in 1...p}$,
           operation : *operation*$_k^{k \in 1...o+p}$)

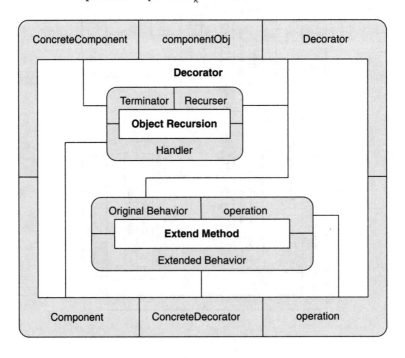

A.9.4 Proxy

FulfillMethod(Abstractor : *Subject*, Fulfiller : *Proxy*,
  operation : *request*)
FulfillMethod(Abstractor : *Subject*, Fulfiller : *RealSubject*,
  operation : *request*)
DeputizedRedirection(Redirector : *Proxy*,
  RedirectSibling : *RealSubject*,
  FamilyHead : *Subject*,
  target : *any*, operation : *request*)

Proxy(Subject : *Subject*, Proxy : *Proxy*, RealSubject : *RealSubject*,
  request : *request*)

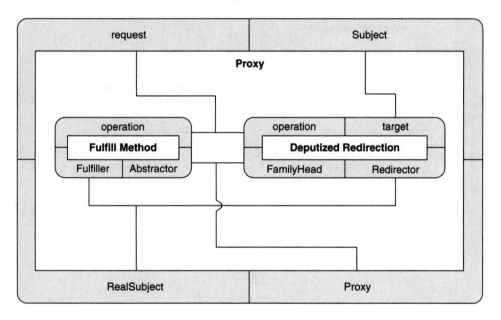

A.9.5 Chain of Responsibility

RedirectedRecursion(Recursor : *Handler*,
                redirectTarget : *successor*, operation : *handleRequest*)
ExtendMethod(OriginalBehavior : *Handler*
           ExtendedBehavior : *ConcreteHandler*,
           operation : *handleRequest*)

    ChainOfResponsibility(Handler : *Handler*,
                   ConcreteHandler : *ConcreteHandler*,
                   handleRequest : *handleRequest*)

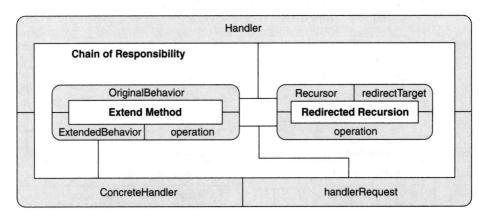

A.9.6 Template Method

FulfillMethod(Abstractor : *AbstractClass*, Fulfiller : *ConcreteClass*,
                operation : *primitiveOperation*)
Conglomeration(Conglomerator : *AbstractClass*,
                operation : *templateMethod*,
                operation2 : *primitiveOperation*)

TemplateMethod(AbstractClass : *AbstractClass*,
                ConcreteClass : *ConcreteClass*,
                templateMethod : *templateMethod*,
                primitiveOperation : *primitiveOperation*)

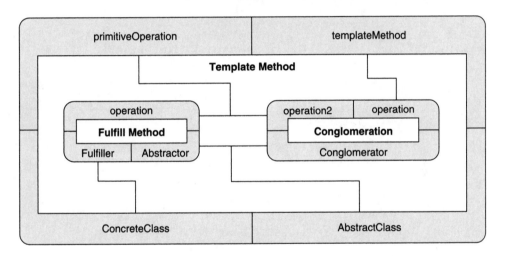

Bibliography

[1] Martín Abadi and Luca Cardelli. *A Theory of Objects*. Springer-Verlag, New York, 1996.

[2] Lee Ackerman and Celso Gonzalez. *Patterns-Based Engineering: Successfully Delivering Solutions via Patterns*. Addison-Wesley, Boston, 2010.

[3] Christopher Alexander, Sara Ishikawa, and Murray Silverstein. *A Pattern Language: Towns, Building, Construction*. Oxford University Press, New York, 1977.

[4] Christopher W. Alexander. *Notes on the Synthesis of Form* (15th printing). Oxford University Press, New York, 1964, 1999.

[5] Kent Beck. *Smalltalk Best Practice Patterns*. Prentice Hall, Upper Saddle River, NJ, 1997.

[6] Pete Becker. Working draft, standard for programming language c++. Technical Report N3242, ISO/IEC JTC/SC22/Working Group 21, 2011.

[7] James M. Bieman and Byung-Kyoo Kang. Cohesion and reuse in an object-oriented system. In *Proceedings of the ACM Symposium on Software Reusability, SSR'95*, pp. 259–262, Apr 1995. Reprinted in ACM Software Engineering Notes, Aug 1995.

[8] James M. Bieman and Byung-Kyoo Kang. Measuring design-level cohesion. *IEEE Transactions on Software Engineering*, 24(2):111–124, 1998.

[9] James M. Bieman and Linda Ott. Measuring functional cohesion. *IEEE Transactions on Software Engineering*, 20(8):644–657, 1994.

[10] Grady Booch. Tribal memory. *IEEE Software*, 25(2):16–17, 2008.

[11] Grady Booch and Celso Gonzalez. Handbook of software architecture. www.handbookofsoftwarearchitecture.com/, Oct 2010.

[12] Jan Bosch. Design patterns as language constructs. *Journal of Object Oriented Programming*, 1(2):18–52, May 1998.

[13] L. C. Briand and J. W. Daly. A unified framework for cohesion measurement in object-oriented systems. In *Proceedings of the Fourth Conference on METRICS'97*, pp. 43–53, Nov 1997.

[14] William J. Brown, Raphael C. Malveau, William H. Brown, W. McCormick Hays III, and Thomas J. Mowbray. *Anti-Patterns: Refactoring Software, Architectures, and Projects in Crisis*. Wiley, New York, 1998.

[15] Shyam R. Chidamber and Chris F. Kemerer. Towards a metrics suite for object-oriented design. In *Proceedings of OOPSLA '91*, pp. 197–211. ACM, 1991.

[16] Shyam R. Chidamber and Chris F. Kemerer. A metrics suite for object-oriented design. *IEEE Transactions on Software Engineering*, 20(6):476–493, 1994.

[17] James Coplien. C++ idioms. In *Proceedings of the Third European Conference on Pattern Languages of Programming and Computing*, 1998.

[18] C++ Standards Committee. Working Draft, Standard for Programming Language C++, Section 20.7.2.2 [util.smartptr.shared]. ISO/IEC Document N3242=11-0012, Feb 2011.

[19] Martin Fowler. *Refactoring: Improving the Design of Existing Code.* Addison-Wesley, Boston, 1999.

[20] Martin Fowler and Kendall Scott. *UML Distilled: A Brief Guide to the Standard Object Modeling Language, 3rd ed.* Addison-Wesley, Boston, 2003.

[21] Erich Gamma, Richard Helm, Ralph Johnson, and John Vlissides. *Design Patterns.* Addison-Wesley, Boston, 1995.

[22] Byung-Kyoo Kang and James M. Bieman. Design-level cohesion measures: Derivation, comparison, and applications. In *Proceedings of the 20th International Computer Software and Applications Conference (COMPSAC'96)*, pp. 92–97, Aug 1996.

[23] Byung-Kyoo Kang and James M. Bieman. Using design cohesion to visualize, quantify and restructure software. In *Eighth International Conference of Software Engineering and Knowledge Engineering, SEKE '96*, Jun 1996.

[24] Joshua Kerievsky. *Refactoring to Patterns.* Addison-Wesley, Boston, 2005.

[25] Howard C. Lovatt, Anthony M. Sloane, and Dominic R. Verity. A pattern enforcing compiler (PEC) for Java: Using the compiler. In Sven Hartmann and Markus Stumptner, eds., *Conferences in Research and Practice in Information Technology*, vol. 43. Appeared at the Second Asia-Pacific Conference on Conceptual Modeling (APCCM2005), 2005.

[26] O. L. Madsen, B. Møller-Pederson, and K. Nygaard. *Object-Oriented Programming in the BETA Language.* Addison-Wesley, Boston, 1993.

[27] Robert C. Martin. *Clean Code: A Handbook of Agile Software Craftsmanship.* Prentice Hall PTR, Upper Saddle River, NJ, 2008.

[28] Scott Meyers. *Effective C++.* Addison-Wesley, Boston, 1992.

[29] Scott Meyers. *More Effective C++.* Addison-Wesley, Boston, 1996.

[30] Jörg Niere, Lothar Wendehals, and Albert Zündorf. An interactive and scalable approach to design pattern recovery. Technical Report tr-ri-03-236, University of Paderborn, Paderborn, Germany, Jan 2003.

[31] S. Patel, W. Chu, and R. Baxter. A measure for composite module cohesion. In *International Conference on Software Engineering*, pp. 38–48, May 1992.

[32] Dirk Riehle. Composite design patterns. In *Proceedings of the 1997 ACM SIGPLAN Conference on Object-Oriented Programming Systems, Languages and Applications*, pp. 218–228. ACM Press, 1997.

[33] James Rumbaugh, Ivar Jacobson, and Grady Booch. *The Unified Modeling Language Reference Manual, 2nd ed.*, Addison-Wesley, Boston, 2004.

[34] M. H. Samadzadeh and S. J. Khan. Stability, coupling and cohesion of object-oriented software systems. In *Proceedings of the 22nd Annual ACM Computer Science Conference on Scaling Up*, pp. 312–319, Mar 8–10, 1994.

[35] Jason McC. Smith. *SPQR: Formal Foundations and Practical Support for the Automated Detection of Design Patterns from Source Code*. Ph.D. thesis, University of North Carolina at Chapel Hill, Dec 2005.

[36] Jason McC. Smith. The Pattern Instance Notation: A simple hierarchical visual notation for the dynamic visualization and comprehension of software patterns. *Journal of Visual Languages and Computing*, 22(5):355–374, 2011.

[37] Jason McC. Smith and David Stotts. SPQR: Flexible automated design pattern extraction from source code. In *18th IEEE International Conference on Automated Software Engineering*, pp. 215–224, Oct 2003.

[38] Jason McC. Smith and David Stotts. *Intent-Oriented Design Pattern Formalization Using SPQR*, chapter 7. IDEA Group, 2007.

[39] Mark Twain. *The Adventures of Tom Sawyer*. Gutenberg Press, www.gutenberg.org/ebooks/74, 2005.

[40] Bobby Woolf. The abstract class pattern. In Neil Harrison, Brian Foote, and Hans Rohnert, eds., *Pattern Languages of Program Design 4*. Addison-Wesley, Boston, 1998.

[41] Bobby Woolf. The object recursion pattern. In Neil Harrison, Brian Foote, and Hans Rohnert, eds., *Pattern Languages of Program Design 4*. Addison-Wesley, Boston, 1998, 41–52.

[42] E. Yourdon and L. Constantine. *Structured Design*. Prentice Hall, Englewood Cliffs, NJ, 1979.

[43] Walter Zimmer. Relationships between design patterns. In James O. Coplien and Douglas C. Schmidt, eds., *Pattern Languages of Program Design*. Addison-Wesley, Boston, 1995, 345–364.

Index

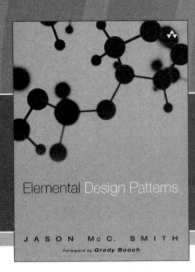

FREE
Online Edition

Your purchase of *Elemental Design Patterns* includes access to a free online edition for 45 days through the **Safari Books Online** subscription service. Nearly every Addison-Wesley Professional book is available online through **Safari Books Online**, along with thousands of books and videos from publishers such as Cisco Press, Exam Cram, IBM Press, O'Reilly Media, Prentice Hall, Que, Sams, and VMware Press.

Safari Books Online is a digital library providing searchable, on-demand access to thousands of technology, digital media, and professional development books and videos from leading publishers. With one monthly or yearly subscription price, you get unlimited access to learning tools and information on topics including mobile app and software development, tips and tricks on using your favorite gadgets, networking, project management, graphic design, and much more.

Activate your FREE Online Edition at
informit.com/safarifree

STEP 1: Enter the coupon code: IPZAXAA.

STEP 2: New Safari users, complete the brief registration form.
Safari subscribers, just log in.

If you have difficulty registering on Safari or accessing the online edition,
please e-mail customer-service@safaribooksonline.com